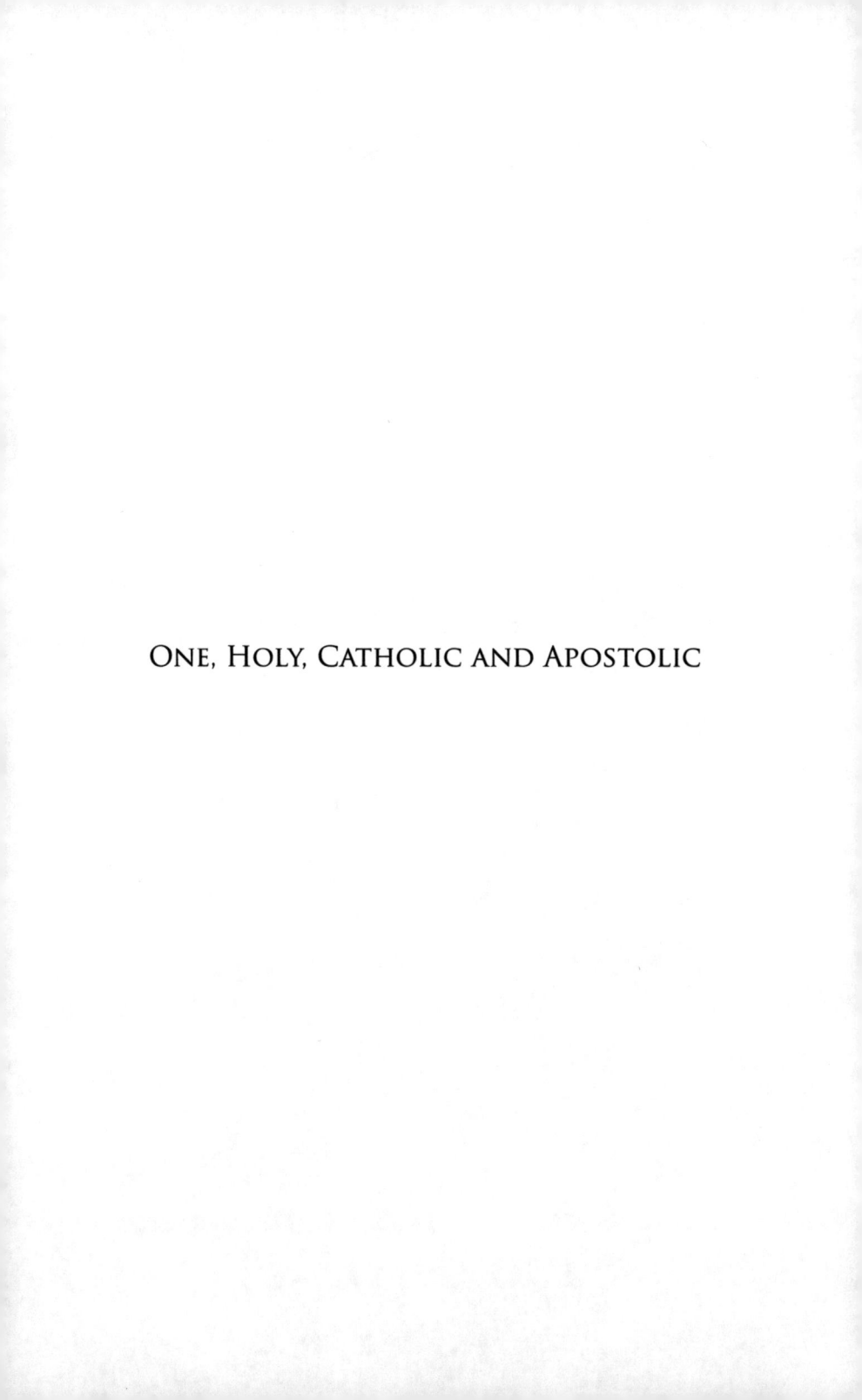

One, Holy, Catholic and Apostolic

ONE, HOLY, CATHOLIC AND APOSTOLIC

ECUMENICAL REFLECTIONS ON THE CHURCH

EDITED BY TAMARA GRDZELIDZE

Faith and Order Paper no. 197

WCC Publications, Geneva

Cover: Greek manuscript 15th century, Church of the Holy Sepulchre, Jerusalem. © Archivo Iconografico, SA/Corbis

Cover design: Marie Arnaud Snakkers

ISBN 2-8254-1440-9

© WCC Publications
World Council of Churches
150 route de Ferney, P.O.Box 2100
1211 Geneva 2, Switzerland
Web site: http://www.wcc-coe.org

Printed in France

Table of Contents

Preface.. VII

Introduction
   by Rev. Dr Alan Falconer 1

1. Does the Church Have a Sacramental Nature? **15**

Does the Church Have a Sacramental Nature? An Orthodox Perspective
   by Rev. Dr Emmanuel Clapsis 17

The Sacramentality of the Church: An Evangelical Baptist Perspective
   by Rev. Dr Timothy George 27

The Sacramentality of the Church: Points of Convergence and Issues to be Addressed
   by Rev. Dr Barbara Schwahn............................. 40

Church and "Sacrament" in Bilateral Dialogues
   by Rev. Antti Saarelma 51

Church as Koinonia / Church as Sacrament
   by Dr Donna Geernaert 62

Koinonia in the Context of Sacramentality of the Church
   by Rev. Dr Hermen P. Shastri 78

Does the Church Have a Sacramental Nature? Report 84

2. Authority and Authoritative Teaching in the Church **89**

Holiness as Content and Purpose of Ecclesial Authority
   by Metropolitan Daniel Ciobotea........................ 91

An Overview of Some Faith and Order Papers on Authority
   by Rev. Dr Gert Jansen................................. 97

Response to an Overview of Some Faith and Order Papers on Authority
   by Dr Mary O'Driscoll 104

Reflections on Authority in the Roman Catholic-Lutheran Dialogue
   by Dr Turid Karlsen Seim 109

Reflections on Authority and Authoritative Teaching in Light of ARCIC II
   by Rev. Dr William Henn............................... 124

VI   *One, Holy, Catholic and Apostolic*

    Authority in Context: Methodist Bilateral Conversations and Councils of Churches
        by Rev. Dr Hermen Shastri 133
    Authority in Contemporary Ecclesiology: Some Reflections
        by Rev. Dr Martyn Percy............................... 141
    Authority in Contemporary *Ecclesio* Theology
        by Mrs Sarah S. Kaulule 148
    Response to "Authority in Contemporary Ecclesiology: Some Reflections"
        by Dr Nicholas Constas............................... 154
    Authority and Authoritative Teaching: Report.................... 162

3. Ministry and Ordination in the Community of Women and Men in the Church................................. 167

    Ministry in Faith and Order: One Woman's Ecumenical Memory
        by Dr Mary Tanner................................... 169
    The Holy Spirit and Ministry: A Lutheran Perspective
        by Dr Bernd Oberdorfer 180
    The Holy Spirit and Ministry: Comments from a Latin American Woman
        by Rev. Araceli Ezzatti................................ 191
    Reflections on "Vocation" and "Ministry"
        by Dr Donna Geernaert 196
    Ministry and Vocation
        by Dr Urs von Arx................................... 203
    The Community of Women and Men in the Church Study: How Did It Come Into Being?
        by Rev. Dr Constance F. Parvey........................ 208
    Women's Ordination: An Extrinsic Issue
        by Dr Dimitra Koukoura.............................. 214
    Women's Priesthood as a Theological and Ecumenical Problem
        by Dr Nikolaos Matsoukas............................. 218
    A Lutheran Perspective
        by Rev. Dr Christine Globig........................... 223
    Ecumenical Developments in Ordination Rites
        by Rev. Dr James F. Puglisi........................... 226
    Ordination in the Eastern Churches
        by Rev. Dr Paul F. Bradshaw.......................... 242
    Ministry and Ordination in the Community of Women and Men in the Church: Aide-mémoire 247

Appendix

    Scriptural Images of the Church: An Eastern Orthodox Reflection
        by Hieromonk Alexander Golitzin....................... 255

Contributors 267

Preface

The main aim of this volume is to introduce theological contributions to the drafting process of *The Nature and Mission of the Church*,[1] the Faith and Order paper on ecclesiology. The process presented through these essays took place over the period 2001-2004. The consultations were intended in the first place to assist in revisions to an initial draft but also to raise important ecclesiological issues within the churches and beyond.

The selection of these papers was accomplished according to certain principles; the first criterion was to answer questions raised by a particular consultation and the second was to answer the challenges of ecumenical life through theological reflection from a particular setting.

The contributors to this volume come from a wide range of denominational backgrounds and countries. Most are themselves constructively engaged in ecumenical theology through their service in the churches and participation in bilateral or multilateral conversations.

We are indebted to the drafting group. Nine to ten high-profile theologians from Orthodox, Roman Catholic, Anglican, Lutheran, Reformed, United, Methodist and Pentecostal traditions worked hard throughout this process to improve the first draft, *The Nature and Purpose of the Church*, according to wisdom gleaned from the consultations as well as from responses to the draft and from the Faith and Order plenary commission meeting in Kuala Lumpur, Malaysia, in 2004.

The papers will help readers to think in a way consistent with ecumenical considerations concerning such fundamental ecclesiological issues as sacramentality, authority and ordained ministry in the church. The main intention of this volume is therefore to accompany and aid reflection on the nature and mission of the church from the ecumenical perspective, and thus to facilitate the reception of the Faith and Order ecclesiology document *The Nature and Mission of the Church*.

Each section of the book follows the same pattern and ends with a report from the consultation. The appendix contains a paper selected from those that were commissioned by the Faith and Order secretariat at various stages of the drafting process.

It was by a particular set of circumstances that I had to edit this volume on my own. The ecclesiology consultations were planned according to the recommendations of the Faith and Order standing commission and were masterminded by the director of Faith and Order at that time, Dr Alan Falconer, who by the time of preparation of the manuscript had moved back to his home country; therefore, I was left to complete the work and revise its content for publication. However, it is appropriate that Alan Falconer write the introduction.

Finally, I would like to thank my colleagues who in various measure helped in preparing this book, in particular Tom Best for his valuable advice, and Renate Sbeghen, Katyarina Pastoukhova and Alexander Freeman for providing valuable technical assistance.

My special gratitude goes to Mary Tanner, the former moderator of Faith and Order, whose passionate and scholarly questioning and wide ecumenical experience have provided a reliable source of support throughout the preparation of *One, Holy, Catholic and Apostolic*.

Tamara Grdzelidze

NOTE

[1] This document, which has grown out of *The Nature and Purpose of the Church* (1998), will be published shortly.

Introduction

REV. DR ALAN FALCONER

The papers and reports in this volume are part of a Faith and Order process to explore the nature and mission of the church. They contribute to this exploration and make a contribution to a fundamental text being developed within the international Faith and Order commission. To situate the contribution of these particular consultations to ecumenical dialogue on the nature of the church, it is important to place them in the context of the overall Faith and Order ecclesiology project.

In the responses of the churches to the Faith and Order study on Baptism, Eucharist and Ministry (BEM), many church commissions detected that there had been an underlying implicit ecclesiology, and called for a more explicit and focused study on the church.[1] While BEM itself had not specifically addressed the nature, purpose or form of the church, affirmations in each section of the statement about the church led readers to suggest that a baptismal or eucharistic ecclesiology was an implicit framework for the text, and that the threefold ministry as evident in some Christian traditions was being proposed as a *sine qua non* of and for the church.

In the light of those reactions, the plenary commission on Faith and Order, meeting in Budapest in 1989, proposed that the overall programme of Faith and Order should focus on "The Nature and Mission of the Church: Ecumenical Perspectives on Ecclesiology".[2] The commission felt that such a study might provide a coherent, comprehensive, ecclesiological framework for the studies on BEM, apostolic faith, and unity and renewal being undertaken by the commission, might respond to some of the critical comments to BEM, and could draw on the increasing ecumenical discussions on the understanding of the church evident in a number of international bilateral dialogues.[3] The recommendation was that previous work on the topic be brought into consideration alongside that on koinonia which was the subject of a number of bilateral dialogues, to provide basic ecumenical perspectives on ecclesiology which could serve as an impetus for the renewal and enrichment of the ecclesiologies of the different Christian traditions and thus for their convergence in the movement towards visible unity. Various themes for the development of the study were suggested – the church as the body of Christ, the temple of the Spirit, the people of God, the kingdom of God and the covenant. The intention was therefore not to develop a detailed ecclesiological system or even an "ecumenical ecclesiology".

The commission also found itself seeking to articulate for the Canberra assembly of the World Council of Churches in 1991 a statement on "The Unity of the Church as Koinonia: Gift and Calling". This statement, which was adopted at the assembly after a number of emendations, had been a response to a request from the central committee of the WCC. The statement begins with a reflection on the purpose of the church, rooted in the action of the Holy Trinity. It notes that the unity of the church to which we are called is a koinonia given and expressed in faith, worship, ministry and life, and then identifies a number of common actions which might help the churches to realize more faithfully the character and purposes of the church.[4]

A further reflection on koinonia also emerged from a series of essays published by the Joint Working Group between the Roman Catholic Church and the World Council of Churches. This was designed as an interpretative study on the Canberra text, setting it in the context of previous ecumenical statements on unity. It was also to be a contribution to the fifth world conference on Faith and Order in Santiago de Compostela in August 1993.[5]

After the Canberra assembly, the major work undertaken by the Faith and Order commission was the organization of the fifth world conference. This was the first such conference for thirty years, and was the first to draw on the fruits of full Roman Catholic participation in the ecumenical movement. The major theme was that of koinonia, and the conference sought to reflect on the theological and biblical understanding of koinonia, and on koinonia in faith, life and witness. A preparatory discussion paper was drafted and then examined in a number of regional conferences.[6] The conference itself explored the importance of an understanding of the Holy Trinity for an understanding of koinonia, and called for a study on the nature of the church – a community confessing the one faith to God's glory, sharing sacramental and ministerial life and engaging in common witness.[7]

In the light of these impulses, then, the Faith and Order standing commission in 1994 began a process of study and reflection on "The Nature and Purpose of the Church".

Faith and Order reflections on the church

The question of the nature of the church has been on the agenda of Faith and Order since its first world conference at Lausanne in 1927.

In the first stage of the ecumenical movement as the churches sought to move from a situation of competition with each other, and to move towards acceptance of each other's existence and co-existence, they adopted an approach which was at root "comparative". Churches compared their stances on doctrinal questions with each other. Thus, in the early Faith and Order conferences a comparative approach to the church was evident. Each tradition presented papers on its confessional understanding of the subject. In Lausanne, papers were presented by His Beatitude Chrysostom (Orthodox – Greece), Dr S. Parkes Cadman (Congregational – US), Rt Rev. Dr Alexander Raffey (Lutheran – Reformed), Dr Friedrich Siegmund-Schultze (Evangelical Lutheran – Germany), Dr H.B. Workman (Methodist – UK), Prof. Fernand Ménégoz (Lutheran – France), Metropolitan Stefan (Orthodox – Bulgaria). The second world conference in Edinburgh in 1937 reflected on "The Church of Christ and the Word of God", using a similar methodology.[8] The same method was also in evidence at the third world conference on Faith and Order in Lund 1952. Papers on "The Nature of the Church" were presented on behalf of the church of Rome (Dr Newton Flew), and from the Greek Orthodox church, the German and Scandinavian Lutheran churches, the Reformed churches in Scotland and other European countries, the Church of England, the Old Catholic Church, Baptists, Congregationalists, the Society of Friends, Methodists, Churches of Christ and the Church of South India. While this was a comprehensive, comparative approach, it became clear that such a methodology was no longer appropriate.[9] This comparative methodology, however, is at root not a method of dialogue, but one of monologue. It can be characterized by the phrase "we will accept you as long as you are the same as us, but we will reject you at the points of difference". Edwin Muir phrased this well in his poem, "The Solitary Place":

> If there is none else to ask or reply
> But I and not I,
> And when I stretch out my hand, my hand comes towards me
> To pull me across to me and back to me,
> If my own mind, questioning, answers me,
> If all that I see
> Woman and man and beast and rock and sky,
> Is a flat image shut behind an eye,
> And only my thoughts can meet me or pass me or follow me,

> O then I am alone
> I, many and many in one
> A lost player upon a hill.[10]

With our own perspectives as the only acceptable positions, it was possible only to affirm the status quo – "the solitary place". The comparative method evident in doctrinal and church and society discussions in the first phase of the ecumenical movement moved interchurch relations from conflict, competition and co-existence to comparative acceptance. However, it was evident that such a method could not effect real relationship – communion. At Lund, therefore, a different methodology was adopted. Theological discussions now proceeded on the basis of an attempt to reach consensus. The conference, as has been noted, received a comprehensive series of confessional papers on the nature of the church. But it noted,

> We cannot build the one church by cleverly fitting together our divided inheritances. We can grow together towards fullness and unity in Christ only by being conformed to him who is the Head of the body and Lord of his people.

The statement then explored the complementarity of the various understandings, identified the one-sidedness of many approaches, and called the church to reassert its nature as the pilgrim people:

> Those who are ever looking backward and have accumulated much previous ecclesiastical baggage will perhaps be shown that pilgrims must travel light and that, if we are to share at last in the great supper, we must let go much that we treasure... We cannot know all that shall be disclosed to us when together we look to him who is the Head of the body. It is easy for us in our several churches to think of what our separated brethren need to learn. Christ's love will make us more ready to learn what He can teach us through them.[11]

This approach to doctrinal questions was matched also by the attempt to act as churches in a cooperative and consensual manner. The Lund world conference adopted what came to be known as the Lund principle:

> Should not our churches ask themselves whether they are showing sufficient eagerness to enter into conversation with other churches, and whether they should not act together in all matters except those in which deep differences of conviction compel them to act separately?[12]

This question addressed to the churches proposed a new relationship between the churches. It in fact became a methodology adopted in doctrinal and church and society discussions. The comparative methodology began to give way to a consensus methodology. In this, the churches sought to do theology together. They sought together out of the riches of their confessional traditions to affirm a common theology. An underlying understanding of the nature of the church was also evident at Lund. The church was described as the pilgrim people of God – a community which learns from each other on the journey and seeks to discern truth. A first stage in this new method was reached through the attempt by the commission to agree on how to do theology together – the discussion on scripture and Tradition at the fourth world conference on Faith and Order in Montreal in 1963 and subsequent discussions on the interpretation of scripture.[13] On the basis of this agreement on method it has been possible to reach consensus on baptism, eucharist and ministry; on the common confession of the apostolic faith; and on a wide variety of doctrinal questions evident in bilateral and multilateral dialogues. The consensus methodology pursued in doctrinal and church and society discussions has encouraged the churches to move beyond the "solitary place".

In the period after the Faith and Order world conference at Montreal, while there was no specific study undertaken on the nature and purpose of the church, a number of ecclesiological questions were the subject of discussion, e.g. catholicity. As noted above, however, it became clear after reviewing the responses to BEM that it was important that this subject be examined.

The nature and purpose of the church

1. Its framework and method

With this background on the impulses for the study on the nature of the church, and on the methodology of the Faith and Order commission, the work towards a convergence text on ecclesiology began. In the course of four years, three different attempts were made to find an appropriate framework.

In the first attempt, at a consultation in Dublin in 1994, discussions focused on perceived church-dividing issues, e.g. apostolicity and catholicity as elements of the life and faith of the church as koinonia; forms of authority and decision-making in the service of the church as koinonia; the place and mission of the church as koinonia in the saving purpose of God. These materials were then placed in a wider framework by a drafting group of the commission at Barbados in November 1994 – the purpose of God; the church of the triune God; the nature and mission of the church; word, sacrament and ministry; local church and the communion of local churches; church and history; church and kingdom, and an attempt was made to identify converging understandings towards mutual recognition.[14] It became apparent that it was not sufficient to address specific issues on ecclesiology, since it was perceived that a number of assumptions were being made on ecclesiology which were not shared by all the traditions in Faith and Order.

In the attempt to find a wider framework for a convergence text, the drafting group of the commission began to use the Canberra statement on koinonia. In doing this, much of the previous work was adapted to the new framework which was to be a "scholion" – to use the term of the late Fr Jean-Marie Tillard – or memorandum and trajectory drafted on the basis of the Canberra text. This text was presented to the meeting of the plenary commission meeting at Moshi, Tanzania, in August 1996.[15] On the basis of discussions there and in subsequent reflections in the drafting group, it was agreed that it was not appropriate to use the Canberra statement as a basis, since it might give the impression either that the text had been adopted at Canberra on the basis of such an understanding, or that the Canberra text provided a sufficient theological outline on ecclesiology.

It was therefore decided to attempt a statement on the church in the style of the BEM methodology, viz. to produce what was felt to be a convergence text, but identifying those questions where it was thought that convergence had still to be reached (material placed in boxes). In all this struggle to find an appropriate framework, the drafters sought to draw on the agreements of international bilateral dialogues, on previous Faith and Order work, on the understanding and images of the church in holy scripture, and on the other studies being undertaken by the commission, e.g. on hermeneutics, worship and ethics. In particular, two discrete projects were drawn on.

After the Canberra assembly, the Faith and Order commission and the Justice, Peace and Integrity of Creation team in the World Council of Churches began an exploration of the relation between ecclesiology and ethics. While this was designed to bring those two streams of work in the WCC into closer relationship, the reports of the study process emphasize the rootedness of discipleship in the sacrament of baptism and the Lord's supper, and that ethical engagement is an expression of koinonia.[16] The very existence of the church makes a statement to society. The study process explored ways in which that statement about and to society is firmly and intentionally rooted in the reflection and life of the Christian community.

Second, in the light of the bilateral dialogues, a request was made to the commission by the meeting of representatives of United and Uniting churches at Ocho Rios, Jamaica, in 1995, that a study on *episcope* and episcopacy be undertaken.[17] The last such study had been published in 1979 and had made an important contribution to the discussion on ministry in BEM.[18] There, two distinctions had proved to be fruitful – viz. that between apostolic succession and apostolic tradition and that between *episcope* and episcopacy. But since that time, a number of bilateral dialogues have considered the question, a number of church unions have been effected and a number of regional ecumenical agreements, e.g. between Anglicans and Lutherans, have come into effect. The consultation on *episcope* and episcopacy in Strasbourg, therefore, presented a comprehensive account of the state of the question and sought to move forward on the issue. While the papers and consultation reports have been published, the study on the nature and purpose of the church drew on the reports for its own section on the ministry of oversight.[19]

The study paper on *The Nature and Purpose of the Church* employed a method similar to that used in BEM, drew on previous work undertaken by the Faith and Order commission and the international bilateral dialogues, and incorporated the results of discrete studies on ecclesiology and ethics and *episcope* and episcopacy in the quest for the visible unity of the church (a similar methodology was to be applied to the subsequent phase of the project – see below).

2. The text of "The Nature and Purpose of the Church"

The study has six chapters. The first, "The Church of the Triune God", explores the nature of the church and God's purpose for the church. In the first part, the major focus is on the church as creation of the Word and of the Holy Spirit (*creatura Verbi et creatura Spiritus*), thus emphasizing that the church belongs to God, is created, nourished and sustained by God and because of God is one, holy, catholic and apostolic. This is further elaborated by an exposition of three central biblical images which refer to the trinitarian dimension of the church – the people of God, the body of Christ and the temple of the Holy Spirit. None of these images is exclusive, but all of them implicitly or explicitly include the other trinitarian dimension as well.

The development of the section on God's purpose for the church is rooted in Ephesians chapter 1 and John 17. The church participates in God's mission of healing, reconciliation, and anticipates the new humanity which is God's intention for creation. An examination of this section shows that it draws on bilateral dialogues, e.g. the Reformed-Roman Catholic statement "Towards a Common Understanding of the Church", and on previous work reflecting on the Canberra statement, and reflects the direction for a statement which the Budapest plenary commission meeting indicated.

The second, and perhaps the most contentious, chapter of the statement focuses on the church in history. This is an attempt to explore the church in its human dimension. The statement declares that the church

> is exposed to change, which allows for both positive development and growth as well as for the negative possibility of decline and distortion. It is exposed to individual, cultural and historical conditioning which can contribute to a richness of insights and expressions of faith but also to relativizing tendencies or absolutizing particular views. It is exposed to the Holy Spirit's free use of its power (John 3:8) in illuminating hearts and binding consciences. It is exposed to the power of sin.[20]

In this carefully worded section, the church is described as a historical reality, exposed to the ambiguity of all human history, and thus not yet the community God desires. And yet – the church is called to be the sign and instrument of God's design. The chapter carefully reflects the tension between that which the church is and that which the church is called to become, and elaborates the further questions to be explored as the churches seek to move towards convergence. Of course, it is too facile to identify the different approaches as simply stances taken by different confessional traditions. The controversies surrounding the actions and words of Pope John Paul II on reconciliation and his pleas for forgiveness particularly in the context of the Jubilee year celebrations (e.g. 12 March 2000) demonstrate differences of approach within the Christian communions also.

The third chapter discusses the church as koinonia. The rich tapestry of the scriptural understanding is presented and summed up in the following paragraph:

> The basic verbal form from which the noun koinonia derives means "to have something in common", "to share", "to participate", "to have part in", "to act together" or "to be in a contractual relationship involving obligations of mutual accountability".[21]

While most of those definitions have appeared in previous discussions on koinonia, the new definition is one which is evident in the New Testament and draws on the business world of contract and of mutual accountability. Koinonia entails and is predicated upon mutual accountability to each other in Christ. Through Christ we are bound to each other, and are involved in a dialogue with each other which invites us to give an account of our stewardship of faith, life and witness. This chapter continues by exploring the relation between unity and diversity, and the church as a communion of local churches, thus emphasizing the importance of understanding the church as a community which exhibits diverse expressions and experiences, and a community which seeks to express koinonia in a variety of diverse cultural circumstances and geographical locations.

Life in communion is the subject of the fourth chapter of the text. God bestows on the church apostolic faith, baptism and eucharist as means of grace to create and sustain the koinonia, and this koinonia is furthered by structures of ministry, oversight and conciliarity. In this section, the reflections of the commission on apostolic faith, baptism, eucharist and ministry provide the basis of the convergent text, and further questions in each area are identified for future work. The chapter seeks to draw on the convergence evident in the responses of the churches to BEM and to take discussion forward on disputed questions. Thus the discussion on oversight places the issue in the context of balancing the communal, personal and collegial dimensions of *episcope*, and notes that in fact the ecumenical movement itself is increasingly leading to a degree of shared oversight in many parts of the world. The chapter points to the importance of conciliarity and primacy but notes that fundamental and basic work needs to be done on this before any common statements can be attempted.

The fifth chapter of the text examines service in and for the world. For a considerable period of the drafting process, there was a move towards including this in chapter four. For some churches, the marks of the church are that the church is the community of word, sacrament and discipline (cf. the Scots confession of 1560), where discipline refers to the care of the poor, the refugee, the health of the community and the nurture of the community through education. Thus certain issues described as ethical may be deemed *status quaestionis*, e.g. inclusion of all people regardless of race or gender. For many churches, however, the church is the community of word and sacrament, and discipline is an explication of the community formed by the word and nourished by the sacrament. This chapter then explores Christian discipleship as bearing witness to God's reconciling, healing and transforming of creation. This discipleship is based on the life and teaching of Jesus of Nazareth.

The final chapter is an encouragement to churches, communions, councils and theological institutes to examine the text and send their reflections to the commission for a further process of drafting.

3. The continuing process

In 1998, the text was sent widely to churches, councils of churches, ecumenical and theological institutes for comment. The new standing commission identified a twofold process for the continuing work. Having received some 45 responses from church commissions, theological institutes and councils of churches, the commission established a drafting group to emend *The Nature and Purpose of the Church*. Many of these responses highlighted certain areas where it was felt that subsequent work was needed – areas which coincided with those already identified by the commission. Among these areas it was clear that for many the relationship between church and mission needed to have a higher focus in the text – perhaps even providing one of its main threads. This had been one of the areas already identified in the Budapest report of 1989. Other concerns related to the question as to whether the church itself has a sacramental nature, the role of authority in the church (the subject of a consultation process in Dublin 1994) and the issue of ordination in the community of women and men in the church.

It was therefore agreed that a series of consultations on these specific themes be held. The consultations would explore the issues in their own right. They were not to be examinations of the issues as they appeared in *The Nature and Purpose of the Church*. Rather, a fresh examination of these issues was sought. The results of the papers and reports of the consultations would then be fed into the work of the re-drafting group who would have discretion as to what would prove to be helpful to their process.

The first of these consultations was held in conjunction with the commission on World Mission and Evangelism in Germany on "Ecclesiology and Mission". The papers and report were published as the April 2001 edition of the *International Review of Mission*, and the results discussed by the re-drafting group.

The other three topics were the results of separate consultations and the papers and reports are presented in this volume.

The methods of the consultations

As in the work of the commission when it produced *The Nature and Purpose of the Church*, the consultations sought to explore the work which had already been undertaken by the Faith and Order commission and by the various bilateral dialogues on the topic under consideration. Scholars were invited to examine the reports of Faith and Order, and to analyze the various dialogues undertaken by Christian world communions, and thus draw on insights gained as churches have sought convergence and agreement. An important aspect of the planning process for the consultations was to invite scholars who had not been members of the dialogues themselves to explore the bilateral and multilateral reports. It was hoped that in this way an objective examination would help to identify important themes and issues for the discussions. In the consultation on authority and authoritative teaching it was also possible to draw on work being undertaken simultaneously on the topic by the Faith and Order commission of the National Council of Churches of Christ in the USA.

A further desire of the planners was to ensure that the results of current reflection on these issues within the theological community would also be presented so that new horizons might be evident. In all the consultations this did indeed prove productive.

In the consultation on authority and authoritative teaching, for example, the issue of authority was placed in the wider context of the holiness of the church, thus making it possible to examine the wider context in which it is necessary to consider the question and to be made aware of the way in which a recognition of authority in other traditions can be made possible. It was also important that the discussion of authority in the church was also explored in the context of discussion of authority in contemporary societies from the perspective of a sociologist.

This widening of the horizon of the topic under consideration was particularly important in the consultation on ministry and ordination in the community of women and men in the church. This was perhaps the issue which had provoked the most heated exchanges within the Faith and Order commission in the planning process. Clearly it was a most sensitive issue, particularly for some churches. This was the first occasion on which the Faith and Order commission had directly addressed the issue of the ordination of women as such. However, it was important that this consultation did not simply rehearse the discussion points which had emerged in bilateral dialogues or within churches as they sought to address the question – important as these were. The consultation therefore explored the topic in the framework of the Holy Spirit and vocation, and through an examination of the ordination rites of the various traditions. When a church ordains a person to ministry of word and sacrament, what is it saying about the nature and character of the office and its place in the total ministry of the church? In the event this consultation, I believe, proved to be alive to the sensitivities of all traditions and positions.

In all the consultations there was a pervasive atmosphere of respect and listening. The reports make clear that the last word on any of the issues has not emerged. But these are useful staging posts in terms both of content and of method for subsequent explorations.

In this introduction, I have not sought to give an analysis of the various contributions or reports. Nor has it been possible to convey the tensions and frustrations of the consultation processes, nor the wonderful atmospheres generated and the relief when agreement became evident. The work of multilateral discussions is imperative for the work of bringing the churches towards unity. It does not concentrate solely on historic disagreements but offers possibilities for new insights which emerge from a wider perspective, drawing on other traditions and the results of contemporary research and reflections. May this volume contribute to the search for ecumenical agreement and bring us closer to that unity which our Lord wills and which is essential if the church is to reflect God's intention for humankind.

NOTES

[1] See Max Thurian ed., *Churches Respond to BEM*, vols I-VI, WCC, 1986-88.
[2] See Thomas Best ed., *Faith and Order 1985-1989: The Commission Meeting at Budapest 1989*, Faith and Order Paper no. 148, WCC Publications, 1990, pp.202ff., 216ff.
[3] See Harding Meyer and Lukas Vischer eds, *Growth in Agreement*, Faith and Order Paper no. 108, WCC, 1984, and Jeffrey Gros, Harding Meyer and William Rusch eds, *Growth in Agreement II*, Faith and Order Paper no. 187, WCC Publications, 2000, for the reports of the various dialogues.
[4] In *Growth in Agreement II*, pp.937ff.
[5] Günther Gassmann and John Radano eds, *The Unity of the Church as Koinonia: Ecumenical Perspectives on the 1991 Canberra Statement on Unity*, Faith and Order Paper no. 163, WCC, 1993.
[6] *Towards Koinonia in Faith, Life and Witness: A Discussion Paper*, Faith and Order Paper no. 161, WCC, 1993, and Thomas Best and Günther Gassmann eds, *Regional Consultations in Preparation for the Fifth World Conference on Faith and Order: Summary Reports*, Faith and Order Paper no. 163, WCC, 1993.
[7] See Thomas Best and Günther Gassmann eds, *On the Way to Fuller Koinonia: Official Report of the Fifth World Conference on Faith and Order*, Faith and Order Paper no. 166, WCC Publications, 1994.
[8] See H.N. Bates ed., *Faith and Order: Proceedings of the World Conference, Lausanne 1927*, New York, George Doron, 1927; Leonard Hodgson ed., *The Second World Conference on Faith and Order: Edinburgh 1937*, New York, Macmillan, 1938.
[9] R. Newton Flew ed., *The Nature of the Church: Papers Presented to the Theological Commission Appointed by the Continuation Committee of the World Conference on Faith and Order*, London, SCM Press, 1952.
[10] Edwin Muir, *Collected Poems*, London, Faber, 1960, p.81.
[11] Oliver Tomkins ed., *The Third World Conference on Faith and Order, Lund 1952*, London, SCM Press, 1953, pp.20f.
[12] *Ibid.*
[13] See P.C. Rodger and Lukas Vischer eds, *The Fourth World Conference on Faith and Order: The Report from Montreal 1963*, London, SCM Press, 1964, and Ellen Flesseman-van Leer ed., *The Bible: Its Authority and Interpretation in the Ecumenical Movement*, WCC, 1980.
[14] See the *Minutes of the Meeting of the Faith and Order Standing Commission*, Aleppo, Faith and Order Paper no. 170, WCC, 1994.
[15] See Alan Falconer ed., *Faith and Order in Moshi*, Faith and Order Paper no. 177, WCC, 1998, pp.97-114, 232-63.
[16] See Thomas Best and Martin Robra eds, *Ecclesiology and Ethics: Ecumenical Ethical Engagement, Moral Formation and the Nature of the Church*, WCC, 1997.
[17] See Thomas Best ed., *Built Together: The Present Vocation of United and Uniting Churches*, Faith and Order Paper no. 174, WCC, 1996.

[18] *Episkope and Episcopate in Ecumenical Perspective*, Faith and Order Paper no. 102, WCC, 1980.
[19] Peter Bouteneff and Alan Falconer eds, *Episcope and Episcopacy and the Quest for Visible Unity*, Faith and Order Paper no. 183, WCC, 1999.
[20] *The Nature and Purpose of the Church: A Stage on the Way to a Common Statement*, Faith and Order Paper no. 181, WCC, 1998, p.18, §37.
[21] *Ibid.*, p.25 §52.

1

Does the Church Have a Sacramental Nature?

6-11 June 2001
Ottawa, Canada

Does the Church Have a Sacramental Nature?

An Orthodox Perspective

REV. DR EMMANUEL CLAPSIS

The question whether the church has a sacramental nature gains legitimacy, at least for Orthodox theologians, from the conversational setting of the ecumenical movement that aims to develop a convergence in ecclesiology that may advance and further deepen the unity of God's churches. The question itself is raised because for some Christian churches and ecumenists the church is the sacrament of God's presence in the world, while others believe that while Christ is the sacrament of God's grace in the world, the church must not be called a sacrament. The church is only a privileged instrument of God's grace that ultimately leads to unity in the church of the whole world with Christ. This differentiation reveals theological convictions and historical sensitivities formative of particular confessional identities and needs to be taken seriously in our effort to craft an ecumenical convergence on ecclesiology.

The ecumenical space in which we are discussing this matter demands a constructive ecumenical ecclesiology faithful to the early apostolic tradition and at the same time sensitive to particular traditions that different Christian churches have developed in their history. The ecclesiology that we are called to develop, after we have heard each other, while it will reflect our unity in a common understanding of what the church is, will challenge us to enhance our particular ecclesiologies, expanding our horizon of understanding of what the church is in such a way that we include the others in our views. Finally, it will not be enough to note the differences that churches continue to have with each other, but we must answer the question of whether such differences, after the assurances we have given to each in our common quest for unity, continue to be divisive or to be different expressions and embodiments of the same truth about the church.

The sacramentality of the church in ecumenical dialogues

The church has been understood as mystery or sacrament by many Christian churches, but it became a central concept in ecclesiology through its extensive use by the Second Vatican Council. *Lumen Gentium* in particular begins its description of the church with the term mystery and *sacrament*. "The church is truly in Christ as a sacrament, that is, as a sign and instrument for achieving the most intimate union with God and also towards the union of all humanity" (no. 1). Other passages in the same constitution employ the term "sacrament" to refer to the church. God "has called together and established his church so that she might be for one and all the visible sacrament of this saving unity" (no. 9,3). Jesus Christ "risen from the dead, he shared his life-giving Spirit with his disciples and through them he made his body, the church, into an all-embracing sacrament of salvation" (no. 48,2; cf. also no. 59). For the elucidation of the term "sacrament", the following is to be found in the documents:

> Normally the term "sacrament" in the widest sense, or "mystery" or sign of "salvation", is used for Jesus Christ... With the church fathers this term often refers to the whole economy of salvation, which includes the various liturgical exercises of the church. For that reason the same church is called "sacrament" or "mystery".[1]

The text makes clear in what sense the church may be regarded as a sacrament, namely, only in its coming from Christ and thus only in dependence upon him. Furthermore, the unity of the human community and of the cosmos with Christ in the church is an event that the Holy Spirit makes possible. The emphasis on the sacramental nature of the church gives primacy to the divine element in the church's life.

The Reformed-Roman Catholic dialogue in its report "Towards a Common Understanding of the Church (1984-1990)" insists that Christ is the primordial sacrament of God and the sacramentality of the church is wholly dependent upon the lordship of Christ and the work of the Holy Spirit. The dialogue participants were not able, however, to agree on the nature of this dependence of the church on Christ and the Holy Spirit:

> We do not yet understand the nature of this salutary activity in the same way. The Reformed commonly allege that Catholics appropriate to the church the role proper to Christ. Roman Catholics, for their part, commonly accuse the Reformed of holding the church apart from the work of salvation and of giving up the assurance that Christ is truly present and acting in his church. Both these views are caricatures, but they can help to focus attention on genuine underlying differences of perspective, of which the themes of *creatura verbi* and *sacramentum gratiae* serve as symbols (no. 112).

In the statement on church and justification of the Lutheran-Roman Catholic dialogue, the interlocutors stated that neither the foundation of the church nor its goal lies in the church itself, and that it therefore does not exist by itself or for itself. Only in and through Christ, only in and through the Holy Spirit is the church effectual as a mediator of salvation" (no. 122). It is part of the logic of such a sacramental concept of the church that the church in its human weakness must "incessantly pursue the path of penance and renewal" and be called to "continual reformation". In response to whether the church is the only mediator of salvation granted to the world by God, the dialogue concludes that this is a matter of difference between wholeness and the partial. It affirms that outside the "visible structure" of the church, "many elements of sanctification and of truth can be found" and God's saving activity is visibly and latently at work at the same time among "those who have not yet received the gospel" (no. 124).

Lutherans in this dialogue will note that it is of paramount importance for their theological tradition to affirm as clearly as possible that God alone bestows forgiveness, life and salvation on every believer through the means of grace, word and sacraments. The church, as the "assembly of all believers", is the place "in" which these means of grace are effectual (no. 125). The church, for Lutheran theologians, is "in a derivative sense an instrument of salvation" (no. 126). "As mediator of word and sacrament the church is the instrument through which the Holy Spirit sanctifies; it is the mother that begets and bears every Christian through the word of God", but in such a way that Jesus Christ himself is working and becomes salvifically present in its preaching and administration of the sacraments (no. 127). Lutherans, while they will not be hesitant to affirm that the church imparts participation in salvation to believers, nevertheless will insist that it is Christ alone and not the church who has gained salvation for the world and who bestows on believers participation in this salvation through word and sacrament" (no. 127). They also warned that viewing the church as "sacrament" must not contradict the fact that the church, "the community of believers", as people justified by God are at the same time holy and sinful.

Lutheran theologians have agreed with the Catholics that the church is instrument and sign of salvation and, in this sense, a "sacrament" of salvation (no. 134). This agreement presupposes their queries about sacramentality. The unfilled lacunae in their theological reflection about the church's sacramentality that needs further reflection is what the Reformed-Roman Catholic dialogue had also recognized as still an unresolved issue: "how Christ and the church are one in sacramental activity without thereby being identified, and how a possible sacramental view of the church therefore has its roots in the fundamental description of Christ as the primal sacrament and is limited by that statement" (no. 131).

Neither the Anglican-Roman Catholic dialogue or the Orthodox-Roman Catholic dialogue has recognized this as a matter for further reflection, although both consider the church to be the sacrament of God's presence in the world entirely dependent on God, established and nourished by the risen Christ and the Holy Spirit for the salvation of the world. The second Anglican-Roman Catholic International Commission in its agreed statement on "Church as Communion" uses scriptural language to affirm the sacramentality of the church. The church serves God's purpose to bring the whole creation into communion with life in God. This is definitively realized in Jesus Christ: Jesus Christ by who he was, by what he taught and by what he accomplished. This communion with God through Christ is "constantly established and renewed through the power of the Holy Spirit". It is through God's Spirit that the richness of God's grace becomes actively present in the church. Since the church by the grace of God reveals and embodies the "mystery of Christ" (cf. Eph. 1:23, 3:4,8-11) it is rightly described as the visible sign which both points to and embodies our communion with God and with one another. It is a foretaste of the fullness of communion to be consummated when Christ is all and in all. It is a "mystery" or "sacrament" (no. 17).

The Eastern Orthodox-Roman Catholic dialogue affirms that the primordial sacrament is Christ himself. It is affirmed that Christ, who is "the sacrament par excellence", given by the Father for the world, continues by the power of God's Spirit to offer to the world unity with God. To refer to the sacramental nature of Christ is to bring to mind the possibility given to humanity, and through humanity to the whole cosmos, to experience the "new creation", the kingdom of God here and now through material and created realities. However, what we receive in sacramental form is "a foretaste", "a pledge" of eternal life and "sign of the kingdom of God". Through and in baptism and the eucharist, the Holy Spirit and Christ indissolubly unite creation with God (no. 4b). The faithful, the baptized Christians, participate in this communion through repentance (metanoia) and confession *(exomologesis)* that allows the Holy Spirit to transform them by cleansing their souls and bring through them the whole world into unity with God in Jesus Christ.

Turning to the theological reflection of Faith and Order, we must note that the sacramentality of the church received particular attention at the Faith and Order consultation in Chantilly in 1985.[2] It is interesting that this study opted to explore the sacramentality of the church through the biblical concept of mystery. The report of this consultation became a section of the study *Church and World* published in 1990. In *Church and World* the word "mystery" is explicated:

> When the word "mystery" is applied to the church, it refers to the church as a reality which transcends its empirical, historical expression – a reality which is rooted in, and sustained and shaped by, the communion of the Father, Son and Holy Spirit.[3]

It signifies what the church already is by the grace of the Holy Spirit that brings the faithful into unity in Christ and in communion with each other as they move towards the fullness of Christ's kingdom: "The unity of the divine-human relationship revealed in Jesus Christ is therefore the foundation of unity and community for God's people" (no. 18). The followers of Christ participate in God's life only through the work of the Holy Spirit that imparts in them participation in God's life. In another more recent statement of Faith and Order what the church is by the grace of God's spirit is clearly affirmed:

> As in the life of Christ the Holy Spirit was active from the conception to the resurrection, so also in the life of the church the same Spirit of God forms Christ in all believers and their community. The Spirit incorporates human beings into the body of Christ through faith and baptism, enlivens and strengthens them as the body of Christ nourished and sustained at the Lord's supper, and leads them to the full accomplishment of their vocation (no. 11).

The *Church and World* study connects the sacramentality of the church with its vocation to the sign that effectively reveals the future of the world in God's love:

> As the body of Christ, the church participates in the divine mystery. As mystery, it reveals Christ to the world by proclaiming the gospel, by celebrating the sacraments (which are themselves called "mysteries"), and by manifesting the newness of life given by him, and thus anticipating the kingdom already present in him (no. 21, p.27).

It suggests that what the church is as mystery must not be seen separately from what the church is for the world. The terms "mystery" and "sign", seen as closely inter-related and complementary expressions of the church's being and mission, are particularly important.

> The mystery of God's presence in the church is already a sign addressed to the world. And the church as a sign is an invitation to the world to let itself be permeated by the divine mystery. These two ecclesiological perspectives are always in tension with the reality of the church as a historical, human commu-

nity. This tension cannot be solved by separating the "divine nature" of the church from its "human nature". Rather, this tension is the deepest challenge to a constant renewal of the life of the church in order that it may better correspond to its divine calling and mission as mystery and sign for the world (no. 23, p.27).

An Orthodox perspective

For Orthodox theology, the church is understood to be primarily an asymmetrical divine-human reality. It is always the pre-eminent active presence of God in the church and what God accomplishes through it for the world that defines its nature. "Orthodox theology never treats the earthly aspect of the church in isolation, but thinks always of the church in Christ and the Holy Spirit."[4]

The church is the mystery in which God unites all creation in Christ through those whom God has chosen by the Holy Spirit for the salvation of the world. It is the mystery of God's salvific presence in the world. The great mystery of salvation, however, is Christ himself, and the communion of Christ with the world in the church is a mystery in a derivative sense. This communion augments the glorified humanity of Jesus with the fullness of God's creation. The church, for Orthodox ecclesiology, is not just the assembly of the faithful who are united in their memory of, adherence to, and proclamation of the gospel. It is the unity of such people with God, made possible through the incarnation, life, death and resurrection of God's Word and the work of the Holy Spirit. As such the church cannot be exhaustively described or defined since it is always more than what we can understand, observe or even experience. It is a mystery, a real event grounded in the incarnation of God's Word and God's redemptive and salvific work in Christ, nourished by the unceasing work of the Holy Spirit. In the words of Fr Dumitru Staniloae:

> Christ is the climactic central mystery from which a power of attraction operates permanently to draw human beings into union with him, making this union of which He is the centre the enlarged mystery of the church. Christ is the source from which the power which continually maintains the divine life in the church unceasingly springs... Because it is a life of love, the life which springs from Christ is communicated to them by another divine Person, the Holy Spirit. The Holy Spirit inspires human beings with love for Christ, makes them responsive to his love as their chief Brother, and breathes into them his filial love for the Father.[5]

Thus, for the Orthodox tradition the church is not an autonomous entity that dispenses salvation through its sacraments. It is rather the expansion of Christ's mystery into the present, while Christ remains as its centre and its founder. The church is "a kind of Christ's epiphany in and through his people in history",[6] "the embodiment of God's saving action in the temporal order". *It is in and through the church, and by the power of the Holy Spirit, that God's salvific work continues in Christ.* While Orthodoxy recognizes the need to affirm that Christ through God's Spirit is the primary mystery of God's presence in the world, its sacramental ecclesiology does not allow any dissociation of Christ from the church.[7]

The church as a divine-human reality is the mystery of God's presence in the world. Mystery refers to God's self-communication through human, created realities. The "sacral" event, as Nikos Nissiotis wrote, "consists in the fact that God has singled out a channel of communication, specific and visible, by using worldly elements in order to penetrate history and restore the broken communion with man, giving his grace anew in a special way".[8] Referring to the church as mystery means that the church as a distinctive concrete event and institution has its origins in God and its members are called out of the world to participate in God's active love for the world. The church does not possess its own being as a self-perfecting community but it exists from God and for the world, being that part of the world that reflects the restored communion between God and the world. The restored communion of God with the world, as we experience it through and in the church, is an anticipation of the coming kingdom of God in which we participate with hope and which exercises an immediate pressure on history. Eschatology in the church's sacramental life becomes a real presence in history.[9] It reveals the future of the world and thus conditions decisively the church's life and witness.

The church, despite the primacy of the sovereignty of God's grace in its life, exists in history and its historical *facticity* is an element of its being that cannot be ignored. The real challenge for an ecumenical convergence on ecclesiology is how we can take seriously the church's earthly, created and human aspects without surrendering the pre-eminent sovereignty of God's grace in defining her nature. If the church is a *theanthropic* (divine-human) reality then its humanity can be understood only as it relates to Christ and the Holy Spirit. Any attempt to study the human or created element of the church's being apart from its unity with God leads to misunderstandings of what the church of God is. Orthodox theologians will insist that the church is a sacramental and sociological community, spiritual and temporal. The church, as Nissiotis stated, "is not only a divine institution but also a human, 'sociological' one in the full sense. Those who forget it are, *in praxis*, monophysites, and their 'sacramental vision' is introverted, seriously defective and therefore fruitless."[10] Perhaps this kind of criticism is addressed to those theologians who detach the church from the world and its historical context, failing to integrate the human aspect of the church in their ecclesiology and advancing a form of sacramentalism that leads to ecclesiolatry. Orthodox theologians will insist that those elements of the world that we discern in life of the church in history are not determinative of the church's nature.

> The church is not to be understood in terms of human worldly power of earthly authority and jurisdiction. In ecclesiology then, we must be exceedingly careful not to take as a "model" some political or cultural forms existing in the secular pluralistic society around us. We must not assimilate the church to monarchist structures like those of the Roman empire, or hierarchies like those of medieval feudalism, or even to the patterns like those of modern democracy.[11]

The church, because it is the unity of the faithful and through them of the whole creation with God, cannot be anything less than holy because it has been cleansed by the Holy Spirit and united with God by participating in the glorified humanity of Christ. Yet, from a human perspective the baptized Christians, the faithful who constituted the visible church by the grace of the Holy Spirit, are not always reflective of God's holiness. The Orthodox church distinguishes baptized Christians in their sinfulness from the church. While Christians may be sinners, the church as the body of Christ is forever holy. Gennadios Limouris suggests that the dogma of Chalcedon can be helpful in understanding the *theanthropic* (divine-human) nature of the church:

> The dogma of Chalcedon must be applied to the church as well as to Christ. Just as Christ the God-Man has two natures – divine and human – so in the church there is *synergia* or cooperation between the two that the one is perfect and sinless, while the other is not yet fully so. Only a part of the humanity of the church – the saints, in heaven – has attained perfection, while here on earth the church's members often misuse their human freedom. The church on earth exists in a state of tension: it is already the body of Christ, and thus perfect and sinless, and yet, since its members are imperfect and sinful, it must continually become what it is.[12]

Orthodox theologians will differentiate the church as body of Christ, temple of the Holy Spirit and new creation from the faithful who may misuse their freedom and commit sins incompatible with their faith in God.

While Christ grants salvation to the world in and through the church, these believers who may constitute the church in history either as particular persons or a collective entity may not live the fullness of the gospel and be in Christ despite their baptism and their participation in the sacramental life of the church. Baptism is not a magical guarantee against the possibility of becoming once again a slave to the devil and thus being excluded from the body of Christ (1 Cor. 5:1-3; 2 Thess. 3:6-14; 2 Tim. 3:5 (St John Chrysostom, 3rd Homily on Ephesians, 4). "On the steep and dangerous road to the Land of Promise, from Sunday to Sunday, and from day to day, one may fall into the hands of Satan and be cut off from the body of Christ."[13] The faithful engrafted into Christ's body through baptism must again and again re-receive the grace of God through repentance and conversion as they hear the gospel of Jesus Christ and invoke the Holy Spirit to guide them into unity with Christ. Other Christian churches do not make this kind of distinction between the church and its sinful members, either as a group or particular persons. This gives them the right to speak about the sinfulness of the church. Orthodox ecclesiology, through the differentiation of the church and its sinful members, maintains that the church is always holy because of the sovereignty in it of God's presence and the purifying grace of the Holy Spirit that cleanses the communion of the faithful from all sin and bring them into unity in Christ's body.

Nikos Nissiotis argued that in the sacramental communion the whole creation is united with God and is redeemed. When we speak about the redemption of the world, it includes those aspects of the world that resist unity with God since nothing can overpower the grace of God.

> In the *ecclesia* and its sacramental reality the negative side is overcome, because the brokenness as a reality in the whole of creation happens outside the Being of God and concerns man's relationship with him. The sin is in the mode of existence and not in the essence of God's being, or in some imperfections in his divine ikon in mankind. Therefore, the sacramental communion is possible as redeeming and restoring the communion of "all things" with God.[14]

However, despite the redemption of the whole creation and in particular of the ecclesial communion from the forces of brokenness, "the negative catholicity continues to be active both inside the church and in the whole universe". The church in history finds itself between the catholicity of love and the catholicity of fall and through the grace of the Holy Spirit is called again and again to bring all things into unity. "The catholicity is a process of God's grace creating, redeeming and saving all men and all things. Grace binds everything together into a strange Oneness." This approach preserves the absolute, overwhelming power of the grace of God over sin and acknowledges at the same time the historical reality of sin and its destructive presence mainly in the world, but also within the ecclesial communion.

It is very important that an ecclesiology should keep this curious and unique dialectic between unshaken communion in essence and brokenness in existence in the whole creation. This is because the *ecclesia* as sacramental communion is absolutely holy, and a sure guarantee for sharing in the full communion with God by his grace, but all men yet remain sinful and in broken relationship both in the *ecclesial* communion and in the world.[15]

NOTES

[1] *Schema constitutionis dogmaticae de Ecclesia*, Vatican, 1963, Parsl, p.15, "5"= Acta Synodalia 2/1, 233, note 5.
[2] Gennadios Limouris ed., *Church-Kingdom-World: The Church as Mystery and Prophetic Sign,* Faith and Order Paper no. 130, WCC, 1986.
[3] *Church and World: The Unity of the Church and the Renewal of Human Community*, Faith and Order Paper no. 151, WCC, 1990, pp.26f.
[4] *Church-Kingdom-World*, p.36.
[5] *Ibid.*, p.53.
[6] *Ibid.*, p.27.
[7] *Ibid.*, p.24.
[8] *Ibid.*, p.110.
[9] *Ibid.*, p.109.
[10] *Ibid.*, p.113.
[11] *Ibid.*, p.25.
[12] *Ibid.*, p.8. While the Christological foundation of the church makes the dogma of Chalcedon a basis for understanding its theanthropic nature, we must not forget that Chalcedon, rather than explaining this unity of the two perfect natures of Christ, a mystery in itself, only defines how this unity must not be understood.
[13] John Romanides, "The Ecclesiology of St Ignatius of Antioch", in *Greek Orthodox Theological Review*, 7, 1961, p.64.
[14] *Church-Kingdom-World*, p.108.
[15] *Ibid.*, p.109.

The Sacramentality of the Church
An Evangelical Baptist Perspective
REV. DR TIMOTHY GEORGE

Does the church have a sacramental nature? More precisely, can we say that the church not only possesses or performs sacraments, but is itself a sacrament? This is a relatively new question on the ecumenical agenda. The key text which forms the basis of recent discussions is from the opening paragraph of the Dogmatic Constitution *Lumen Gentium*, approved on 21 November 1964 at Vatican Council II:

> By her relationship with Christ, the church is a kind of sacrament or sign of intimate union with God, and of the unity of all humankind. She is also an instrument for the achievement of such union and unity.[1]

As an evangelical and a Baptist, I belong to an ecclesial tradition for whom the language of the church as sacrament is problematic, or at least not so congenial. I shall examine several specific challenges posed to evangelical Baptist ecclesiology by the concept of the church as sacrament. I shall also attempt to offer some constructive points of contact in our continuing quest to define and proclaim the mystery of that community of faith which Jesus loves, for which he gave himself up, and which he continually sustains by the power of the Spirit and the good news of the gospel.

The challenge of sacramental language

In his helpful survey of the reception of the language of the church as "sacrament, sign and instrument", Günther Gassmann traces a growing openness to use these terms to describe the place and vocation of the church and its unity in God's plan of salvation. He admits that there is no uniform understanding of what these terms mean in the various ecumenical texts in which they occur. Of the three terms, "sacrament is the most unambiguous being used in the sense of effective mediation, representation, or anticipation".[2] At the same time, sacrament is also the least frequently cited of these three terms. Apparently, it is less of an ecumenical stretch to describe the church as "a persuasive sign of God's love", or as an instrument for accomplishing God's purpose in Christ, than to claim that the church is the "sacrament of God's saving work".

At times, however, "sign" and "sacrament" seem to be used interchangeably, as in the report of the WCC's world conference on mission and evangelism in Melbourne in 1980. Here the church is defined as the body of Christ, "the sacrament of the kingdom in every place and time", and elsewhere in the same report, "a sign of the kingdom of God because it is the body of Christ on earth".[3] While Baptists and evangelicals have been largely absent in this discussion, they are likely to find "sign" and "instrument" more congenial terms for describing the reality and mission of the church than the more historically freighted word "sacrament". Here we shall explore some of the ecclesiological reservations for applying sacramental language to the church. Following this, we shall look at some possible points of contact between the evangelical tradition and more sacramental models of the church.

At the heart of Baptist and evangelical ecclesiology is a distinction which seems to play little role in recent ecumenical texts, namely, the Augustinian distinction between the church visible and invisible. Within the Baptist tradition, the classic definition of the invisible church comes from the Second London Confession, a Particular Baptist statement of faith, published in 1677, which echoes the language of the Westminster Confession:

> The catholic or universal church which with respect to the internal work of the Spirit, and truth of grace, may be called invisible, consists of the whole number of the elect, that have been, are, or shall be gathered into one, under Christ, the Head thereof; and is the spouse, the body, the fullness of him, that filleth all in all.[4]

The church, then, is the body of Christ extended throughout time as well as space, consisting of all persons everywhere who have been placed in vital union with Jesus Christ through the ministry of the Holy Spirit. As Georges Florovsky used to say, the church is characterized by a temporal as well as a spatial catholicity, a catholicity not reducible to, nor strictly verifiable by, historical continuity, numerical quantity or geographical extent.

In the New Testament the church invisible and universal is depicted as a heavenly and eschatological reality, not as an earthly institution to be governed and grasped by mere mortals. The only text in the New Testament which directly refers to the church as the mother of believers is Galatians 4:26 where, in contrast to the earthly city in

Judea, the church is called "the Jerusalem that is above, the heavenly Jerusalem". Another text of major importance which extends this idea is Hebrews 12:22-24:

> But you have come to Mount Zion, to the heavenly Jerusalem, the city of the living God. You have come to thousands upon thousands of angels of joyful assembly, to the church *(ecclesia)* of the first-born, whose names are written in heaven. You have come to God, the judge of all men, to the spirits of righteous men made perfect, to Jesus the Mediator of a new covenant, and to the sprinkled blood that speaks a better word than the blood of Abel.[5]

As a reality beyond our ken, this universal church is not at our disposal and thus we can only believe it *(credo ecclesiam)* – not believe *in* it as we believe in God the Father Almighty, Jesus Christ his only Son, and the Holy Spirit. Rather, when we confess that we "believe the church", we are bearing witness to its reality. We mean to say that we believe that it exists; that we ourselves by God's grace have been placed within it, along with all others who "bow their necks under the yoke of Jesus Christ" (Belgic Confession, art. 28); and that the gates of hell shall never prevail against it.

One objection, though perhaps not the strongest, against defining the church as a sacrament is that it seems to obscure the full celestial and eschatological reality of the church depicted in Hebrews, the book of Revelation and other apocalyptic texts. This, despite the fact that sacraments are understood as efficacious signs, that is to say, signs that point beyond themselves to a greater reality, a reality which in some sense the sacraments themselves produce or convey. But if, with the council of Trent, we can describe a sacrament as "the visible form of an invisible grace", then it seems to say too little about the church to call it a sacrament.

Put otherwise, sacramental language about the church seems to privilege unduly *ecclesia militans* at the expense of *ecclesia triumphans* and, for those who believe in purgatory, *ecclesia dormans* as well. While there is much about the heavenly state that we do not know, and about which it is unwise to speculate, surely the fullness of the church's communion with the triune God then and there is much more than an intensification of its pilgrim experience here and now. The eucharist is indeed a foretaste of that eschatological banquet called the marriage feast of the Lamb, and the continuity between the two is central to the meaning of *sursum corda* in the liturgy, but to quote St Paul, "When wholeness comes, the partial will vanish... my knowledge now is partial; then it will be whole like God's knowledge of me" (1 Cor. 13:9-12). However we explain divine action in the sacraments, including the real presence of Christ in the eucharist, the Christian *sacramenta* are signs of that ultimate *mysterion* that is "not yet" fully revealed or conveyed amidst the groanings of this present age (cf. Rom. 8:24-26).

It should be said at once that the concept of the invisible church can be (and sometimes has been) distorted into a kind of ecclesiastical docetism according to which the earthly and historical form of the church has been negated and its mission in the world reduced to a "spiritualized" fellowship with no more gravity than a discussion group or a social club. Already in the 16th century, the Reformers were aware of this criticism and vigorously denied the charge that by the church they meant only a *civitas platonica*. Indeed, they sought to reconstruct a purified form of catholic Christianity, a real life and blood community of faith that would bear the "marks of the true church" *(notae verae ecclesiae)*. The *notae* do not replace the traditional Nicene attributes *(una, catholica, apostolica, sancta)*, but they rather call into question the unity, catholicity, apostolicity and holiness of every congregation which claims to be a church, thus subjecting it to an outward, empirical examination.[6] In this way, as Calvin says, "the face of the church" emerges into visibility before our eyes (*Inst.* 4.1.9).

The early Baptists follow Luther and Calvin in regarding the word purely preached and the sacraments duly administered as the two irreducible marks of the visible church, although they, along with others in the Reformed tradition (cf. the Scots Confession, 1560), expanded and formalized the *notae*-concept to include discipline as an indicator of a true visible church. By thus elevating discipline as a distinguishing mark of the church, the Baptists (along with other puritans and later pietists) defined the true visible church as a covenanted company of gathered saints, separated from the world in its organization and autonomy and separating back to the world through congregational discipline those members whose lives betrayed their profession.

The church visible

Many of these themes were brought together in the response of the Baptist World Alliance (BWA) to the Faith and Order document *Baptism, Eucharist and Ministry*. While affirming the invisible church as the whole number of the elect, inclusive of all "spiritual, regenerate believers", that is, "all of the redeemed of all ages", the visible church here on earth is defined in this way:

> It will thus be seen that the organized church as an institution is not, for Baptists, primary but secondary, functional and instrumental. It was intended to be, and exist as, the functioning agency of the kingdom of God on earth and

of its gospel. Ideally, it should concretely and socially embody the universal spiritual church as the body of Christ in each community. It is the declarative agency of that power that has no direct saving authority or power. It proclaims salvation and offers it to man in the name of the Redeemer; it does not definitely administer or withhold salvation. It has no vicarious mediatorial function, but is committed to the proclamation of the complete, exclusive priesthood and sacrifice of Jesus Christ as the Lamb of God that taketh away the sin of the world. Baptists thus find no place in, and no place for, any hierarchy and no saving value in any sacrament.[7]

In this understanding of ecclesiology, there are several factors that mitigate against applying sacramental language to the visible church.

1. The church as herald. In speaking of the "declarative agency" of the church whose primary function is to "proclaim salvation... in the name of the Redeemer", the BWA response to BEM identifies Baptists as those for whom the "word" is primary and the "sacrament" secondary. On this view, the church is essentially a herald of the lordship of Jesus Christ. Its essence is essentially proleptic: its message does not terminate upon itself but rather anticipates and to some extent precipitates (cf. Matt. 24:14) the coming reign of God. As Avery Dulles has shown, this view finds a parallel in Roman Catholic theology in Hans Küng who stresses the kerygmatic role of the church:

> It is the reign of God which the church hopes for, bears witness to, proclaims. It is not the bringer or the bearer of the reign of God which is to come and is at the same time already present, but its voice, its announcer, its *herald*. God alone can bring his reign; the church is devoted entirely to its service.[8]

This is not to say, of course, that the event of proclamation is devoid of sacramental power. Quite the contrary. In declaring that "the preaching of the word of God is the word of God", the Second Helvetic Confession (1566) exalted the *ex opere operato* character of Christian proclamation. As the Lord says through the prophet Isaiah, "It is my word that goes forth from my mouth: it will not return to me empty" (Isa. 55:11). Or, in the language of St Paul, the preaching of the gospel has an irrevocable effect: it conveys either the sweet fragrance of salvation or the noxious odour of perdition (2 Cor. 2:14-16). The dominical sacraments of baptism and the Lord's supper also have a heraldic function in the economy of salvation. They are "the visible words of God" proclaiming in visual, tactile and olfactory ways what the preacher has declared audibly in the exposition of holy scripture.

One of the questions posed here is this: Can the kerygmatic and sacramental understandings of the church reinforce and support, rather than cancel out, one another? The most helpful effort in this direction thus far has come from the second phase of the Reformed-Roman

Catholic dialogue in the document *Towards a Common Understanding of the Church (1984-1990)*. Here the two conceptions of the church as *creatura verbi* and "sacrament of grace" are seen as possibly "expressing the same instrumental reality under different aspects, as complementary to each other or as two sides of the same coin". At the same time, it is noted that these two conceptions provide a basis of creative tension between Roman Catholic and Reformed communities, a tension that comes to the fore on issues of ecclesial continuity and ministerial order.

2. *The primacy of Jesus Christ.* In describing the non-sacramental character of the visible church, the BWA statement declares that the church in its terrestrial form "has no vicarious mediatorial function, but is committed to the proclamation of the complete, exclusive priesthood and sacrifice of Jesus Christ as the Lamb of God that taketh away the sin of the world". No ecclesial community in Christendom would deny that this latter statement is also true of its ministry and witness.

However, to describe the church as sacramental seems to many Baptists and evangelicals to qualify the primacy of Christ in a way that compromises his essential lordship over the church both visible and invisible. We see this, for example, in the famous encyclical of Pope Pius XII *Mystici Corporis* (1943), in which the church is referred to *quasi altera Christi persona* ("as if it were another person of Christ").[9] True enough, in some expressions of popular evangelical piety, the church is seen as the direct continuation of the incarnation in an almost crass way. As one popular ditty has it, "Jesus has no hands but our hands to do his work today, no feet but ours to help folks on their way." Quite apart from the Pelagian and deistic overtones of such a statement, evangelicals at their best recoil from directly identifying Christ and the church, lest the latter be made into an object of faith alongside of its Lord. Paul Tillich, among others, saw the temptation of putting the historical church in the place of God as a step towards unwitting idolatry.[10] In the New Testament the metaphor of the body of Christ describes the relationship of believers to one another (in 1 Cor.) and to Christ (in Ephesians and Colossians, where the body is distinguished from Christ, its Head), but not to the surrounding world. In other words, "the body image looks inwards and upwards but not outwards".[11] This is not to project some monstrous dichotomizing of head and body, but rather to insist on a proper distinguishing of the two.

3. *The sovereignty of the Holy Spirit.* In describing the visible church as "not primary but secondary, functional and instrumental", the BWA statement reflects the conviction, rooted in the Augustinian and Calvinist traditions, that the church and its sacraments never become

eminent subjects of causality, that God the Holy Spirit remains sovereign even over the means God has chosen to draw men and women unto Godself. Christ neither shares his glory nor gives his lordship to anyone else, not even to the church. The wind of the Spirit blows wherever it pleases (cf. John 3:8). This means that the church is the body of Christ, created and continually renewed by the awakening power of the Holy Spirit. It is the Holy Spirit who imparts faith to the believer and thus makes effective the *opus operatum* of the sacraments. The sacraments are thus seals of assurance and may not be dispensed with without spiritual detriment. But while we are bound to the sacraments, God is not. By no means should we disparage the external means of grace God has given to the church in its earthly pilgrimage, but neither should we be surprised when, by the Holy Spirit, God works in ways that go beyond our understanding – *etiam extra ecclesiam*!

In thus shying away from sacramental language about the church, often preferring the word "ordinances" instead of "sacraments" when referring to the Lord's supper and baptism, the Baptist and evangelical traditions have made a conscious protest against a kind of sacramental imperialism that seems to endow the sacraments with an importance such that without them salvation is not possible, a view undergirded by an exaggerated ecclesiology that treats the church as though it were itself divine. At the least, statements such as "the church contains Christ" and "the sacraments make the church" seem to call into question the sovereign freedom of the Spirit no less than the lordship of Christ.

4. *The provisionality of the visible church.* Within the Baptist tradition, and especially within the Southern Baptist Convention, there are some who teach that there is an inviolate continuity of true visible churches, an unbroken ecclesial succession, extending back across the centuries to Jesus, John the Baptist or "the First Baptist Church of Jerusalem", as the primitive Christian community described in Acts is anachronistically called. According to this view, no other true churches have ever existed except those that have received valid "orders" and authentic "sacraments" through this palpable, pipeline succession. Often enough, "the trail of blood", as this view of church succession is sometimes called after a popular tract of the early 20th century, leads through various dissenting and frequently quite heretical groups such as the Montanists, the Donatists, the Cathari, the Petrobrusiani, etc. While no credible Baptist historian supports this thesis, it is still widely held in some quarters. Most Baptist theologians, however, reject this view as not only historically incredible but also theologically unnecessary. While Jesus promised that the gates of

Hades would not prevail against his church, nowhere does scripture guarantee the permanence or perpetuity of any local congregation. In fact, in speaking to the churches of Asia Minor in Revelation 2 and 3, the Risen Christ calls on them to repent lest their lampstands be removed (Rev. 2:5).

Evangelicals do not define the apostolicity of the church in terms of a literal, linear succession of duly ordained bishops, but point rather to the inscripturated witness of the apostles and the succession of apostolic proclamation. This is why failure to be faithful to the gospel is not a minor offence to be lightly passed over, but rather a life-threatening disorder to be constantly on guard against. Still, God has never left himself without a witness, even though it be the witness of a small remnant, sometimes persecuted, perhaps unseen and unknown to the chroniclers of church history (cf. Luther's *ecclesia latens*). In this sense, the Blessed Virgin Mary can indeed be *mater ecclesiae* for Baptists and evangelicals no less than for Orthodox and Roman Catholic Christians: Mary received the word of annunciation in faith ("She would not have conceived had she not believed", said Luther) and she was at the centre of those faithful few who stood vigil under the cross while others scurried for safety.

5. *Protests against impersonalism.* For Baptists and evangelicals, to say that the sacraments are constitutive of the church is to misunderstand our common sharing in holy things *(communio in sanctis)*. The Pentecostal discussion partners in the Pentecostal-Roman Catholic dialogue speak for all evangelicals when they declare that "the central element of worship is the preaching of the word. As persons respond to the proclamation of the word, the Spirit gives them new birth, which is a presacramental experience, thereby making them Christians and in this sense creating the church."[12] Baptists, of course, carry this principle even further by delaying baptism until there is some evidence of conversion, with the result that this sacrament is really a testimony to a faith already openly professed.

Baptists and other evangelicals are leery of defining the church as sacramental, in part because this appears to make the church and its sacraments automatic dispensers of salvation, thus undercutting the necessity of a personal appropriation of grace in the experience of the "new birth". Gerald Bray has posed four questions which evangelicals bring to the ecumenical conversation concerning their understanding of conversion:

> (1) Why is the evangelical experience of salvation so important to those who have had it that they are often ready to discount other forms of Christianity as inauthentic? (2) Can the evangelical experience not be found in other Chris-

tian traditions, expressed in a different way? (3) And if it can, why do evangelicals stand apart from the rest of the church? (4) On the other hand, if it cannot, what claim do evangelicals have to be authentically Christian, especially in a way that implies that exclusion of others?[13]

These are questions that bear further investigation, but the Evangelical-Roman Catholic Dialogue on Mission (ERCDOM), a series of meetings which took place over a period of seven years (1977-84), represents the most sustained engagement with these issues thus far.

Ecumenical implications
From what has been said thus far, it is clear that most Baptists and evangelicals hold serious reservations about the ecumenical usefulness of describing the church itself as a sacrament. The reasons for this include, among others, the following points:
1. As a term of ecumenical consensus, "the church as sacrament" is of recent vintage, lacking sufficient biblical and patristic warrant.[14] One well-known text from Cyprian is sometimes cited to the contrary: "The church is the indissoluble sacrament of unity."[15] But these words which come from a letter of Cyprian dealing with the Novatian controversy are not without ambiguity and certainly cannot serve as a *Stichwort* for contemporary ecclesiology. Other concepts for the church such as "the people of God", "the body of Christ", and "the temple of the Holy Spirit" do not suffer from this disadvantage, being firmly rooted in both scripture and Tradition.
2. Quite apart from ecclesial traditions which find sacramental language problematic, there are different, and perhaps contradictory, understandings of what a sacrament is not only among, but also within, distinct communities of faith.
3. Despite protests against ecclesiastical triumphalism and organizationalism, to define the church as sacrament serves in an ironic way to demystify it, that is, to make it less, rather than more, of a mystery. Historically, this has sometimes reinforced a sacramental will-to-power and resulted in an ecclesiology of glory, a temptation admittedly faced by all denominations and church traditions, not merely the so-called sacramental ones.
4. Finally, to define the church as sacrament obscures the sole sufficiency and sovereignty of Jesus Christ who remains supremely free and does not surrender his royal prerogative even to the community that bears his name, nor to the signs and seals with which he blesses, nourishes and sanctifies his body. Christ, not the church, is both the *sacramentum* and the *res sacramenti*, both the sign and the reality signified: Christ alone is the *Ursakrament*.

Without surrendering these fundamental convictions, is it possible for Baptists and evangelicals to learn from and even appropriate the sacramental imagery of the church? In exploring such ecumenical challenges and opportunities, it is well to remember that we have come a long way since the time of Emil Brunner who remarked in his controversy over the church with Otto Karrer, "It always remains improbable that a genuine Catholic will ever allow himself to be persuaded by a genuine Protestant."[16] Baptists and evangelicals still have far to go before we can talk meaningfully about a reconciliation of memories with our ecumenical partners, but we can applaud this statement from the Reformed-Roman Catholic dialogue: "Shared memories, even if painful, may in time become a basis for new mutual bonding and a growing sense of shared identity."

Cardinal Joseph Ratzinger offers a possible way forward in our present discussion in his description of the origin of the word *sacramentum* as a designation for the church in Vatican Council II. Ratzinger points out that the language of the church as sacrament, originally introduced to the council's fathers from a draft composed by German theologians, was significantly altered by the Belgian theologian Gérard Philips:

> The German theologians state plainly and without more ado that the church is the sacrament of the union of men among themselves and with God. The Belgian text is more cautious in its approach. It begins by defining *sacramentum* as "a sign and an instrument" but even then introduces the word itself with circumspection and a qualifying *veluti* ("as it were"), thus characterizing the usage as figurative by comparison with the usual use of the term and explaining it at the outset.[17]

The Latin *veluti* is frequently used to introduce a hypothetical comparative clause; it means "as if", "as though", "just as", "like as". In rejecting the straightforward equation of church and sacrament in favour of the more considered, qualified expression *veluti sacramentum*, the council fathers showed great wisdom in recognizing the fundamentally analogous nature of this designation. The church *is* the people of God, the church *is* the body of Christ, but the church is "like a sacrament", or "a sort of sacrament". If Ratzinger's explanation of this textual history is correct, then perhaps concerns raised by Baptists, evangelicals and other Protestants may be addressed in ways that benefit our common ecumenical quest. In conclusion, I suggest four possible avenues of further investigation along this line.

1. Without actually defining the church as the continuation of the incarnation, evangelicals can appreciate and affirm the incarnational character of Christ's presence and ministry in the work and witness of

his people on earth. The language of the church "embodying" the gospel helpfully points in this direction, as seen in this statement from the *Manila Manifesto* (1989), a document produced by a gathering of evangelicals committed to "calling the whole church to take the whole gospel to the whole world":

> The church is intended by God to be a sign of his kingdom, that is, an indication of what human community looks like when it comes under his rule of righteousness and peace. As with individuals, so with churches, the gospel has to be embodied if it is to be communicated effectively. It is through our love for one another that the invisible God reveals himself today, especially when our fellowship is expressed in small groups, and when it transcends the barriers of race, rank, sex and age which divides other communities.[18]

2. One of the most important pre-conciliar theologians who emphasized the sacramentality of the church was Henri de Lubac. For him the designation of the church as a sacrament stood in opposition to a kind of sacramental individualism that in essence reduced the Christian faith to a modern mystery religion.[19] Regrettably, many Baptists and evangelicals interpret their own conversion as a supreme act of individualism, a private response detached, if not divorced, from the corporate community of faith. Without diminishing the call for personal repentance and faith, evangelicals need to develop an authentic churchly spirituality drawn from the riches from the whole Christian tradition. And we might well begin this journey by recognizing the sacrament-*like* character of our own historic confessions, covenants and catechisms.[20]

3. In the 1984 apostolic exhortation *Reconciliatio et Paenitentia*, Pope John Paul II delineated three ways in which the church can be spoken of as sacrament: first, as a reconciled community which witnesses to the work of Christ in the world; second, as the custodian and interpreter of holy scripture, calling the entire world to the good news of reconciliation in Christ; and, finally, by reason of the seven sacraments each of which in its own way "makes the church" and serve as means of "conversion to God". For reasons already stated, Baptist evangelicals have great difficulty accepting the third explanation given by the Holy Father.[21] However, the first and second interpretations of sacramentality are surely consonant with Baptist and evangelical understandings of the church's mission and witness. Committed as they are to the sufficiency of holy scripture and the Reformation principle of *sola scriptura,* evangelicals do not accept the infallible teaching authority of any ecclesial jurisdiction. They do regard the Bible itself as *veluti sacramentum* and believe that the scriptures are to be read and interpreted in the context of a covenanted community of faith. Indeed,

Baptist evangelicals would likely respond more warmly to ecumenical initiatives and projects centred on the common study of holy scripture than to theological investigations of the nature of the church.

4. One aspect of regarding the church "like a sacrament" assumes its character as a community that necessarily points beyond itself. Put otherwise, the church *veluti sacramentum* may serve, when and where God so wills it and permits it by his grace, as a sign that conveys that which it signifies (e.g. the "real presence of Christ in the eucharist"), but the church is always a sign that does not rest in itself; it is always on the way to something else. Here on earth, the church is always *ecclesia in via*. This means that the church always exists in a state of becoming, buffeted by struggles, under the sign of the cross. As Luther says in *The Large Catechism*, the church on earth is

> God's little holy flock... it is called together in one faith, one mind and understanding. It possesses a variety of gifts, yet it is united in love without sect or schism... until the last day the Holy Spirit remains with the holy community or Christian people.[22]

NOTES

[1] LG 1. In Latin the text reads: *Cum vero Ecclesia sit in Christo signum et instrumentum seu veluti sacramentum intimae totuis generis humani unitatis eiusque in Deum unionis.*

[2] Günther Gassmann, "The Church as Sacrament, Sign and Instrument: The Reception of this Ecclesiological Understanding and Ecumenical Debate", in *Church, Kingdom, World*, WCC, 1986, p.14.

[3] "Message to the Churches", in *Your Kingdom Come,* report on the world conference on mission and evangelism, Melbourne 1980, WCC, 1980, pp.235-36.

[4] In 1742 this same confession was published in America, with slight alterations, as the Philadelphia confession of faith. Cf. Timothy and Denise George eds, *Baptist Confessions, Covenants, and Catechisms,* Nashville TN, Broadman & Holman, 1996, pp.84-85. The visible/invisible church distinction is mentioned in the document, "Towards a Common Understanding of the Church (1984-1990)", from the Reformed-Roman Catholic dialogue where the point is to affirm the indissoluble link between the two "sides" of the one ecclesial reality.

[5] This passage has been called "the most majestic panorama of the transcendent eschatological reality that is the communion of saints, the eternal fellowship of pilgrims past and present". Markus Bochmuehl, "The Church in Hebrews", in Markus Bochmuehl and Michael B. Thompson eds, *A Vision for the Church: Studies in Early Christian Ecclesiology,* Edinburgh, T. & T. Clark, 1997, p.149.

[6] This concept is more fully developed in Calvin than in Luther. See Heinrich Heppe, *Reformed Dogmatics,* London, 1950, pp.657-64. See also Timothy George, *Theology of the Reformers,* Nashville TN, Broadman & Holman, 1988, pp.172-93.

[7] William R. Estep, "A Response to Baptism, Eucharist, and Ministry: Faith and Order Paper no. 111", in William H. Brackney and Ruby J. Burke eds, *Faith, Life, and Witness: The Papers of the Study and Research Division of the Baptist World Alliance, 1986-1990,* Birmingham AL, Samford UP, 1990, p.3. The words quoted here are actually those of Baptist missiologist W.O. Carver. See his essay, "The Baptist Conception of the Church", printed under the title, "Denominational Statements of Baptist Churches", in R. Newton Flew ed., *The Nature of the Church,* New York, Harper, 1951, p.289. I take this statement and the paper in which it was quoted as fairly representative of Baptist views, although it was not endorsed officially by the Baptist World Alliance.

[8] Hans Küng, *The Church*, New York, Sheed & Ward, 1968, p.96. See also Avery Dulles, *Models of the Church*, New York, Doubleday, 1974, pp.76-88.
[9] Quoted from Paul Schrotenboer ed., *Roman Catholicism: A Contemporary Evangelical Perspective*, Grand Rapids MI, Baker Book House, 1988, p.21. However, the following statement in *Lumen Gentium*, 8, does not equate, but only compares the church and the incarnation: "For this reason the church is compared, not without significance, to the mystery of the incarnate Word. As the assumed nature, inseparably united to him, serves the divine Word as a living organ of salvation, so, in a somewhat similar way, does the social structure of the church serve the spirit of Christ who vivifies it, in the building up of his body (cf. Eph. 4:15)."
[10] Paul Tillich, *Systematic Theology*, Chicago, Univ. of Chicago Press, 1963, p.162-82.
[11] P.T. O'Brien, "The Church as a Heavenly and Eschatological Entity", in D.A. Carson ed., *The Church in the Bible and the World: An International Study*, Grand Rapids MI, Baker Book House, 1993, pp.113-14.
[12] "Final Report of the Pentecostal-Roman Catholic Dialogue", in William G. Rusch and Jeffrey Gros eds, *Deepening Communion: International Ecumenical Documents with Roman Catholic Participation*, Washington, US Catholic Conference, 1998, p.416.
[13] Gerald Bray, "Evangelicals, Salvation, and Church History", in Thomas P. Rausch ed., *Catholics and Evangelicals: Do They Share a Common Future?*, New York, Paulist, 2000, p.79.
[14] See two recent treatments of this theme and its ecumenical potential: Eberland Jüngel, "Die Kinche als Sakrament?", in *Zeitschrift für Theologie und Kirche*, 80, 1983, pp.432-57; Robert W. Jenson, *Unbaptized God: The Basic Flaw in Ecumenical Theology*, Minneapolis, Fortress, 1992, pp.90-103.
[15] Cyprian, "On the Unity of the Church", ANF 5:422.
[16] Emil Brunner, *The Christian Doctrine of the Church, Faith and the Consummation*, Philadelphia, Westminster, 1960, p.60.
[17] Ratzinger, *Principles of Catholic Theology*, San Francisco, Ignatius, 1987, pp.44-45.
[18] John Stott ed., *Making Christ Known: Historic Mission Documents from the Lausanne Movement, 1974-1989*, Grand Rapids MI, Eerdmans, 1996, pp.241-42.
[19] Ratzinger describes de Lubac's concern in this way: "The concept of a Christianity concerned only with *my* soul in which I seek only *my* justification before God, *my* saving grace, *my* entrance into heaven, is for de Lubac that caricature of Christianity, that, in the 19th and 20th centuries, made possible the rise of atheism." Ratzinger, *Principles*, 49. See also Henri de Lubac, *Catholicism: A Study of Dogma in Relation to the Corporate Destiny of Mankind*, trans. Lancelot C. Sheppard, London, Burns, Oates & Washbourne, 1950.
[20] See Timothy George, "An Evangelical Reflection on Scripture and Tradition", in *Pro Ecclesia*, 9, 2000, pp.184-207.
[21] An extract from this text is printed in J. Neuner and J. Dupuis eds, *The Christian Faith*, New York, Alba House, 1996, pp.316-17.
[22] Theodore Tappert ed., *The Book of Concord*, Philadelphia, Fortress, 1981, p.417.

The Sacramentality of the Church
Points of Convergence and Issues to be Addressed
REV. DR BARBARA SCHWAHN

Let me start with two personal remarks.

First of all I would like to remind us of our many convergences in the area of ecclesiology today. When my husband, a Roman Catholic who is very interested in theology even though he is not a theologian, had a short look at the background material for this consultation, he asked me, "Why do you have to talk about this? Why do people write pages and pages on the purpose and nature of the church? It seems to me so evident, what I read here." What he meant were all the biblical descriptions and images of the church that we have in common. And indeed in some papers of the background material, one reads many pages until a controversial question arises. And as the Lutheran-Roman Catholic document on "Church and Justification" states, "Regarding the most important elements in our task as churches – evangelization, worship and service to humanity – no essential differences divide us."[1]

I think that it is good to bear this in mind in our discussions about issues that are still difficult between us. Because this is the perception of many people in our churches and in society. And how the church is seen by the people has a lot to do with the way people attribute sacramentality to the church.

It seemed a little strange to me to look at ecumenical documents of the last decades in our material in order to discern the convergences and open questions, because in the process of writing the paper on *The Nature and Purpose of the Church* this work had already been done. Some of the proposals for further work have already been taken into account. Most of the controversial topics are analyzed, and open questions are marked as such. So I think I will not present anything new. What I will try to do is to sum up the main issues that came up in the reports of some bilateral dialogues and to read these passages with the sacramentality of the church in mind.

In some places I will try to formulate, according to my understanding, the questions we need to address now.

The church as sign, instrument and sacrament

1. THE COMPLEMENTARY CHARACTER OF THESE TERMS

To ask "Does the church have a sacramental nature?" is a very general question. In a way, even theologians of the Reformation churches could – some with certain reservations – answer "yes".

It depends on how we define a sacrament and on which understanding of this term we base the answer. In the document "Church and Justification", for example, Lutherans and Roman Catholics agree on the position that the church is not in the same way sacrament as baptism and the Lord's supper. The Lutheran view is, "The church itself is in a derivative sense an instrument of salvation", and they formulate questions regarding the Catholic understanding that follows the scholastic thinking in describing sacraments as "visible signs and instruments of invisible grace".[2]

Therefore in the convergence texts we have read a clear definition of the terms we use. But whatever the meaning of the term "sacrament", there is always a danger that the church glorifies itself and acts as if meaning and goal of the church and of its unity would lie in themselves.[3]

So it was helpful to use not only the single term "sacrament", but also to speak about the church as sign and instrument, so that the terms illuminate each other and lead to a kind of "balanced ecclesiology".

Günther Gassmann has pointed to the reception of these three terms in Vatican II and in ecumenical discussions. It seemed evident to all the partners in dialogue that only one term not be used to describe the nature and function of the church in analogy to the plurality of pictures that are used for the church in the scriptures.[4]

For the same reason, and because it is important for some confessional families, there was no serious discussion about eliminating the term "sacrament" for the church at all. It was, however, strongly recommended to use an unambiguous language for describing the church. Therefore the Faith and Order document on ecclesiology does not use the term "sacrament" for describing what can be said by the churches together.

2. THE CHURCH AS WITNESSING SIGN FOR THE WORLD

It seemed to me quite interesting to look at the connection between the sacramentality of the church and its character as a witnessing sign for the world. In Lima 1982 it was urged "that the sacramental and socio-ethical dimension implied in the sign concept should be held together".[5]

Manas Buthelezi sees the visibility of the church in its "ecclesiastical life-style", in so far as it points to the cross. The church should be "ready to become nothing so that others may become important".[6]

This means that the question of the church's sacramentality is not only one of its nature and of self-understanding, but one of its visibility and its engagement in the world.

Questions for further consideration

The term "sacrament" as a description for the church is ambiguous in the ecumenical discussion, even though it is interpreted by the description of the church as sign and instrument. Therefore a clear definition is needed every time we use the term. This is not in the first place meant as a common definition of a consensus, but everybody should make clear how the term is used in the specific context.

Then we might ask: Do we really agree that the church has a sacramental nature? And when this is the case, do we define the church's sacramental nature in the same way?

It was proposed in the context of the study on the "Unity of the Church and Unity of the Humankind" to incorporate the concept of the church as sacrament or sign into a trinitarian framework.[7] This seems helpful to avoid triumphalism and to describe the relationship between the sacramentality of the church and its task in the world.

The sacraments, the gospel and the sacramental character of the whole church

The ecumenical documents of recent years show, especially for Orthodox and Roman Catholic theology, that the celebration of the eucharist is central for their ecclesiology. It is the place where the sacramentality of the church is visible, where its relationship to Christ is manifested. It is the moment of incorporation into Christ.

Gennadios Limouris writes, "The church is a reality revealed in the act of the eucharist, even fulfilling itself visibly in time through the constant celebration of the Lord's mystical supper."[8]

When referring to the article by Nikos Nissiotis "The Church as a Sacramental Vision and the Challenge of Christian Witness", John Hind states, "The eucharist is the most characteristic act of the church."[9]

The Anglican-Roman Catholic statement on "Church as Communion" comes to the same conviction: "The sacramental nature of the church as sign, instrument and foretaste of communion is especially manifest in the common celebration of the eucharist."[10]

And in the Eastern Orthodox-Roman Catholic document *The Mystery of the Church* we read: "...the holy eucharist, the sacrament, which incorporates us fully into Christ". "Starting from the communion the church manifests what it is, the sacrament of the trinitarian koinonia."[11]

Lutherans emphasize that even preaching in worship has a sacramental character. Gospel and celebration of sacraments (eucharist and baptism) characterize for them the church as a communion of salvation. In preaching and in celebrating the eucharist the church becomes "sacramental".

The reason they focus on preaching is their understanding of the church as recipient of salvation. Through the gospel Christ speaks to the congregation of the faithful and thereby it becomes clear that he confronts the church.[12] For the same reason the Reformed speak of the church as *creatura verbi*. Jesus Christ is the word of God, the primordial sacrament, the Lord over the church and the sacraments.[13]

The other traditions emphasize the church's role as mediator of salvation and the sacramental character that it has in itself by its relationship with Christ.

Nevertheless it seems a matter of common sense for both of the groups that the church's "sacramentality" has to be understood completely "in Christ". And a result of the Lutheran-Roman Catholic dialogue is the common conviction that "the church stands under the gospel and has the gospel as its subordinate criterion".[14]

Questions for further consideration

Can we accept the different positions as different foci in our traditions or do they exclude each other because the church is seen in different roles?

Perhaps we still have to discuss the relationship between the biblically founded sacraments, the other sacraments and the church as sacrament.

The question then would be: Where in the church can we find the holiness of God? What gives the church a sacramental character? The preaching of the gospel, the celebrating of the scriptural sacraments or of others, or even the holiness of people or of episcopacy (which they receive through the sacraments)?

Christ and the church: criteria for a common understanding of the church

One conviction, central in all the dialogues, was that the church has a subordinated role under Christ. When we talk of the church as sacrament it must be clear that the church does not have salvation in itself but refers to Christ.

The Second Vatican Council defines the church generally as "a kind of sacrament or sign of intimate union with God, and of the unity of all mankind", "by her relationship with Christ".[15] It emphasizes that the church's sacramentality has to be subordinated under the saving work of Christ. Roman Catholic theology therefore talks about Jesus as "primal sacrament" *(Ursakrament)*.[16]

Evangelical positions are more specific. In 1973 Ernst Käsemann avoided the term sacrament and talked of the cross as the true sign of the church. It is only when the church takes seriously the sign of the cross that it is like Christ himself "a sign in the perspective of the resurrection of the dead and the dawn of a new creation".[17]

In the Reformed-Roman Catholic dialogue this was stated very clearly: "All language concerning the sacramentality of the church, then, must respect the absolute lordship of Christ over the church and the sacraments."[18]

The Lutheran-Roman Catholic dialogue then led to the common basic conviction that justification as the central theological content of scripture should be the criterion for the self-understanding of the church that is totally dependent on the justifying work of Christ. It is stated, "It must be evident that salvation can never be effected by human beings or be at their disposal, but even in the activity of the church it remains the gift of God." Therefore it is easier to come to a consensus by talking of the church as sign and instrument of salvation. But in this sense the dialogue even talks about the church as "sacrament" of salvation.[19]

Even though this common basic formulation was reached, there remain open questions between Lutherans and Reformed on the one side and Roman Catholics on the other.

There is still the impression that in the Roman Catholic self-understanding structures and elements of church order seem to be "holy" in themselves, which means that they are God-given and therefore have divine character.

Reformed theologians therefore ask whether Roman Catholics do not allocate to the church the role that is proper to Christ.[20]

Because of this supposition some Reformation churches criticized the Joint Declaration on Justification in October 1999. For them the open ecclesiological questions did not allow the recognition of the common understanding of justification. They could not see an agreement concerning the critical character of justification even for the self-understanding of the church (as sacrament). And the Vatican declaration *Dominus Iesus* increased that impression by emphasizing that one has to be a member of the Roman Catholic Church to belong to the one holy, catholic and apostolic church in the true sense.

On the other hand, there is still the question of Roman Catholic theologians who ask whether or not the Reformed in particular give up "the assurance that Christ is truly present and acting in his church".[21]

Questions for further consideration

As a consequence of what I have said above, there still seem to remain questions concerning the relationship of the visible and invisible church, the relationship between church and sin, and of course the mutual recognition as church, as will be mentioned in the next pages. But having in mind the agreements about the predominant role of Christ for the nature and life of the church, we perhaps have to ask one general question: Is the self-understanding of a church in its relation to Christ still a theologically controversial issue? Do we have to discuss what is the meaning of a church being subordinated to Christ? Or is it rather a question of the reception of this ecumenical convergence and of mutual accountability in the practice and teaching of the churches?

Consequences of using the Christological criterion for a self-understanding as a really sacramental church

In talking about common criteria for a mutual recognition of ecclesiologies, important questions are: What are the visible elements of a truly sacramental church that does not see salvation in itself but refers to an invisible reality? What elements are God-given and therefore necessary for salvation? Are they the preaching of the gospel and the celebrating of the Lord's supper or certain ministries and structural elements of the church or even the personal holiness of people?

The controversial questions in this area are summarized in "Church and Justification" as follows:

> (1) the institutional continuity of the church, (2) the ordained ministry as ecclesial institution, (3) the teaching function of the church's ministry, and (4) the jurisdictional function of the church's ministry. Each of these areas relates to the above-mentioned reciprocal questioning by Catholics and Lutherans: whether the Lutheran doctrine of justification diminishes the reality of the church; whether the catholic understanding of the church obscures the gospel as it is explicated by the doctrine of justification.[22]

The shared Lutheran-Roman Catholic conviction is that the structure of the ministries developed in history is not only the result of human factors, such as sociological or political circumstances, but is not thinkable without the help of the Holy Spirit. Both sides agree on the position that word and sacrament are necessary for salvation and that the ministries serve the right preaching and celebrating of the sacraments. So they state, "The question is rather one of a clear gradation in the evaluation of this ministry, which can be and has been described on the Catholic side by predicates such as 'necessary' or 'indispensable', and on the Lutheran side as 'important', 'meaningful', and thus 'desirable'."[23]

The Reformed tradition ultimately refers to the "Spirit-guided character of preaching", to the authority of scripture, not however to a God-given ministry.[24] But as a result of the discussions it is said very clearly that in Reformed teaching there is no invisible church that is known by God alone and that is totally separated from the community which is gathered by the word and sacrament. But the visible and invisible church belong together. "The invisible church is the hidden side of the visible, earthly church."[25]

The Orthodox and Anglican traditions however see their ministerial structure as God-given. Gennadios Limouris mentions as a criterion to distinguish the true church from "pseudo-assemblies" "to what bishop or authority they are joined".[26]

John Hind mentions as one characteristic of Anglican ecclesiology the God-given nature of episcopacy. He even describes the belief that the actual sanctity of some of its members demonstrates the holiness of God.[27]

Question for further consideration
The role of episcopacy and other structural elements for the sacramentality or holiness of the church.

Church and sin
Whether the diverse positions are seen as mutually exclusive or only gradually different, as the Lutheran-Roman Catholic document states, depends also on the way the ministries are exercised in the light of the common criterion, how the church fulfils its task in the world. This becomes very clear when the relationship between church and sin is discussed.

It is a common basic conviction that the church is more than the sum of its members, because of the sacramental presence of Christ. However, this is the result of interpretation.[28]

But there are differences between the Reformation churches and the others when it comes to the question whether the church is in danger of sin or not.

What is the relationship between the church and the world? To what extent does the church participate in the brokenness of the world while having a sacramental nature as the body of Christ?

Lutherans and Roman Catholics agree on the fact that the church constantly needs repentance and forgiveness of sin. The Lutheran position is that the church is holy insofar as it is rooted in the triune God. As such it is indestructible. Martin Luther made the distinction between the teaching of the church and its life. In its life the church needs justification. This corresponds to the Catholic distinction between the church as a whole that cannot fall in sin and the members of the church who always need renewal.[29]

Both churches agree that the church's indestructibility should not be understood in a static way as a kind of possession. Differences emerge while answering the question: "Where does the idea of the church's need for renewal or of its sinfulness find its necessary limit, by reason of the divine pledge that the church abides in the truth and that error and sin will not overcome it?"[30]

Lutherans ask where the "God-given indestructible holiness" is "so objectivized in specific ecclesial components, that they appear to be exempt from critical questioning" (p.126). In other words, Lutherans find it problematic that the specific structure, for example of ministries, is seen in the Roman Catholic Church as God-given in such a way that it seems impossible to ask critical questions about their self-understanding and their way of acting. The Catholic side finds it hard to see "why the effects of divine decisiveness should be intrinsically open to criticism".[31]

Interesting and important for the situation of all the churches is the perspective which John A. Baker brought into the discussion. He asked: What is the consequence of the way we understand and describe ourselves? Baker stated that the more we describe the church as holy and as different from the world, the higher are the world's expectations of the church. The church should understand itself as a part of the world that is open to God. But on the other hand, there is a danger of "crossing over to the world's side", where no kind of resistance on the part of the church would be accepted by society.[32]

In this context Reformed and Roman Catholics state, "... we do not think in the same way about the relation of the church to the kingdom of God. The Reformed insist more on the promise of a 'not-yet'; Catholics underline more the reality of a gift 'already there'."[33]

Nevertheless both sides agree on the fact that "the holiness of the preaching of the word and of the administration of the sacraments endures... In this sense the church is holy..."

Does the Church Have a Sacramental Nature?

Question for further consideration
However there is still an open question: Where does the idea of the church's need for renewal or of its sinfulness find its limit so that the promise that it will stay in the truth still applies?

Acceptance of other churches as church

The question that lies behind the different positions on the visibility of the church, of the relationship between church and sin and therefore of the church's continuity, seems to be the following: can we find elements of sanctification outside of the visible structure of our church? Do we recognize the sacramental nature of the structures of the other churches?

This is the key question in the ecumenical dialogue and the basis for the mutual recognition of the churches. Therefore every church should ask itself this question.

The issue was discussed explicitly, e.g. in the Reformed-Roman Catholic dialogue group. The result was:

> We diverge, however, on the matter of the closer identification of the church with its visible aspects and structure. Roman Catholics maintain that the church of Christ "subsists" in the Roman Catholic Church... The question is, therefore, to what degree they can recognize that the church of Christ also exists in the Reformed churches. The Reformed for their part do not understand the church as reducible to this or that community, hierarchy or institution. They claim to belong to the church and recognize that others also do. Their chief difficulty is not in extending this recognition to the Roman Catholic Church, but in the view that the Roman Catholic Church has of its special relation to the church of Jesus Christ.[34]

It was also mentioned that according to the different understanding of the relationship between church and sin the interpretations of the division in the 16th century are not the same.

> The Reformed consider that the Reformation was a rupture with the Catholic "establishment" of the period... this does not mean that the resulting division was a substantial rupture in the continuity of the church. For Catholics, however, this break struck at the continuity of the Tradition derived from the apostles.[35]

Question for further consideration
What are the consequences of the 16th-century division for the sacramentality of the one church of Christ and of the diverse churches?

Final remarks

I would like to summarize my observations in answering the first question that the Faith and Order commission asked the churches through *The Nature and Purpose of the Church:* How far can we recognize in this text an emerging convergence on the nature and the purpose of the church? I will concentrate especially on the issue of the church's sacramentality.

When I compare the results of the recent dialogues, for example, with results of the Lutheran-Roman Catholic dialogue in Germany after the second world war, then it becomes quite clear that a great deal of work has been done in clarifying the differences.

On the one hand, the gap seems to become smaller between the position that sees the sacramental character of the church founded in its ontological relationship to Christ and the one that binds sacramentality with the celebration of the sacraments and the preaching of the gospel. One position was trying to understand the other out of its own thinking, and one could find astonishing parallels between their respective theological systems (cf. the parallel between Martin Luther's distinction between teaching and practice of the church and the Roman Catholic distinction between the church and its members).

One could overcome the above-mentioned gap and obviously come to an ecumenical consensus between many churches by developing in particular a common understanding of the church as sign and instrument, and by developing common criteria for recognizing other and different ecclesiologies. When it is a common ground that a church, because of its sacramental nature, always refers to Christ, who can make us new, and that no church has salvation in itself, then diverse ecclesiologies with different foci can and have to be mutually recognized. The criterion is accepted by the churches. The question is then how it finds its expression in their teaching and practice.

On the other hand, there is a possibility of a divergence between theologians who have been in the common process of interpretation and others who have not. Some members of a church may interpret sacramentality in the way they speak of a sacramental nature of the church, some may interpret it in another way.

The issue to be mentioned here is whether all Baptist churches or Pentecostal churches would talk about a sacramental nature of the church. In the report of the Pentecostal-Roman Catholic dialogue 1985-89, Pentecostals do not accept the Roman Catholic understanding of sacraments and of the church as sacrament. But "in their own way they do affirm that the church is both a sign and an instrument of salvation".[36] But the Pentecostal churches seem to have different understandings of the sacraments within themselves. Some see the Lord's supper as reminder of Jesus' death and resurrection, some consider it to be a means of grace.[37] We should not forget the position of these churches in our ecumenical discussions.

NOTES

[1] "Church and Justification", in *Growth in Agreement II: Reports and Agreed Statements of Ecumenical Conversations on a World Level, 1982-1990*, J. Gros, H. Meyer and W.G. Rusch eds, WCC Publications, 2000, p.541.
[2] *Ibid.*, pp.518,517.
[3] Günther Gassmann, "The Church as Sacrament, Sign and Instrument", in *Church, Kingdom, World: The Church as Mystery and Prophetic Sign*, Gennadios Limouris ed., WCC, 1986, p.2.
[4] "Church and Justification", p.520.
[5] "The Church as Sacrament", p.11.
[6] *Church, Kingdom, World*, p.143.
[7] *Ibid.*, p.5. Cf. the definition of sacramentality by the Anglican-Roman Catholic Commission: "The church as a divine gift, grounded in Christ himself and embodied in human history, through which the grace of Christ is mediated for the salvation of humankind" ("Church as Communion", in *Growth in Agreement II*, p.328).
[8] *Church, Kingdom, World*, p.26.
[9] *Ibid.*, pp.127-28.
[10] "Church as Communion", p.334.
[11] "The Mystery of the Church and of the Eucharist in the Light of the Mystery of the Holy Trinity", in *Growth in Agreement II*, pp.652-53.
[12] "Church and Justification", pp.513,515-16.
[13] "Towards a Common Understanding", in *Growth in Agreement II*, p.802.
[14] "Church and Justification", p.515. See also the first chapter of *The Nature and Purpose of the Church: A Stage on the Way to a Common Statement*, Faith and Order Paper no. 181, WCC Publications, 1998.
[15] *Church, Kingdom, World*, p.2.
[16] "Church and Justification", p.516.
[17] Cf. G. Gassmann and M. Buthelezi in *Church, Kingdom, World*, pp.8,139.
[18] "Towards a Common Understanding", p.804.
[19] "Church and Justification", p.519.
[20] "Towards a Common Understanding", p.805.
[21] *Ibid.*
[22] "Church and Justification", p.527.
[23] *Ibid.*, p.532.
[24] "Towards a Common Understanding", p.805.
[25] *Ibid.*, p.809.
[26] *Church, Kingdom, World*, p.23.
[27] Cf. *ibid.*, pp.128,131.
[28] *Ibid.*, pp.23,132.
[29] "Church and Justification", p.524.
[30] *Ibid.*
[31] "Church and Justification", p.525.
[32] *Church, Kingdom, World*, pp.160-61.
[33] "Towards a Common Understanding", p.808.
[34] *Ibid.*, p.809.
[35] *Ibid.*, p.808.
[36] "Perspectives on Koinonia", *Growth in Agreement II*, p.748.
[37] *Ibid.*, p.727.

Church and "Sacrament" in Bilateral Dialogues

REV. ANTTI SAARELMA

When preparing for this consultation, I came across the home-page of the Anglican diocese of Ottawa on the internet. The mission statement of the diocese reads as follows:

> **How the diocese of Ottawa works**
>
> Our mission statement: The Anglican diocese of Ottawa is a serving community of Christ-centred people empowered by the Holy Spirit. It is called to be a sign, foretaste and instrument of the reign of God through prayer, celebration, proclamation, ministry, compassion, justice and faithful stewardship in l'Outaouais and Eastern Ontario, Canada, and the rest of the world.

This seems to be a local adaptation of our theme. The church as a sign, instrument and foretaste of the kingdom of God is also the topic of my presentation. It is my task to present four dialogue documents from bilateral dialogues on this issue. These bilateral documents are:

- the Eastern Orthodox-Roman Catholic "The Mystery of the Church and of the Eucharist in the Light of the Mystery of the Holy Trinity" = MC;[1]
- the Anglican-Roman Catholic, as seen in "Church as Communion" = CC;[2]
- the Reformed-Roman Catholic "Towards a Common Understanding of the Church" = TCUC;[3]
- the Lutheran-Roman Catholic "Church and Justification" = CJ.[4]

The intention of the presentation is to offer some clues as to where common perspectives are evident and where discussion needs to take place as the discussion is taken forward. The hope is that it will be possible to find some elements which may enhance the convergence between the churches.

Within the Faith and Order study document *The Nature and Purpose of the Church* (TNPC), this paper takes as starting point the box which can be found on page 23. The box is related to sub-chapter II.B "Sign and Instrument of God's Design" (§§42-47). The box on page

23 points out that "several churches" sum up the nature of the church as sign and instrument of God's design in the expression "the church as sacrament". "Other churches do not apply the concept of sacrament to the church" in order to clearly distinguish between church and sacraments and to keep in mind the reality of sin in the church.

You have been given a paper which is a compilation of passages where these documents address common issues of agreement or diversity. I have grouped these issues as follows:
1) Holy Trinity;
2) Christ as the sacrament *par excellence*;
3) the church as a place of God's action;
4) the church as an instrument of God's action;
5) the church as a foretaste of God's reign;
6) mission to the world;
7) notions of sign and sacrament;
8) necessity of the church;
9) visibility of the church;
10) the church human and divine.

The four above-mentioned documents present us with an essential variety of theological and spiritual traditions. The Roman Catholic Church was involved in all these dialogues. The other partners are from Eastern Orthodox, Lutheran, Anglican and Reformed churches.

Reading these texts is an exciting exercise because of the diversity of theological languages they contain. All dialogue partners have their own languages, some have many. In addition comes the language of ecumenical consensus. Let us enter this ecumenical jungle of theological languages. Key words for this enterprise are church, sacrament, sign, instrument and mediation.

Holy Trinity

Holy Trinity is the first issue on our list. This is more or less self-evident. Faith in the triune God is the fundamental basis also for theological reflection on the nature of the church. The Lutheran-Roman Catholic "Church and Justification" puts it like this: "The church is the communion of believers called into existence by the triune God." It is "anchored in the divine life of the triune God". "God allows the church to share in the triune divine life... The church's unity partakes of and reflects the unity of the triune God" (49).

ARCIC II expresses this divine participation more briefly but quite as clearly: "At the centre of this communion is life with the Father, through Christ, in the Spirit" (CC 15). In the Reformed-Roman Catholic document (TCUC 74-75) the tone is more Christological, but the trinitarian basis is necessary where the Holy Spirit needs to be put in relation with the Son:

> Finally, the work of Jesus, the Son, reveals to us the role of the Spirit of God who is common to him and to the Father: it reveals to us that God is triune. The Holy Spirit is present and active throughout the history of salvation. By the life, death and resurrection of Jesus, the Holy Spirit becomes the common gift of the Father and the Son to humanity.

One would perhaps expect that the Orthodox-Roman Catholic document would have the strongest trinitarian approach. That is, however, not the case. Main issues are the mystery of Christ and the eucharist (MC I.5.d): "Starting from there, the church manifests what it is, the sacrament of the trinitarian koinonia, the 'dwelling of God with men' (cf. Rev. 21:4)."

As one can expect, the Orthodox-Roman Catholic document is rich in trinitarian language (MC II,1). The church's model, its origin and its purpose are in the mystery of the triune God: "One of the chief texts to remember is 1 Corinthians 10:15-17: one sole bread, one sole cup, one sole body of Christ in the plurality of members. This mystery of the unity in love of many persons constitutes the real newness of the trinitarian koinonia communicated to men in the church through the eucharist... This is why the church finds its model, its origin and its purpose in the mystery of God, one in three persons."

This applies to individual Christians as well. In the communion of the church in the eucharist they "grow in mystical divinization" which makes them participate in the life of the Holy Trinity (MC 4): "The Spirit united to the Son for carrying out the Father's work. ... Believers are baptized in the Spirit in the name of the Holy Trinity to form one body. ... By the communion in the body and blood of Christ, the faithful grow in that mystical divinization which makes them dwell in the Son and the Father, through the Spirit."

Christ as the sacrament *par excellence*

The Holy Trinity, however, is not the starting point in any of these documents. The starting point is the mystery of Christ. Christ is "the sacrament *par excellence*" (MC I.3), the necessary basis for all other sacraments.

In the Orthodox-Roman Catholic document, the link between Christ and the eucharist is extremely close. Eucharist becomes (MC I.1-4) "the sacrament of Christ himself. The sacrament of the Christ event thus becomes identical with the sacrament of the holy eucharist."

Also the Holy Spirit is linked closely to Christ (MC I.2): "Christ continues to give himself in the Spirit, who alone gives life (John 6). The Lord Jesus enters into the glory and into his sacramental *tropos* in this world. The eucharist and the church, body of the crucified and risen Christ, become place of the energies of the Holy Spirit." Finally, "the mission of the Spirit remains joined to that of the Son" (MC I.5). At least this notion of the church binds the Holy Spirit so closely together with the mystery of Christ that there seems to be no separate, independent role left for the Spirit.

ARCIC II links the sacramentality of the church with the eucharist. It reminds that the origin of the communion of the church is Christ. In the celebration of the eucharist, the church points to this origin and ultimately to the Father, because Christ is in communion with him (CC 24): "The sacramental nature of the church as sign, instrument and foretaste of communion is especially manifest in the common celebration of the eucharist. Here, celebrating the memorial of the Lord and partaking of his body and blood, the church points to the origin of its communion in Christ, himself in communion with the Father; it experiences that communion in a visible fellowship; it anticipates the fullness of the communion in the kingdom; it is sent out to realize, manifest and extend that communion in the world."

A strong Christological emphasis is clear in all these documents. In "Church and Justification" the first main chapter (2) dealing with "the abiding origin of the church" is almost entirely Christological, e.g. subtitle 2.1, "Jesus Christ as the only foundation of the church".

The Reformed-Roman Catholic document TCUC 20 mentions the relationship between Christ and the church as one of the motives of the Reformation: "The Reformers rejected all in the life of the church which, in their understanding, obscured the unique mediatorship of Jesus Christ and seemed to give to the church an excessive role alongside him."

On the other hand, in ecclesiology even a strong emphasis on Christ remains in balance in relation to the rest of the Trinity. After all, it is the Holy Spirit who enables and empowers Christ's presence in the church after the ascension. The Reformed-Roman Catholic document (TCUC 80) links Christ and the Holy Spirit like this:

> Fundamental for us all is the presence of Christ in the church... Christ himself acts in the church in the proclamation of the word, in the celebration of the sacraments, in prayer and in intercession for the world. This presence and this action are enabled and empowered by the Spirit, by whom Christ calls to unite human beings to himself, to express his reality through them, to associate them in the mystery of his self-offering for them.

It is interesting to compare the role of the Holy Spirit in the Reformed-Roman Catholic and the Orthodox-Roman Catholic documents. There are obvious differences in the understanding of the relationships within the Holy Trinity and in the doctrine of eucharist. Yet, from the perspective of ecclesiology, the relationships between the Holy Spirit and Christ seem surprisingly similar. Could this be a point of contact from where further convergence would be possible?

The church as a place of God's action

Trying to grasp the idea of the church as "sacrament" in these dialogue documents, the first steps have now been taken. Trinitarian basis and Christological focus are common features to all these documents. I would now like to proceed from the area of greater convergence to issues of greater diversity.

Even those churches which have difficulties in saying that God acts "through" the church can admit that God acts "in" the church. This latter idea can be expressed the church as "a place of God's action". In CJ 108 this notion is put in opposition with the idea of the church as the instrument of God's action:

> A comparison of Lutheran and Catholic views of the church cannot disregard the fact that there are two fundamentally inseparable aspects of being church: on the one hand the church is the place of God's saving activity (the church as an assembly, as the recipient of salvation) and on the other it is God's instrument (the church as ambassador, as mediator of salvation).

The idea of the church as a place of God's action is present also in the Reformed-Roman Catholic document (TCUC 85-86):

> The church is called into being as a community of women and men to share in the salvific activity of Christ Jesus... Justification by grace through faith is given us in the church. This is not to say that the church exercises a mediation complementary to that of Christ or that it is clothed with a power independent of the gift of grace. The church is at once the place...

In the church God acts through the Holy Spirit in the word of God and in the sacraments. Both TCUC and CJ deepen this idea of hearing of God's word. The notion of "the creation of the word" *(creatura verbi)* gives expression to a classical Reformation concern. The word of God "creates" the church, when it brings about faith in human beings. According to TCUC (70) the church is "the beneficiary and the herald" of the gospel of Christ. "The church, like faith itself, is brought into being by the hearing of God's word in the power of God's spirit; it lives *ex auditu*, by hearing" (98).

CJ underlines (36-38) the criteriological concern behind this focus on the word of God. The church is subordinate to the gospel and always dependent on the word of God. It is interesting that in 1990 TCUC presents this notion *creatura verbi* as a Reformed position. Only three years later, in CJ the Roman Catholic partner subscribes the main concern (CJ 37-38):

> The conviction that the church lives out of the gospel also determines the Roman Catholic understanding of the church. In Vatican II's Dogmatic Constitution on the church we read, "... the gospel... is for all time the source of all life for the church"; [LG 20] and the Decree on the Church's Missionary Activity says that the "chief means of this implantation [i.e., of the church] is the preaching of the gospel of Jesus Christ". [AG 6]. In the Malta report Catholics and Lutherans together said that the church "as *creatura et ministra verbi*... stands under the gospel and has the gospel as its superordinate criterion" [Malta 48]... There was agreement that "the authority of the church can only be service of the word and... it is not master of the word of the Lord" [Malta 21]... The definition of the church as *creatura evangelii* therefore means that the church lives on the basis of the gospel that is communicated in word and sacrament and accepted through faith.

It is clear that in an Orthodox document the emphasis is on the eucharist. In this context it is, however, interesting to point out MC I.6, where the Lutheran-Roman Catholic commission talks about hearing of the word and the use of the Bible in the liturgy:

> The eucharistic celebration makes present the trinitarian mystery of the church. In it one passes from hearing the word, culminating in the proclamation of the gospel – the apostolic announcing of the word made flesh – to the thanksgiving offered to the Father and to the memorial of the sacrifice and to communion in it thanks to the prayer of epiclesis uttered in faith. For the epiclesis is not merely an invocation for the sacramental transforming of the bread and cup. It is also a prayer for the full effect of the communion of all in the mystery revealed by the Son.

Church is "a place of God's action" in all these documents. In terms of defining the fashion of God's action in the church, "a place" is in a way the smallest common feature. As ecumenism is an art of small steps, it would often be helpful to start with this kind of basic observation. Moreover, if such a basic observation takes place in another church's liturgy, it becomes a basic experience that God acts in the liturgy of that other church.

The church as an instrument of God's action

In addition to being a mere place of God's action, the church is also its instrument. God uses the church as medium of his saving work. There is a surprising degree of agreement about this.

The Reformed-Roman Catholic document underlines the active role of the faith community. When the gospel is preached, the community hears and responds (TCUC 101):

> The community of faith is thus not merely the community in which the gospel is preached; by its hearing and responding to the word of grace, the community itself becomes a medium of confession, its faith a "sign" or "token" to the world; it is itself a part of the world transformed by being addressed and renewed by the word of God.

The same Reformed-Roman Catholic document uses still other expressions for the church in God's service (TCUC 85-86): The church does not exercise "a mediation complementary to that of Christ" nor does it have "a power independent of the gift of grace. The church is at once the place, the instrument, and the minister chosen by God to make heard Christ's word and to celebrate the sacraments in God's name throughout the centuries."

The introductory paragraph CJ 108 was already quoted because of the notion of "place". At the end of the paragraph, there is a remarkable sentence:

> A comparison of Lutheran and Catholic views of the church cannot disregard the fact that there are two fundamentally inseparable aspects of being church: on the one hand the church is the place of God's saving activity (the church as an assembly, as the recipient of salvation) and on the other it is God's instrument (the church as ambassador, as mediator of salvation). But it is one and the same church which we speak of as the recipient and mediator of salvation.

As a "place" of God's action, the church is a Christian "assembly" which is "recipient of salvation". In addition to that passive role, the church is also God's "instrument" and "ambassador". Moreover, CJ calls it "mediator of salvation".

This latter notion is interesting in this context. To talk about the church as "mediator of salvation" might give the impression that the church has been given a more active role in God's design. Elsewhere in the CJ there is a strong emphasis on the mediatorship of Christ: "Christ, the mediator of all salvific gifts" (64).

A similar statement was important also in the Joint Declaration on the Doctrine of Justification (JD 18): "Lutherans and Catholics share the goal of confessing Christ, who is to be trusted above all things as the one Mediator (1 Tim. 2:5-6) through whom God in the Holy Spirit gives himself and pours out his renewing gifts." Many people were delighted by this statement because it was considered to remove the unclarity regarding the proposed "*co-mediatrix*". Does the language of

CJ make the church a *co-mediatrix*, instead of being a *ministra, instrumentum* and *signum*?

CJ 122 retains the term "mediator" but links it to Christ and the Holy Spirit:

> The term "sacrament", as a sign and instrument of salvation, gives expression to the universal mission of the church and its radical dependence on Christ. It thus becomes clear that neither the foundation of the church nor its goal lies in the church itself and that it therefore does not exist by itself or for itself. Only in and through Christ, only in and through the Holy Spirit is the church effectual as a mediator of salvation.

Later on CJ explains that the church is "instrument" only "in a derivative sense" (CJ 126):

> But if the church is the place where these means of grace become effectual it follows that the church itself is in a derivative sense an instrument of salvation. On the one hand it is called into being as a *congregatio fidelium*, a church, through the event of the "means of grace" so that it is itself a *creatura evangelii*; on the other, it is the place where people participate in salvation – there is no alternative.

When my own church gave a response to CJ, this passage received some criticism. Our church suggested that instead of "being sacrament" the notion of "sacramental nature" be employed:

> Section 4 discusses the church as the recipient and mediator of salvation. These two characteristics are first presented as the respective emphases of the two partners (§108). Then both the Lutheran perspective (4.1.1) and the Catholic one (4.1.2) are discussed more comprehensively. The presentation of the Lutheran perspective focuses on describing the church as the "congregation of the faithful" *(congregatio fidelium/sanctorum)*. The individualistic view of the congregation of the faithful as a mere sum of its individual members is rejected; what is chosen as the fundamental point of departure is the community brought into being and sustained by the Holy Spirit, to which individuals then belong (§109). Article 7 of the CA and the apology passage related to it are interpreted on the basis of the previous articles of the CA, and this stresses the criteriological significance of the doctrine of justification (§110). It is important that the text which follows does not limit itself to emphasizing the church as the recipient of salvation, but also presents the necessity of the church for salvation as a Lutheran view (§111).
>
> In the same context, CJ also discusses the question of the priesthood of all believers (the universal priesthood). This section should agree more clearly with what was said earlier in the document (53, 56, 68-71) and emphasize that baptism, justification and the priesthood of all believers belong together. What CJ presents later as the Catholic view of this matter (113-116) could, for the most part, also represent the joint position of both partners. Scandinavian Lutheranism agrees on this point with the ancient tradition of the church.

Subsection 4.2 focuses on the notion of the church as "sacrament of salvation". What are taken as pivotal starting points are §48 of the Malta report, §85 of *Facing Unity*, and §20.1 of the Dogmatic Constitution on the Church of Vatican II, which all emphasize the primacy of the gospel over the church. The church is described as "sacrament" in quotation marks, in order to differentiate this usage of this concept from what are normally called the sacraments. Later, CJ makes this differentiation clearer from a Lutheran point of view (126-128). The sacramental nature of the church is also depicted by means of the concept "sign" (118).

However, the relationship between the church as "sacrament" and the "normal" sacraments remains somewhat unclear in this sub-section. This presentation makes it possible to bend the interpretation of the concept of sacrament. It would be more important to say that the church has a sacramental nature, and to interpret it on the basis of the instruments of salvation, than to actually call it a sacrament. This would make it much easier to reach and express a consensus concerning the matter itself.

According to CJ, the Catholic understanding of the church as "sacrament" is based on an even more fundamental view of Christ as the "primal sacrament" (*Ursakrament*, 120). The text also presents as a Catholic view the notion that the church is "sacrament" in a manner which is different from, even if analogous to, the way in which baptism and the eucharist are sacraments (123). Both these notions provide very strong points of contact with Lutheran thinking, as shown in 128.

The Anglican-Roman Catholic document feels (CC 17) even freer to call the church a "mystery" or a "sacrament". As a matter of fact, the intention is not at all far from the Reformed-Roman Catholic expressions "instrument", "sign", "minister" or "medium":

> Thus the Church "which is Christ's body, the fullness of him who fills all in all", reveals and embodies "the mystery of Christ" (cf. Eph. 1:23, 3:4,8-11). It is therefore itself rightly described as a visible sign which both points to and embodies our communion with God and with one another; as an instrument through which God effects this communion; and as a foretaste of the fullness of communion to be consummated when Christ is all in all. It is a "mystery" or "sacrament".

The TNPC box on p.23 mentions different understandings of sacraments, among them "visible sign" and "effective sign". In these bilateral documents, "effective sign" is used only in CC 19. It is, however, in current ecumenical use e.g. in the Porvoo Common Statement (48). "Visible sign" is more frequent, e.g. CC 17; TCUC 108 (for the Catholic position):

> As Christ's mediation was carried out visibly in the mystery of his incarnation, life, death and resurrection, so the church has also been established as visible sign and instrument of this unique mediation across time and space. The church is an instrument in Christ's hands because it carries out, through the

preaching of the word, the administration of the sacraments and the oversight of communities, a ministry entirely dependent on the Lord, just like a tool in the hand of a worker.

The concept of "sign" is an old theological term, which has been used for sacrament. In classical Western theology, sacrament has been defined as the visible sign of an invisible grace of God and causes what it signifies *(efficit quod figurat)*. The term "sign" gained high ecclesiological relevance when it was included in the Dogmatic Constitution on the Church *Lumen Gentium* of the Second Vatican Council (LG 1): "Since the church is in Christ like a sacrament or as a sign and instrument both of a very closely knit union with God and of the unity of the whole human race, it desires now to unfold more fully to the faithful of the church and to the whole world its own inner nature and universal mission."

The church as a foretaste of God's reign

The terms "sign and instrument" have been fixed together as a current concept for a sacramental understanding of the church. Recently a third term has been added to the expression. This ecclesiological slogan reads now: "a sign, instrument and foretaste [of the kingdom of God]".

In our four dialogue documents, this formula can be found only in CC (17):

> It is therefore itself rightly described as a visible sign which both points to and embodies our communion with God and with one another; as an instrument through which God effects this communion; and as a foretaste of the fullness of communion to be consummated when Christ is all in all. It is a "mystery" or "sacrament".

It is, however, in frequent use in other ecumenical documents (e.g. Porvoo 18: "Therefore the church is sent into the world as a sign, instrument and foretaste of a reality which comes from beyond history, the kingdom of God") and ecclesial texts.

Reading these ecumenical texts, the history of that slogan raises curiosity. Is the father of the formula Lesslie Newbigin with his famous article "A Local Church Truly United"?

Conclusion

We have read four dialogue documents from the perspective of the box on p.23 of TNPC. Some of the questions raised in the box could not be discussed here (e.g. distinction between the church and sacraments, sin in relation to the church and sacraments conceived as means of the self-actualization of the church).

This reading gave in any case the impression that there is a great degree of understanding towards a sacramental notion of church in these bilateral documents. It might be partly due to the fact that the Roman Catholic Church was involved in all these dialogues. On the other hand, recent dialogues, e.g. with Anglican and Lutheran involvement, have produced texts with similar perspectives.

In terms of ecumenical terminology, "sign and instrument" seems to be a helpful concept in ecumenical ecclesiology. Only some churches feel comfortable talking about the church as a "sacrament". It is nevertheless clear that "other churches do not apply the concept of sacrament to the church". They may, however, accept the intention and even want to enrich their ecclesiological thinking with these ecumenical insights. If the main difficulty is the term "sacrament", "sign and sacrament" can be a relevant alternative.

"We believe the church as the mother of our new birth, and not in the church as if she were the author of our salvation."[5]

NOTES

[1] In *Growth in Agreement II: Reports and Agreed Statements of Ecumenical Conversations on a World Level, 1982-1998*, Jeffrey Gros, Harding Meyer and William G. Rusch eds, WCC Publications, 2000, pp.652-59.
[2] ARCIC II, "Church as Communion" = CC. Dublin 1990. In *Growth in Agreement II*, pp.328-43.
[3] Second phase 1984-1990, in *Growth in Agreement II*, pp.780-818, esp. pp.802-809).
[4] Third phase 1986-93, in *Growth in Agreement II*, pp.485-565, esp. pp.495-525).
[5] CCC 169 Faustus of Riez, *De Spiritu Sancto* 1, 2: PL 62, II.

Church as Koinonia / Church as Sacrament

DR DONNA GEERNAERT

While the concepts of "church as koinonia" and "church as sacrament" are readily identified with the Vatican II renewal of ecclesiology, Catholic theologians have been consistent in recalling the traditional basis for this development. In his 1974 *Models of the Church*, for example, Avery Dulles offers a survey of the biblical and patristic roots of both concepts. Yet, the adoption of these terms by the Second Vatican Council has made their usage almost a commonplace in Roman Catholic thought. Further, there is a linking of koinonia and sacrament in the Dogmatic Constitution on the Church which sees the church, because of its relationship with Christ, as "a kind of sacrament, or sign of intimate union with God, and of the unity of all humankind".[1] The church is described as the "universal sacrament of salvation" (*LG*, p.48; *GS*[2], p.45; *Ad Gentes*[3], p.1), and the "visible sacrament of this saving unity" (*LG*, p.9). In some cases the conciliar text indicates the deep roots of this concept of the church in patristic thinking by referring to various expressions of Cyprian, who speaks of ecclesial unity as a sacrament (*LG*, p.9 and *Sacrosanctum Concilium*[4], p.26). A similar linking of terms is found in Pope John Paul II's recent apostolic letter, *Novo Millennio Ineunte*.[5] Here the text begins by making reference to "the domain of communion (koinonia)" as embodying and revealing "the very essence of the mystery of the church". It then goes on to state, "It is in building this communion of love that the church appears as 'sacrament', as the 'sign and instrument of intimate union with God and of the unity of the human race'."[6]

For this presentation on "the inter-relationship between the church as koinonia and church as sacrament", I will begin with a definition of terms and a review of the inter-relatedness of koinonia and the celebration of the sacraments. The text will then attempt to apply the definition of sacrament to the concept of church as koinonia by exploring both what the concept signifies and how the church may effect what is signified. Finally, the paper notes the "not yet" quality of the church as koinonia and suggests some implications for ongoing reflection on the church as sacrament. In addition to materials drawn from Roman Catholic sources, the paper will make use of various discussions of "koinonia" and "sacrament" in several of the bilateral dialogues which have had Catholic participation.

Definition of terms

1. Church as koinonia

Although "koinonia" is never equated with "church" in the New Testament, it is the term that most aptly expresses the mystery underlying the various New Testament images of the church: people of God (1 Pet. 2:9-10), flock (John 10:14; Acts 20:28-29; 1 Pet. 5:2-4), vine (John 15:5), temple (1 Cor. 3:16-17), bride (Rev. 21:2), body of Christ (1 Cor. 12:27, 10:17; Rom. 12:4-5; Eph. 1:22-23). All of these express a relationship with God and also imply a relationship among the members of the community. In the epistles of Paul, koinonia is used in various ways. It describes the eucharist (1 Cor. 10:14-20) where Christians who share in breaking the bread and blessing the cup have koinonia with the body and blood of Christ. The communities which contributed to the collection for the saints in Jerusalem are bound in koinonia with them through the sharing of material goods (1 Cor. 8:3-4; Rom. 15:26-27; Phil. 1:5). Yet another use of koinonia stresses the fellowship of those who walk in the light because they are in communion with the Father and the Son and consequently with one another (1 John 1:3,7). In the New Testament, the basic verbal form of koinonia means "to share", "to participate", "to have part in", "to have something in common", or "to act together". The noun can signify fellowship or community. It usually signifies a relationship based on participation in one and the same reality (1 John 1:3; cf. 1 John 1:7).

To speak of koinonia is to speak of the way human beings come to know God as God's purpose for humanity is revealed. God in Christ through the Holy Spirit calls human beings to share in fellowship within the divine life, a call to which they respond in faith. Thus, koinonia refers first to fellowship with God and subsequently to sharing with one another. The Spirit of God acting in history is the main agent of that koinonia which is the church. Persons are brought into living relationship with the Father through the Son by the power of the Spirit. The new creation is a foretaste of what will come in fullness through the Spirit at the end of time and human relationships are set in a new context so that people may recognize one another as equally God's children and come to acknowledge the bonds that link them as a gift from God. God's redeeming act in Christ demands that all humanity be united.

The extraordinary synod of bishops held in 1985 to assess the implementation of Vatican II states that it was on the basis of an ecclesiology of communion (koinonia) that "the Catholic church at the time of the Second Vatican Council fully assumed its ecumenical responsibility".[7] From a Catholic perspective, three aspects of an ecclesiology of communion are particularly helpful in promoting ecumenical relations: (1) this understanding of the church is rooted in a trinitarian theology which sees distinctions of Persons maintained through mutual relatedness; such a notion of communion will continue to affirm unity in diversity and diversity in unity; (2) the concept of "communion" allows for varied degrees of relationship and implies that communion will have a certain visibility; (3) an ecclesiology of communion asserts that sharing a common life with God in Christ entails communion with one another and the whole created world.

2. Church as sacrament

Even before the Second Vatican Council, many Roman Catholic theologians had described the church as a "sacrament", because this term is associated with the biblical term "mystery". Such a sacramental description highlights the comparison between what the church is and what is enacted in the celebration of the sacraments. Just as the sacraments in scholastic thinking are described as visible signs and instruments of invisible grace, Vatican II sees the church as "one interlocked reality which is comprised of a divine and a human element" in which "the communal structure of the church serves Christ's Spirit, who vivifies it by way of building up the body (cf. Eph. 4:16)".[8] But this view of the church as "sacrament" also stands in the context of the effective imparting of salvation to all people: "The one Mediator... communicates truth and grace to all" through the church.[9] The council sees the establishment of the church as rooted in the whole mystery of Christ (cf. *LG* 2-5) but links the identification of the church as "sacrament" in a special way with the resurrection of Christ and the sending of the Spirit: "Rising from the dead (cf. Rom. 6:9), He sent his life-giving Spirit upon his disciples and through this Spirit has established his body, the church, as the universal sacrament of salvation" (*LG* 48; cf. *LG* 7, 59). Speaking of the church as "sacrament" in the context of salvation for all people and of mission theology shows that the council did not simply take over earlier theories but developed its own theological position.

The term "sacrament", as a sign and instrument of salvation, gives expression to the universal mission of the church and its radical dependence on Christ. The church does not exist by itself or for itself. It is only in and through Christ, only in and through the Holy Spirit, that the church is effectual as a mediator of salvation. In Catholic thought the concept of sacrament is constantly applied to the church analogically. Thus the term "sacrament" is always placed within quotation marks when related to the church in order to draw attention to the analogous use of language. In the Dogmatic Constitution on the Church, this is expressly highlighted when talking of the church as "a kind of *(veluti)* sacrament... a sign and an instrument..." (*LG* 1). In fact, the incarnate Christ is the primordial sacrament of God. Jesus is the full revelation of grace (cf. John 1:14) and "the image of the invisible God" (Col. 1:15), the one who has become "the source of eternal salvation to all who obey him" (Heb. 5:9). For Thomas Aquinas, the original sacraments of our salvation are the "mysteries of the flesh of Christ"; in particular, the passion and the resurrection of Christ are sacraments by reason of their double character of being exemplary sign as well as instrumental and effective cause.[10] Christ is the unique foundational sacrament, the active and original source of the whole economy of salvation visibly manifested in the world.

The application of the term "sacrament" to the church is analogical not only with respect to Christ but also in relation to the celebration of the sacraments. This is evident in the functioning of the individual sacraments which develop their saving efficacy "on the basis of their being celebrated" *(ex opere operato)*. Since it is Christ who effects salvation in the sacraments, their efficacy is not dependent on the worthiness of the minister or the recipient. This cannot be said in the same way about the church as "sacrament". The concept of sacrament is applied to the church to assist theological reflection, to clarify the inner connection between outward, visible structure and hidden, spiritual reality. Thus, when Catholic theologians speak of the sacraments as self-actualizations of the church, their hope is to prevent a purely outward understanding of the church as simply the steward of sacraments, and to affirm an inner affinity between the church and the sacraments, both being seen as signs and instruments of salvation. Constituted by God's saving grace, the church becomes the instrument for extending the divine offer as widely as the scope of God's eternal purpose for humankind. In such an approach, the sacraments of the church may be considered as particular instances of the divine mystery being revealed and made operative in the lives of the faithful. Instituted by Christ and made effective by the Spirit, the sacraments bring the mystery home to those in whom God pleases to dwell. The church is a sacrament founded by Christ and entirely dependent on him. Its being and its sacramental acts are the fruit of a free gift received from

Christ, a gift in relation to which he remains radically transcendent, but which, however, he commits to the salvation of humankind.

Koinonia and celebration of the sacraments

The mystery of salvation is a mystery of koinonia. While this koinonia will be complete only in the reign of God at the end of time, it is already visibly present in the community of faith and love which is the church. In the church,

> Christ now acts through the sacraments he instituted to communicate his grace. The sacraments are perceptible signs (words and actions) accessible to our human nature. By the action of Christ and the power of the Holy Spirit they make present efficaciously the grace that they signify.[11]

As those visible realities through which God is communicated to the church and through which the church responds to God's self-communication, sacraments are directly ecclesial in character. They are expressions of the nature and mission of the church. Sacraments are acts of worship and signs of Christ's presence, as well as signs of faith and of the unity of the church. There is a two-way relationship between the church and the sacraments. On the one hand, the sacraments build up the church as the body of Christ until its members come to their full stature; on the other hand, the church is at work in the sacraments by virtue of the mission received from the Holy Spirit.

The particular sacraments flow from the sacramental nature of God's self-communication in Christ. They are specific ways in which by the power of the Holy Spirit the risen Jesus makes his saving presence and action effective in the world. Every sacrament presupposes and expresses the faith of the church which celebrates it. In a sacrament the church does more than profess and express its faith: it makes present the mystery it is celebrating. The human person is integrated into the body of Christ by his or her koinonia with this visible church which nourishes faith by means of the sacramental life and the word of God. Every sacrament of the church confers the grace of the Holy Spirit because it is inseparably a sign recalling what God has accomplished in the past, a sign manifesting what God is effecting in the believer and in the church, and a sign announcing and anticipating the eschatological fulfilment.[12] In the sacramental celebration the church thus manifests, illustrates and confesses its faith in the unity of God's design. The sacraments are the privileged place where the faith is lived, transmitted and professed.

By the celebration of the sacraments, the church proclaims, transmits and assimilates its faith. Further, in the celebration of the sacraments, each local church expresses its profound nature. It is in continuity with the church of the apostles and in koinonia with all the churches which share one and the same faith and celebrate the same sacraments. In the sacramental celebration of a local church, the other local churches recognize the identity of their faith with that church's and by that fact are strengthened in their own life of faith. Thus, the celebration of the sacrament confirms the koinonia of faith between the churches and expresses it. This is why a member of one local church, baptized in that church, can receive the sacraments in another local church. This koinonia in the sacraments expresses the identity and oneness of the faith which the churches share.

The sacramental nature of the church is especially evident in the common celebration of the eucharist. In celebrating the eucharist, the church points to the origin of its koinonia in Christ who is in koinonia with the Father and the Spirit. In the eucharistic celebration, the church experiences this koinonia in a visible fellowship, anticipates the fullness of the koinonia in the eschatological reign of God, and is sent out to realize, manifest and extend that koinonia to the world. As stated by the council of Trent, the eucharist is not simply one of the sacraments but is pre-eminent among them because of the presence of Christ. At the Second Vatican Council, the eucharist was identified as "the source and summit of the entire Christian life".[13] In and through the eucharistic koinonia with Christ, ecclesial koinonia is established and strengthened. Celebrating the eucharist, the church becomes fully itself. This bond between the church and the eucharist is expressed in a well-known summary of the patristic tradition, "the eucharist makes the church". The eucharist is the proclamation of faith from which is derived and to which every confession is ordered. In the eucharistic concelebration between representatives of different local churches identity of faith is particularly manifested and reinforced by the sacramental act itself.[14] Identity of faith, then, is an essential element of ecclesial communion in the celebration of the sacraments. However, a certain diversity in its formulation does not compromise the koinonia between the local churches when each church can recognize in the variety of formulations the one authentic faith received from the apostles.

According to Catholic understanding, koinonia is rooted in the bonds of faith and sacramental life shared by congregations united in dioceses pastored by bishops. Through their bishops the churches are in communion with one another by reason of the common faith, the common sacramental life and the common episcopacy. Among the fellowship of bishops, the bishop of Rome is recognized as the successor of Peter and presides over the whole Catholic communion. Through their day-to-day teaching, more specifically through local and universal councils, bishops have responsibility to articulate clearly the faith and discipline of the church. Church order is thus grounded in the koinonia of faith and the sacraments; church order is at the same time an active expression of koinonia in its service of unity as well as in the way it is exercised.

Koinonia signifies restored relationships in the reign of God

In Catholic understanding, a sacrament "effects what it signifies". From a survey of discussions in various bilateral dialogues, there is evident agreement that koinonia is a sign of the eschatological reign of God. Specifically, church as koinonia signifies the centrality of restored relationships in God's kingdom. As a way of exploring this aspect of the concept of koinonia, a summary of current theological reflection on the concept of community will be helpful.

From a theological perspective, Christian community flows from and reflects the triune life of God. Thus, trinitarian theology provides a basis for identifying the essential characteristics of Christian community. Christians, like the followers of many other faith traditions, maintain that God is incomparable, incomprehensible, beyond all human words and knowing. Yet, Christians also claim that in Jesus Christ a special revelation about God has been given. What is distinctive about Christianity is not so much monotheism per se but a trinitarian understanding of God. As trinitarian theology developed, moreover, two different approaches emerged. Where one approach sought to define the Trinity on the basis of God's being known in human history as Creator, Redeemer and Sustainer, a second type of definition attempted to describe the internal or immanent reality of the God who is known in this threefold encounter. In descriptions of God's immanent reality, the trinitarian Persons are defined not only in relation to their shared nature but also in terms of their mutual relatedness. It is, in fact, this mutual relatedness which identifies each Person as distinct.[15]

In light of this trinitarian understanding of God, it is not surprising that the call to community is integral to the whole created world and especially to its human inhabitants who are made in the image and likeness of their Creator. Recent exegetical studies have been particularly helpful in elucidating this point. While earlier interpretations of the Genesis narratives had focused on woman's secondary creation as the reason for her being subordinate to man by nature, contemporary exegesis emphasizes the simultaneous creation, inter-relatedness and interdependence of male and female. The assertion of male dominance which occurs within the context of a divine judgment on human disobedience is seen as a consequence of sin, a distortion of the harmonious relationship envisioned in the covenant formula of Genesis 2:23. A rethinking of the dominance of male over female suggests a similar re-evaluation of humanity's relationship to the rest of the created world. In the Genesis text, the linking of "image and likeness" to "dominion" identifies humanity's role as that of the steward who does not own but administers, who cares for the world in God's name as God would have it cared for. Thus, rather than endorsing the supremacy of either the male or the human, these creation accounts implicitly condemn the whole domination/subjugation pattern of relating. A unity between equal and differentiated persons in a trinitarian God models the relational character of the created world.

When the God who creates the world chooses to intervene in human history, the call to community is specified in covenant terms which identify right relationships with the neighbour as a way of expressing fidelity to God. In fact, when the prophets of Israel accuse the people of breaking their covenant with God, it is injustice towards the neighbour that is most frequently cited as evidence. Within the covenant framework, moreover, it is the poor who have a special claim to the community's care. Just treatment of the poor is seen as a clear expression of obedience to the law of God. Thus, when Jesus links love of neighbour to love of God in his statement of the great commandment, his teaching is in continuity with covenant law. Yet, the closeness of the linking established by Jesus radicalizes the love commandment by affirming that God cannot be loved without love of neighbour and, more positively stated, that it is God who is loved in loving the neighbour. In addition to making the commandment more radical, Jesus' teaching also universalizes it. Where covenant tradition had tended to limit the neighbour to members of the Jewish community, Jesus removes all limitations to the neighbour's identity and even insists that enemies be loved. Further, in the injunction to love one's enemies, it is God who serves as the model for this kind of loving. Human beings are invited to love as God loves, to live the kind of community God lives.

From the pattern of divine intervention established at the time of the exodus, it is evident that God chooses to interact with a people. God calls a people and even in the most personal of prophetic calls it is the good of the people that predominates. The choice of a people is continued and extended in the activity of Jesus. While scholars question the historicity of many of the events recorded in the gospels, the gathering of a group of disciples around Jesus seems an undeniable historical fact. Further, it also seems evident that Jesus, in contradistinction to the contemporary rabbinic tradition, was prepared to include women among his followers. In fact, the inclusion of women, along with tax collectors and sinners, among the disciples seems indicative of both the world-reversing character and the nearness of the reign of God that Jesus proclaims is "at hand". While the parables present the reign of God as a world of right relationships in which compassion, mercy and forgiveness are structural realities, Jesus' interaction with the outcasts of his society so actualizes these alternate realities that the representatives of the worldly power which is being reversed sentence him to death. For the followers of Jesus, however, the resurrection again reverses this worldly condemnation so that the reign of God can be lived by anticipation in the present world.

In light of their experience of the resurrection which enables them to see the crucifixion as an event of salvation, Jesus' disciples find renewed faith and come to understand themselves as the eschatological community of God, the church *(ecclesia)*. For the early church, the outpouring of the Spirit at Pentecost is an established fact which fulfils the ancient prophecies concerning the last days (Acts 2:16-17). Transformed by the presence of the Spirit, the community becomes the temple of God (1 Cor. 3:16), capable of proclaiming the gospel with convincing power (1 Thess. 1:5). Although they were dramatically changed by their experience of the resurrection, the disciples did not understand themselves to be taking the place of Jesus. They did not simply continue to proclaim the reign of God as they had during his life-time. Instead, the post-resurrection period is marked by a clear transition from Jesus the proclaimer of God's reign to the disciples the proclaimers of Christ. According to Edward Schillebeeckx, the very pattern of Jesus' calling of the disciples suggests the origins of a relationship consistent with this change. Specifically, he asserts that the conversion-model in the call narratives is used to show "that turning to Jesus to follow him is the metanoia (complete about-turn) demanded by the coming kingdom of God". "In that conversion the nevertheless still-to-come rule of God becomes an already present reality." Further, the habitual practice of Jesus' close disciples of being his companions "is the pre-Easter model of what was reckoned after the Easter events to be simply 'Christian living'".[16]

In continuity with the disciples' experience of call, the Christian community after Easter sees conversion to Jesus as the condition for membership in the community of salvation. "In the New Testament the explicit message conveyed by the idea of 'following Jesus' is that fulfilment of the Law... is no longer sufficient for salvation. What now mediates salvation is one's relation to Jesus."[17] In this context, the church becomes the place of contact with Christ and his message, the place where authentic discipleship is possible. "The preaching of the gospel is not merely an account of the historical saving act of God in Christ; Christ himself is at work in the word which is preached."[18] Sacramental worship is a key moment in the life of the church when Christ is present according to his promise. The focus of mission and ministry in the church is to enable Christians to enter into an immediate relationship with Jesus in the Holy Spirit.

Convinced that "Jesus is Lord", members of the early Christian community saw the reign of Christ continued in the church through the charismatic gifts of the Holy Spirit. Further, since all of these gifts have their source in the Holy Spirit, there may be tension but there can be no radical opposition between charismatic and administrative ministries (Rom. 12:6-8; Eph. 4:11-12). In later theological reflection, this understanding of church structure suggests a concept of administrative office as instituted charism with the specific task of safeguarding creative fidelity to the gospel. This view of church structure highlights the mutual relatedness of all charisms within the community of disciples. Since all members of the church remain disciples together, no one's gift may be despised. All charisms are to be respected and every gift is to be judged by its contribution to the integrity of the church's life and mission.

God's eternal purpose, which has been revealed in the person and work of Jesus Christ, is a saving design which embraces Jew and Gentile alike in the goodness of God's final kingdom (Mark 4:11; Eph. 3:5; Col. 1:20,25-27). This good news is signified in the life of the church, for its vocation is to embody and reveal the gospel's redemptive power. What Christ achieved through his cross and resurrection is communicated by the Holy Spirit in the life of the church. In its life, the church is a sign God's gracious purpose for creation, a sign of the right relationships which are central to the reign of God.

How does koinonia effect restored relationships?

The church as koinonia requires visible expression because it is intended to be the sacrament, the sign and instrument, of God's saving work. The koinonia is a sign that God's purpose in Christ is being realized in the world by grace. By proclaiming the truth of the gospel, witnessing to it by its life, and thus entering more deeply into the mystery of the kingdom, the church is also an instrument for the accomplishment of God's purpose. In this perspective, the church is the visible form of God's grace. It opens the way to salvation through preaching, sacraments, and other institutions derived from apostolic authority. Participation in these means of grace constitutes the deeper koinonia that unites members of the church together in true fellowship in the Spirit. Through their common life and koinonia the members of the church witness to salvation as they pray and worship together, forgive, accept, and love one another, and stand together in time of trial. Their koinonia is made possible by a deeper koinonia in the means of grace that come from God who makes the people of the church a new creation in Christ.

The Holy Spirit reveals to the world the presence of the kingdom in creation. The liberty promised to the children of God is nothing less than participation, with Christ and through the Holy Spirit, in the life of God. The gift of the Spirit is the pledge and foretaste here and now of the ultimate fulfilment of God's purpose for the whole created world; it is the first instalment of the coming kingdom (2 Cor. 1:21-22). The unity, holiness, catholicity and apostolicity of the church derive their meaning and reality from the meaning and reality of God's kingdom. They reflect the fullness of the life of God. They are signs of the universal love of God, Father, Son and Holy Spirit, the love poured out upon the whole creation. To speak of the church as sacrament is to affirm that in and through the koinonia of all those who confess Jesus Christ and who live according to their confession, God's plan of salvation for the world is realized. This is why the church, in which God's grace is at work, is itself the sacrament of salvation, the foretaste of God's kingdom, the anticipated manifestation of the final realities.

While the action of the Spirit of God is not limited to the community of Christians, it is within the church, where the Holy Spirit gives and nurtures the new life of the kingdom, that the gospel becomes a manifest reality. As the koinonia of believers with God and with each other, the church is the community where the redemptive work of Jesus Christ has been recognized and received, and is therefore being made known in the world. Koinonia with God in Christ is constantly established and renewed through the power of the Holy Spirit. By the power of the Spirit, the incomparable riches of God's grace are made present for all time through the church. The church as koinonia is called to be a living expression of the gospel, evangelized and evangelizing, reconciled and reconciling, gathered together and gathering others.

In its ministry to the world, the church seeks to share with all people the grace by which its own life is created and sustained. By its communal life, the church bears witness to that society of love in which the reign of God will consist. This is made evident in the Christian community's affirmation of a world reversing understanding of authority and of a leadership which is to be exercised in a way that is radically different from that of "the rulers of the Gentiles" (Matt. 20:20-28). When the church, through its exercise of authority, displays the healing and reconciling power of the gospel, then the wider world is offered a vision of what God intends for all creation. The koinonia of the church demonstrates that Christ has broken down the dividing wall of hostility to create a single new humanity reconciled to God in one body by the cross (cf. Eph. 2:14-16). Confessing that their koinonia signifies God's purpose for the whole human race, the members of the church are called to give themselves in loving witness and service to their fellow human beings.

The church participates in Christ's mission to the world through the proclamation of the gospel of salvation by its words and deeds. Those who are sustained in the life of Christ through word and sacrament are liberated from self-centredness and thus empowered to act freely and live at peace with God and with one another. The church is called to embody the good news that forgiveness is a gift to be received from God and shared with others (Matt. 6:14-15). It is called to affirm the sacredness and dignity of the person, the value of natural and political communities and the divine purpose for the human race as a whole; to witness against the structures of sin in society, addressing humanity with the gospel of repentance and forgiveness and making intercession for the world. In fulfilling its vocation the church is called to follow the way of Jesus Christ, who being the image of the Father took the form of a servant and was made perfect by suffering. When for Christ's sake the church encounters opposition and persecution, it is then a sign of God's choice of the way of the cross to save the world.

Committed to serving the gospel, the church is the recipient and mediator of salvation. The biblical images of the people of God, the body of Christ, and the temple of the Holy Spirit show the church to be a koinonia founded in the life of the triune God from whom it receives life and salvation. In addition, the church imparts life and salvation in faithfulness to its task of mission, which it has received from God. The gospel by which the church was created and lives is mediated by word and by sacrament. Both modes of mediation are linked in a fundamentally indissoluble fashion without doing away with their specific characteristics. Thus, the word proclaimed is an audible sign, the sacraments are a visible word. These are the two modes in which the transmission of the gospel is saving in its effect. Salvation is ultimately a matter of reconciliation and koinonia with God, a sharing in God's life which is effected through real union with Christ. As an instrument of the unique mediation of Christ, a sign of the efficacious presence of that mediation, the church is constituted as a sacrament. In brief, the church is the bearer of the tradition of the word, that is, the sacrament of the word of God; and bearer of transmission of salvation, that is, the sacrament of Christ and of the Spirit. If the church is seen in relation to its source, it may be described as the sacrament of God, of Christ and of the Spirit, as a sacrament of grace. If it is seen in relation to its mission and vocation, it may be called the sacrament of the kingdom, or the sacrament of salvation. Since the concept of koinonia may be affirmed in relation to each of these various designations, it seems equally appropriate to identify the church as the sacrament of koinonia.

Although it is his body, the church is not simply identified with Christ. It is taken into Christ's service to mediate salvation to all people and needs the constant vivifying power of the Holy Spirit. It is Christ as head who grants participation in this Spirit and who thus causes the life and growth of the body. It is part of the logic of such a sacramental concept of the church that the church in its human weakness must be called to "continual reformation".[19] The church is servant, not master, of what it has received. Its power to affect the hearer comes entirely from the Holy Spirit, who is the source of the church's life and who enables it to be truly the steward of God's design. The Holy Spirit uses the church as the means through which the word of God is proclaimed afresh, the sacraments are celebrated, and the people of God receive pastoral oversight, so that the life of the gospel is manifested in the life of its members. Through word and sacrament, Christ acts in the church which is the recipient of the Holy Spirit's activity. The presence of Christ marks the church as the place where salvation takes place. The gift of salvation, however, becomes the task and mission of the church as the community which has received salvation.

Real but imperfect koinonia: the reign of God is "not yet"

The terms "sacrament" and "sign" imply coherence and continuity between diverse moments of the economy of salvation. They depict the church as instrument and minister of the unique mediation of Christ. Of this unique mediation, the church is the servant but never the source. As Christ's mediation was carried out visibly in the mystery of his incarnation, life, death and resurrection, so the church has also been established as visible sign and instrument of this unique mediation across time and space. Like a tool in the hand of a worker, the church is an instrument in Christ's hands as it carries out, through the preaching of the word, the administration of the sacraments and the oversight of communities, a ministry which is entirely dependent on the gift of God. The instrumental ministry of the church is confided to sinful human beings. It can therefore be disfigured or atrophied, mishandled and exaggerated. But the reality of God's gift always transfigures human failure, and God's fidelity to the church continually maintains it, according to the promise (Matt. 28:20) which sustains it in its mission of salvation across the ages. Paradoxically it is pre-eminently in its weakness, suffering and poverty that the church becomes the sign of the efficacy of God's grace (cf. 2 Cor. 12:9, 4:7-12). The power of God to sanctify the church is revealed in the scandal of the cross where Christ in his love gave himself for the church so that it might be presented to him without spot or wrinkle, holy and without blemish (Eph. 5:26-27). God was in Christ reconciling the world to Godself, making him who knew no sin to be sin for us so that in him we might become the righteousness of God (cf. 2 Cor. 5:19-21).

The church is called to be, and by the power of the Spirit actually is, a sign, steward and instrument of God's design. For this reason, it can be described as sacrament of God's saving work. However, the credibility of the church's witness is undermined by the sins of its members, the shortcomings of its human institutions, and not least by the scandal of division. The church is in constant need of repentance and renewal so that it can be more clearly seen for what it is, the body of Christ. Yet, the gospel contains the promise that, despite all failures, the church will be used by the Holy Spirit to draw humanity into koinonia with the life of God and with one another. The church which in this world is always in need of renewal and purification is already here and now a foretaste of God's kingdom in a world still awaiting its consummation, a world full of suffering and injustice, division and strife. Thus, the church as koinonia is called to transcend the seemingly insuperable divisions of the world. Christian koinonia testifies to a world where all, because of their equal standing before God, must be equally accepted by one another; where all, since they are justified by the grace of God, may learn to do justice to one another; where racial, ethnic, social, sexual and other distinctions no longer cause discrimination and alienation (Gal. 3:28). In brief, the church is required to carry out its mission in such a way that the gospel may be heard as good news in differing ages and cultures.

The concept of koinonia challenges the church to live the communion it celebrates with God, with one another, and with the whole created world. Specifically, the church as koinonia witnesses to the world-reversing character of the reign of God. Based on a trinitarian understanding of God, Christian koinonia is to be lived in a simultaneous affirmation of mutuality and difference. This concept of differentiating union endorses neither uniformity nor individualism. In the living of koinonia, there can be no priority of one over another but only mutual concern for the good of each. Further, it seems evident that such a way of life would reverse many contemporary categories of judgment and allow for the paradoxical forgiveness, mercy and compassion illustrated in the parables of Jesus. In a world that is increasingly marked by individualism, isolation and alienation, the church's witness to koinonia could make a significant contribution to the evangelization and transformation of current social structures.

The message of the church is not a private pietism irrelevant to contemporary society, nor can it be reduced to a political or social programme. Only a reconciled and reconciling community in which human divisions are being overcome can speak with full integrity to an alienated, divided world, and so be a credible witness to God's saving action in Christ and a foretaste of the reign of God. Yet, until the kingdom is realized in its fullness, the church is marked by human limitation and imperfection. It is the beginning and not yet the end, the first-fruits and not yet the final harvest. The source of the church's hope for the world is God, who has never abandoned the created order and has never ceased to work within it. It is called, empowered and sent by God to proclaim this hope and to communicate to the world the conviction on which this hope is founded. It is called to be an agent of justice and compassion, challenging and assisting society's attempts to achieve just judgment, never forgetting that in the light of God's justice all human solutions are provisional. While the church pursues its mission and pilgrimage in the world, it looks forward to "the end, when Christ delivers the kingdom to God the Father after destroying every rule and every authority and power" (1 Cor. 15:24).

Conclusion

Since the 16th century, bilateral dialogues have been used to overcome or avoid church division. At the time of the Reformation, for example, bilateral conversations took place between Catholics and Lutherans, Lutherans and Anglicans, Reformed and Lutherans. In the 1960s, however, there was a new emphasis on and sudden surge of bilateral dialogues on both international and national levels. While bilateral dialogues allow for focused conversation on specific issues of division, the danger of isolating the individual dialogues from each other and of losing sight of the indivisibility of the ecumenical movement has been an ongoing concern. To address this concern, the Faith and Order commission and the Christian world communions have co-sponsored a series of forums on bilateral dialogues (1978, 1979, 1980, 1985, 1990, 1995, 1997, 2001).

The research for this presentation on "the inter-relationship between the church as koinonia and church as sacrament" led to a survey of the themes of "koinonia" and "sacrament" in the bilateral dialogues which had Catholic participation. In light of this survey, it is interesting to note the high degree of coherence between the various bilaterals and with the multilateral Faith and Order discussions on these two topics. Similar approaches, understandings and even wordings are evident. A more detailed study of the dialogues might suggest a number of reasons for these similarities. In fact, an energetic PhD student might well explore this question from the perspective of dialogue membership, and also trace the chronological emergence of specific concepts.

NOTES

[1] *Lumen Gentium,* Dogmatic Constitution on the Church, promulgated 21 Nov. 1964, p.1, further referred to as *LG.* See Walter M. Abbot ed., *The Documents of Vatican II,* New York, America Press, 1966.
[2] *Gaudium et Spes.*
[3] *Ad Gentes,* Decree on the Missionary Activity of the Church, promulgated 2 Dec. 1965.
[4] *Sacrosanctum Concilium,* Constitution on the Sacred Liturgy, promulgated 4 Dec. 1963.
[5] *Novo Millennio Ineunte,* The Coming of the New Millennium, promulgated 6 Jan. 2001.
[6] *Novo Millennio Ineunte,* p.42; *Lumen Gentium,* p.1.
[7] "The Final Report of the 1985 Extraordinary Synod", in *Origins,* 15, 19 Dec. 1985, pp.444-50, II, C.7; see also *The Extraordinary Synod,* 1985, Boston, St Paul's Eds, 1985.
[8] *LG,* p.8.
[9] *Ibid.*
[10] St Thomas Aquinas, *Summa Theologica* (translated by fathers of the English Dominican Province), in 5 vols, Ave Maria Press, complete English translation from Latin ed., 1981, IIIa, 62, 5 and *primum,* further referred to as *STh.*
[11] *Catechism of the Catholic Church,* Publ Service, Canadian Conference of Catholic Bishops, Ottawa, Ontario, 1994, p.1084.
[12] *STh.* III,60,3.
[13] Cf. SC, 10; *LG,* 11; *AG,* 9.
[14] Several rites such as the *fermentum* and the *conmixtio* draw attention to the connection between the one bread and the assembling of the church.
[15] H. Denzinger-A. Schönmetzer, *Enchiridion Symbolorum, Definitionum et Declarationum de rebus fidei et morum,* Freiburg im Breisgau, 1965, 1330, further referred to as *DS.*
[16] Edward Schillebeeckx, *Jesus: An Experiment in Christology,* New York, Seabury, 1979, pp.224-29.
[17] *Ibid.,* p.226.
[18] Hans Küng, *The Church,* New York, Doubleday, 1976, p.305.
[19] *Unitatis Redintegratio,* Decree on Ecumenism, promulgated 21 Nov. 1964. Taken from *The Documents of Vatican II.*

Koinonia in the Context of Sacramentality of the Church

REV. DR HERMEN P. SHASTRI

Koinonia: the emerging model of unity
In the history of the Faith and Order movement there are basically two approaches to the search for the visible unity of the church. The first takes the present divided stage of the churches as the starting-point, where the emphasis is placed on the need for the churches to enter into dialogue, to reach deeper mutual understanding and, if possible, to formulate agreed common perspectives. The second starts with the communion which has been established by Christ and continues to exist through the renewing power of the Spirit despite divisions which have arisen in the course of history.

Perhaps it can be said that visible unity can and will only be achieved when unity as "gift" and "task" meet, that is, when the church succeeds in removing the obstacles which for centuries have stood in the way of unity by reaching a sufficient common understanding of "church as communion", which God has given in Christ and reflected in the fellowship of churches to each other.

The statement on "The Unity of the Church as Koinonia: Gift and Calling", adopted by World Council of Churches' seventh assembly (Canberra 1991), directly inspired the work of the fifth world conference on Faith and Order (Santiago de Compostela 1993), which met under the theme "Towards Koinonia in Faith, Life and Witness". Since then, the perception of the understanding of the church as koinonia has become the central focus of the efforts to formulate ecumenical perspectives on ecclesiology. The church as koinonia has provided a necessary entry-point for moving away from an institutional and structural understanding of the church to a more relational character of the life of churches in its vertical and horizontal dimensions of fellowship.

Koinonia is not primarily about the church. It is about the gift of God's own life in relation to the world. It speaks to us of that which God wills for the whole of humanity and the whole of creation. Koinonia also underscores the quality of the divine communion between the three Persons of the Holy Trinity; the giving and receiving love, where in the relational life God is uplifted as undivided and diverse, yet there is complete communion of three distinct Persons sharing one nature. Hence, unity and diversity are inseparably inter-related dimensions within the triune life of God.

Koinonia as it is described in *The Nature and Purpose of the Church* seeks to hold together the vertical dimension of the trinitarian basis of communion with the horizontal dimension of the visible gathering and common life of God's people on earth. The church is not simply the human receiver of revelation but is in itself a dimension of that which is revealed, sharing in the trinitarian life. As Charles Wesley put it, "You whom he ordained to be, Transcripts of the Trinity." The divine love shared inward and outward is sustained by the church's intimate share in the life and witness of the three Persons. So, Trinity is not only the pattern ("that all of them may be one, Father, just as you are in me and I am in you", John 17:20-21), but also the potential for the new community.

So the vision of the church as koinonia challenges the co-existence of the churches in their division. It constantly calls the churches to look beyond themselves and see in each other the faith expressions of the one apostolic and catholic church.

Konrad Raiser argues that the relational emphasis underscored by the concept of koinonia opens new approaches to understanding unity and diversity among the churches.[1] He highlights three features. First, interpreting the church and its unity as koinonia opens up new possibilities to appreciate continuing diversities and differences within the community and to come to terms with the experience of plurality. Second, there is a renewed interest in exploring the links between ecclesiology and ethics, as the church is understood as a community within the wider human community. And, third, the church is *in viam*, engaged in a pilgrimage that leads to conversion as it shares in the way of the cross of Christ, when exposed to the fragmentation of the church's life in the world.

Hence, unity as koinonia is not a goal for its own sake. It is located in the context of the saving purpose of God for all humanity. Therefore, there will always be a double task. On the one hand, we must manifest concretely and visibly the koinonia which is given and which we still maintain to some degree. On the other hand, the struggle to restore the koinonia that is broken must also be viewed within the wider framework of the unity of the whole of humankind.

The inter-relation of church as koinonia and church as sacrament

Being in koinonia with God implies working for the renewal and reconciliation of humanity and the sustainability of creation. The church is in the world witnessing to the fulfilment of God's plan; but it is not of the world (John 15:19). Only in the perspective of the kingdom do the church and the world appear in their eschatological togetherness and fulfilment.

If visible unity is about bearing witness to the world by living God's own trinitarian life, then the church as koinonia must look beyond itself and participate in the reality of God's kingdom of which it is called to be the first-fruit. The study *Church and World* has attempted to show how the vision of visible unity must relate directly with priorities of God's kingdom in the world through the church.[2] The revised working document, *Towards Koinonia in Faith, Life and Witness* maintains, "The church as koinonia is called to share not only in the suffering of its own community but in the suffering of all. In so doing it shows its vocation to invite all people to respond in faith to God's love."[3]

We can speak of the church as the "sacrament" of God's saving work when it is "sign" and "instrument" for the full realization of God's salvific plan for the world. The church as the koinonia of believers with God and with each other is a sign of the new humanity God is creating and a living witness of the renewing work of the Holy Spirit, as it exercises its prophetic role for the transformation of the world.

The sacramental nature of the church as sign, instrument and first-fruit (or foretaste) is especially manifest in the celebration of the eucharist. The eucharistic vision of the church in *Baptism, Eucharist and Ministry* includes the following:

> The eucharist embraces all aspects of life. It is a representative act of thanksgiving and offering on behalf of the whole world. The eucharistic celebration demands reconciliation and sharing among all those regarded as brothers and sisters in the one family of God and is a constant challenge in the search for appropriate relationships in social, economic and political life... As participants in the eucharist, therefore, we prove inconsistent if we are not actively participating in this ongoing restoration of the world's situation and the human condition.[4]

It is in the celebration of the eucharist that koinonia and the church as sacrament are linked. By partaking in the body and blood of Christ and participation in holy communion, the church points to the origin of its communion in Christ within the Trinity, and experiencing that communion as a visible fellowship it anticipates the fullness of the communion in the kingdom, of which the church is a foretaste. If we understand the church in this way, as an eschatological community existing in history, taking upon itself Christ's cross, suffering in this world, celebrating its true identity in the eucharist, then the sacramentality of the church can only be properly manifested in the relationality and mutuality of a lived-out koinonia. As the body of Christ, the church participates in the divine koinonia and lives and reveals it for the world, becoming the mystery and the ferment of the new koinonia of humanity in a new creation. In its brokenness and division, the church experiences the consequences of the brokenness of the world; and through its sacramental life it can serve as an example and ferment of the unity of humankind.

Towards fullness of koinonia in Asia

Ecumenism as it is being articulated in many Asian theological discourses and writings seems to focus on the relational aspects of being church. Ecumenism is not just a matter of programmes, structures or activities; it is first and foremost "a way of being church". It is that set of perspectives on the faith, that quality of relationships with other Christians and other faith communities, that openness to the whole church across the nations and cultures, within which the fundamental question of common obedience is wrestled with.

Based on the documents of the federation of Asian bishops conferences of the Catholic church, the sacramentality and koinonia of the church is understood in the following way:

> If the church in Asia decides to be sign and sacrament of union with God and unity of all mankind, she has to become the church of the poor, live and work with them in order to promote a life worthy of the children of God. The bishops say that she "must live in companionship, as true partners with all Asians as they pray, work, struggle and suffer for a better human life, and as they search for the meaning of human life, and as they search for the meaning of human life and progress". Involvement in such a project will further demand that the church rethinks and makes her sacramental celebrations signs of liberation and transformation in our world, particularly in the Asian context of poverty and oppression.[5]

It is obvious that the stress is on the ethical aspects of koinonia, but it is underscored by developing a relational unity cradled in the context of Asian multi-religiosity. The ecumenical endeavour is not a matter of being churches in Asia but of becoming Asian churches. To be one in Christ, and to be one in solidarity with the poor, is to rediscover the Asian face of Christ. As A. Pieris maintains, "The church-to-church ecumenism could also be the spontaneous outcome of a common endeavour to discover the Asian face of Christ, that is to say, inter-ecclesial ecumenism here in Asia ought to be a by-product of the new praxis which is trans-ecclesial, Christ-centred and world-oriented."[6] The search for a new way of being church is a way of entering and experiencing the koinonia of Christ in the wider context of a fully committed fellowship of churches in dynamic common witness in the Asian scene. In the search for a proper expression of the unity of the church in Asia, Wesley Ariarajah proposes that perhaps the question can be put differently:

> Knowing that our churches are indeed divided over doctrine and church order (which still needs to be addressed), what can we as Christian peoples and churches in Asia do that would not compromise the integrity of our churches and yet help to make more visible the unity we have in Christ, so that the world may believe?[7]

It is also apparent that koinonia and mission are interconnected dimensions of the way of being church in Asia. The church is called to be an effective instrument for the renewal of humanity and a sacramental sign for the unity of humanity. The church is called to live as that force within society through which God's will for the renewal, justice and peace, community and harmony of all people is witnessed to. In a report from a theological round-table sponsored by the Christian Conference of Asia (CCA) and the Council for World Mission that took place in Hong Kong, the vision of unity in relation to the mission context was to support churches towards the sharing of spiritual resources, concrete collaboration in serving humanity, seeking new structures to promote Christian unity, and the recognition of each other as being faithful communities of the kingdom. The emphasis lies in going beyond traditional boundaries of denominationalism. The report points out,

> Despite all that still divides us, we dare to speak of our "common witness", a witness in unity and solidarity with all of humankind. Aware of our individual and institutional weaknesses and of the many compromises of our mission that we have made and accepted in the past, but conscious also of the power of God, "who is strong when we are weak", we – as Orthodox, Protestant and Catholic Christians – reaffirm our commitment to move beyond confessional differences and the social barriers of our own making, as we accept with joy the mission of active faith which Jesus Christ bequeathed to his disciples. In this way, we can understand ourselves to be the people of God among all God's peoples.[8]

It is clear that in Asia, one cannot speak of the church as though its inner unity can be considered completely apart from the larger human solidarity. Or as though it were completely transcendent with no concrete, historical and changing dimensions as it encounters a multi-religious context.

Conclusion

The church consists in sacramental communities of Christians who love each other, existing simultaneously as local churches and as embodiments of the church universal. Koinonia is an essential aspect that can foster unity in the local church and forge connections with all of the other churches, manifesting a real but incomplete commune.

The transformation of Christians and the transformation of the world go hand in hand. The eucharist is the celebration of koinonia in its deepest sense where the sacramental nature of the church is lived out in the ordinary lives of Christians in the world.

The church as koinonia is not simply an ideal vision, but can be viewed historically as the church is also a multi-dimensional and many-layered reality. Such an understanding of the church has ecumenical implications in that its concrete manifestation lies in people living out their lives in interconnectedness, not only with other Christians but also with a wide variety of people. Christian koinonia should be complemented by human koinonia.

Koinonia ecclesiology must make intelligible the mystery of the multi-coloured rainbow – separate colours yet one bow, and together symbolizing the one everlasting covenant of God's koinonia with all of humanity and creation.

> Triune God, mysterious being
> undivided and diverse
> deeper than our minds can fathom
> greater than our creeds rehearse
> help us in our varied callings
> your full image to proclaim
> that our ministries uniting
> may give glory to your name.[9]

NOTES

[1] Konrad Raiser, *To Be the Church: Challenges and Hopes for a New Millennium*, WCC, 1997, pp.43-45.
[2] *Faith and Order Paper no. 151*, WCC, 1990. See rev. version, 12 Feb. 1993, §17, p.13.
[3] *Ibid.*
[4] *Faith and Order Paper no. 111*, WCC, 1982, p.14, §20.
[5] A. Alangararn, *Christ of the Asian Peoples: Towards an Asian Contextual Christology*, Bangalore, Asian Trading Corporation, 1999, p.37.
[6] P.A. de Achutegui ed., *Towards A Dialogue of Life: Ecumenism in the Asian Context*, Manila, Ateneo Univ. Publications, 1976, p.162.
[7] "Making Visible the Unity in Christ That Already Exists", in *Asian Movement for Christian Unity*, joint publication FABC/CTC Bulletin, Hong Kong, CCA, 1996, p.37.
[8] Philip L. Wickeri ed., *The People of God among all God's Peoples: Frontiers in Christian Mission*, Hong Kong, CCA, 2000, p.53.
[9] Carl P. Daw Jr, "God the Spirit, Guide and Guardian", in *The United Methodist Hymnal*, Nashville, United Methodist Publ. House, 1989, p.648.

Does the Church Have a Sacramental Nature?
Report

The possibility of using sacramental language for the church is best approached by an analysis of where the churches stand historically and theologically in reference to this question. It would seem that there are three groups of churches with varying positions on this question.

The churches that accept the concept of church as sacrament do so with some significant qualifications – often unrecognized by others. For example, the church may be described as *veluti sacramentum* (a kind of sacrament). The theological utility of the term for these churches is found in its suggestion that the church points to, and effectively conveys, a participation in the trinitarian koinonia of the Father and the Son and the Holy Spirit.

The sacramentality of the church buttresses the belief in the visibility of the means of grace of those churches that find elements of this conceptuality helpful. Further, it undergirds a strong corporate sense of the body of Christ as over against an individualistic salvation.

There are Christians that reject the sacramental language outright, or else find it extremely problematic; they do not even have sacraments or prefer the terminology of "ordinance". The personal relationship between the individual and God attenuates the corporate sense of church. Thus, the question arises to what extent any descriptor of the church carries meaning.

Behind the divergences or outright dissension about the sacramental nature of the church lies this question: Does God bind Godself to particular recognizable presences and activities in space and time? If between the above-mentioned first two groups convergence, if not consensus, exists on this question, the answer of the third group is characteristically no, and it appears that this is a church-dividing issue.

Jesus Christ is the way, the truth and the life

"I am the way, the truth and the life" (John 14:6). The resolution of all the tensions involved in the question of the sacramentality of the church, in the very idea of sacrament, and indeed in the mystery of human life torn between present experience and future hope is to be found here. Because Jesus Christ is the way, the truth and the life, we know that the one whom we know as our companion *in via*, whether in the brokenness of this world or as our consoler, is the truth of God and our own true life. Our hope is for a future in Christ.

See this vine, O God (Ps. 80:14,15)

The church is like a sacrament of God's salvation not apart from, or even alongside or with Christ, but in Christ, who is the Head and Lord of the church. It is church where the gospel of Christ, the *mysterion*, God's plan of salvation (1 Cor. 2:1,2; Eph. 1:9,10) is proclaimed and through the power of the Holy Spirit people are liberated and converted to share in the new creation and in the communion of the body of Christ.

We considered several pairs of polarities or tensions which appear to be given features of the manifestation of the church in the world and which may be experienced either as creative opportunities or as threats to unity and integrity. We noted that holding different realities together belongs to the nature of sacrament and so considering these polarities is important for any discussion of the appropriateness of applying sacramental language to the church.

As examples of what we have described as "polarities", although they are not necessarily tensions, we identified the following:

The church as divine	The church as human
The church as invisible	The church as visible
The church's essence	The church's existence
The church as gift of God	The ethical calling of the church
The fulfilment to which the church is called	The church *in via*
The church as holy	The sinfulness of Christians and structures.

The church on earth is by definition "in the world". This is not an ambiguous expression. The world may be understood to be the good world of God's creation (Gen. 1:31), or the world defaced by sin, which cannot receive the Spirit of truth which it neither sees nor knows (John 14:17).

The "world" in both senses is the inescapable context within which the church *in via* lives, witnesses, worships and serves. It is not always easy to distinguish between these two "worlds", or rather between these two perspectives on the one world. It is therefore important for Christian communities and their members to be formed for humble and confident witness and service. It is also necessary that we be aware of how far societal values and structures influence our own ways of being the church.

Kyrie eleison

The gospel and the sacraments are God's unconditional gifts to his people for the sake of the salvation of all humankind. God has entrusted his divine gifts to our human hands; however our faithfulness does not match God's faithfulness. Nothing we do or say can weaken the unshakeable fidelity of God. Equally we should recognize that our witness to God's life-giving truth is always in danger of distortion through our sins.

Disciples of an incarnate Lord, members of the body of an ascended Lord, cannot remain apart from the common human quest for a better society and for the more responsible care for creation. Here, too, as Christians we cannot merely prophesy from the sidelines and pretend that in our own lives and communities we are already totally converted to God.

We are constantly in need of repentance and renewal.

Come, Holy Spirit

God's faithfulness to his church is unquestioned, and we know that God always honours the invocation of the Spirit *(epiclesis)* when the gospel is rightly preached and the sacraments duly administered. Nevertheless, every particular Christian community should recognize its own fragility and seek the gift of discernment for faithful witness to the divine truths that called it into being. This is all the more necessary because the whole creation, with its plurality, is to be united in Christ.

We return to Jesus' words, "I am the way, the truth and the life", with the awareness that our commitment to the gospel and the church involves a constant dialogue with Him who is the Way.

The Spirit makes Jesus present, or rather raises us in the eucharistic assembly to the presence of Jesus, to the life in him. To say this is neither to deny God's ability to act however and wherever he chooses, nor is it to undervalue the significance of the continuity of the church as an institution in history (Matt. 28:20).

Nevertheless, since it is the task of the church to proclaim the saving acts of God in the death and resurrection of Jesus, and since in the eucharist we "show forth the death of the Lord until he comes" (1 Cor.

11:26), they have a common role as *epiphanies* (disclosures, manifestations) of the mystery of salvation. All the characteristics of the church are seen in the eucharist. As both church and eucharist reveal the mystery of salvation through the cross and point to its eschatological fulfilment, it is appropriate to recognize that the church has a sacramental nature.

Authority and Authoritative Teaching in the Church

1-7 June 2002
Durau, Romania

Holiness as Content and Purpose of Ecclesial Authority

METROPOLITAN DANIEL CIOBOTEA

The issue of ecclesial authority and authoritative teaching has been a permanent challenge for the life and mission of the church in the world, and it has become a serious concern in the ecumenical debate concerning the understanding of the nature of church unity.

Very often theological reflection on ecclesial ideology is marked by the temptation of an ecclesiastical ideology of power, or of justifying a self-sufficient confessionalism.

The secularization of society today, the religious pluralism and spiritual crisis of our civilization, multiplies such temptations and makes more difficult the perception of the very content and purpose of ecclesial authority. However, a careful study of the origin, content, manifestation and purpose of ecclesial authority and authoritative teaching reveals the fundamental perception of the consciousness of the one, holy, catholic church of the apostles and church fathers that the content and purpose of ecclesial authority is holiness, and that holiness alone makes authority authentic. In this respect, we understand why the manifestations, the means and the servants of ecclesial authority and authoritative teaching are the one, holy, catholic and apostolic church, the holy scriptures, the holy councils and synods, the holy fathers of the church, the holy lives of the saints.

When the search for holiness diminishes in the life of the church, the intensity of authentic ecclesial authority also diminishes, precisely because the holiness of life is the main purpose of exercising ecclesial authority.

For a deeper understanding of the link between holiness and ecclesial authority, there is an urgent need to ask and to respond to the question: What is, or who is, the true source and purpose of ecclesial authority? In the New Testament we see that the authority in the church is inextricably and intimately connected with the authority of Christ, the head of the church.

Authority as a liberating service from sin and death: the New Testament on the authority of Christ

If we look attentively at the authoritative teaching of Christ, we understand that the way in which Jesus Christ exercises his authority reveals that authentic authority is rooted in the mystery of the life of the Holy Trinity. In other words, authority issues from the Father, is manifested and instituted in the church by the incarnate Son, Jesus Christ, and is constituted and communicated in the life of the church throughout the centuries in the Holy Spirit. Since the authority of Christ is exercised in fellowship and cooperation with the Father and the Holy Spirit, the purpose of this authority is precisely the manifestation and communication of the divine eternal trinitarian love for and life in the world.

Christ's power and authority is manifested in his teaching (Matt. 7:29; Mark 1:22, 6:2; Luke 4:32, 24:19; John 7:46), in his miracles (Matt. 8:26,27; Mark 4:39, 6:51; Luke 8:24; Acts 10:38), in his resurrection from the dead (John 2:9-22, 10:17,18), in his granting of eternal life (John 6:27, 10:28, 17:2), in his casting out of demons (Matt. 8:29,31-32; Luke 4:34, 8:28,32) and in his acts "which none other man did" (Matt. 9:33; John 15:24). But all these show that he receives his power from the Father and communicates it, through the Holy Spirit, to the church.

Through the words of Christ's gospel the plan and the work of the Holy Trinity for the salvation of the world is manifested; in Christ's miracles and healings the beginning of humankind's salvation as participation in the love and eternal life of the Holy Trinity is manifested. That is why the instituting of apostolic authority in the church (Matt. 28:19) also contains the commandment to make disciples from all nations, and to baptize them in the name of the Father, of the Son and of the Holy Spirit, and to lead them in the way of salvation, towards life eternal.

The power and authority of Christ, as authority received from the Father and communicated through the Holy Spirit to the church, reveals that within God's own being authority means sharing, co-responsibility and cooperation. Christ's authority shares in the authority of the Father and reveals the authority of the Father (John 5:17,19,21,26; John 10:28-30,36-38). The authoritative power of Christ is the power of saving authority (Luke 23:42,45; John 10:28, 14:2,3; Heb. 7:25). The salvation of humankind is the restoration of the communion between humanity and God who created human beings according to God's own image and likeness, i.e. according to the model of the trinitarian communion (Gen. 1:27). The sharing of the

Holy Spirit in the saving work of Christ is clearly mentioned in holy scripture, first in the incarnation of Christ (Matt. 1:18,20; Luke 1:35), then in Christ's miracles (Matt. 12:28; Acts 10:38), and finally in the resurrection of Christ (Rom. 1:4, 8:11; 1 Pet. 3:18).

The Holy Spirit communicates the truth of the mystery of Christ to the church and leads the church into the fullness of truth, bearing witness to Christ (John 14:26, 15:26). The Holy Spirit is the Spirit of truth and communion (2 Cor. 13:13) between humankind and the Holy Trinity. The saving power or authority exercised by the Persons of the Holy Trinity is the power of love, of self-giving, one to another, and cooperation for the life of the world.

Jesus Christ, as one person of the Holy Trinity, through himself united the whole of humanity with God (John 14:20; Luke 22:25). He gave his life for the salvation of humanity (Mark 10:42). Therefore all power (authority) was given to him in heaven and on earth (Matt. 28:18).

Following the example of Christ and bearing his spirit as service to God and humans (1 Thess. 2:6-10) the church should manifest its authority not as a dominating power upon humanity but as a liberating service from sin and death, from all kinds of egotism, isolation, oppression and marginalization. For the apostles' authority is first of all the gift of God and a duty to serve, the duty of preaching the gospel, the duty of preserving the faith, the duty of keeping the unity of ecclesial communities (1 Cor. 1:16-19; 1 Tim. 6:20), the duty to work for the salvation of all nations and all categories of people, having the deep conviction that the church as people of God, body of Christ and temple of the Holy Spirit is the "pillar and bulwark of the truth" (1 Tim. 3:15).

The content of the authoritative teaching of the apostles as servants of the gospel of Christ (Eph 3:7; Col 1:23) is primarily the search for communion with God (1 John 1:1-2), the search for the holiness of life (Heb. 12:14; 1 Pet. 1:14-16) expressed in prayer, sacramental life and fraternal love towards all people (1 Tim. 6:17; Tit. 3:1,8,14; Eph. 4:2; Phil. 1:9; Heb. 13:1; 2 Pet. 1:7). The pastors of ecclesial communities, bishops and priests, are servants of the authority of Christ in the church, sharing in his saving love for humanity.

The seal of the Holy Spirit

The apostles receive authority as service, being called by God (Acts 9:15; Eph. 3:7,8), and they are instituted as pastors of the church by the Holy Spirit (Acts 20:28, 21:4; 2 Tim. 1:14). They are consecrated to serve and to witness to the authority of God in the church

(2 Tim. 2:21; 1 Thess. 4:8); they are, like the apostles, co-workers with God for the salvation of humankind (1 Cor. 3:6,9, 5:10; 2 Cor. 6:1).

When the pastors of the church (the apostles, bishops and priests) were gathered in councils and synods and, being inspired by the Holy Spirit, proclaimed the true faith, their teaching thus became an authoritative teaching and their gatherings were called holy synods or councils.

However, the synodal teachings which were not inspired by the Holy Spirit and did not reflect faithfulness to the apostolic Tradition were not recognized as being authoritative teaching and remain only uninspired synods and teachings, because it is the true orthodox faith that makes the ecumenical councils holy and their teaching authoritative.

The church as pillar of truth is precisely manifested throughout the centuries as the interpreter of the apostolic Tradition, starting with the establishment of the canon of scripture:

> Fixing the canon of the New Testament thus involved discrimination between those books seen as authoritative and so part of the sacred tradition and those that were not. It was felt to be a case not of the church's conveying authority but recognizing an intrinsic authority already present. As Origen (ca. 185-254) put it, "The sacred books were not the works of human beings; they were written by the inspiration of the Holy Spirit at the will of the Father of all through Jesus Christ" (*De Principiis* 4:9). Just as the writings bear witness to the acts of God in history, so the church points to the Bible, preaching and teaching from its pages and subjecting itself to its guidance. But it also interprets it, providing the mainstream of tradition. The church recognizes in the scriptures the classical, normative account of Christian origins. So a sense of identity between the present and the church's roots is guaranteed and a measure of stability secured.[1]

Based on the authoritative teaching of Christ and the apostles contained in the canon of the holy scriptures, the holy fathers of the church through their writings and the bishops of the church gathered in the holy councils served the church by rejecting the errors and proclaiming the truth of the faith as creeds or holy dogmas and the truth of Christian life in the holy canons (or rules).

However, only that definition of the faith and rules for Christian life which have the same content as the gospel of Christ and are relevant at different stages and in various contexts of history receive authority in the consciousness of the church.

At the same time, many of the leaders of the church, as authoritative teachers in their passion for the saving truth, for the unity and holiness of the life of the church, were inspired by the faith and sacrifice of the holy martyrs and by the holy lives of monks and nuns, and sustained by the faith, prayer and holiness of the laity.

In this respect their authority was exercised as authoritative teaching for keeping the way of holiness and salvation for the ecclesial communities.

Spiritual authority emerging from the holiness of life of all the people of God, not only of bishops and priests, through the exercise of humility and compassion, penitence and renewal, reconciliation and diaconal work in society, remains not only a complementary authority to the pastoral and magisterial authority but also a reminder that authentic authority is service for saving the communion with God and with one another, service for saving the unity of the church as the communion of the saints.

Thus we consider that not only inside every church, but also in the ecumenical encounter and dialogue concerning ecclesial authority, it is necessary to avoid the separation of authority from the concern for spiritual conversion, renewal and reconciliation as manifestations of the search for holiness of life and unity of the church.

If holiness does not remain the content and purpose of ecclesial authority and authoritative teaching, there is a paradoxical risk for simultaneous secularization and sacralization of the ecclesial authority, transforming it into a drive for power as a goal in itself.

Therefore, the knowledge of the life of the apostles, martyrs, saints and the encounter with humble and holy people is essential for the authentic understanding and exercise of ecclesial authority in the life of the church today, as it has always been in history.

Conclusions

Authority is entrusted and received for that mission which serves communion with God and with one another, the holiness of life and the unity of the church.

Authority is a gift and a duty, a gift to be cultivated and shared with others and exercised in a communal way, according to the model of the Holy Trinity, and a duty to be accomplished as co-responsibility with others and for others.

Authority grows or diminishes according to its content and manifestations: authority is service and struggle for truth and justice, for healing and reconciliation, for strengthening fellowship and unity and for bringing the joy of the Holy Spirit in the life of the church in the life of society.

Authority is not a goal in itself but a way and a means for praising the love of God for humankind, for defending human dignity and the beauty of holiness expressed in the communion of the great diversity of persons, nations and generations gathered in the church of Christ.

The exercise of ecclesial authority is at the same time difficult and necessary; it is called to fight against all fragmentations, divisions and alienations produced in humanity by the forces of sin and death.

Ecclesial authority is also the experience of the power of Christ's grace, of the love of God and of the communion of the Holy Spirit, especially when human knowledge and power are recognized as limited, uncertain and unable to heal, to save and to sanctify the lives of persons and communities.

NOTE

[1] Raymond Hammer, "Authority of the Bible", in Bruce M. Metzger and Michael Coogan eds, *The Oxford Guide to Ideas and Issues of the Bible*, New York, Oxford UP, 2001, p.52.

An Overview of Some Faith and Order Papers on Authority

REV. DR GERT JANSEN

The basis and starting-point of my paper is the fourth world conference of Faith and Order at Montreal (1963). As the primary source of authority, Montreal speaks of the history of God's revelation to his people of Israel and God's self-communication in Jesus Christ. This history of God's revelation is not freely accessible: it comes to us through scripture and church tradition. In the words of the now famous Montreal formula: "Thus we can say that we exist as Christians by the Tradition of the gospel (the *paradosis* of the *kerygma*) testified in scripture, transmitted in and by the church through the power of the Holy Spirit."[1]

The Tradition (with a capital "T") of the gospel, the source of God's revelation, is embodied in church traditions (with a small "t"). However, God's revelation and church traditions do not coincide. The norm for distinguishing the true Tradition in church traditions is scripture "rightly interpreted".[2] But what is right interpretation?

This question served as the basis of the hermeneutics study at a consultation in Bristol in 1967. The report from the Bristol consultation points out that the different principles of interpretation of the various confessional traditions play a significant role not so much in biblical exegesis as in the overall interpretation. Some principles of interpretation lay special emphasis on scripture, others on unbroken church tradition, and still others on the current context.[3] According to the Bristol report, all three emphases must be viewed in their interrelation. The questions concerning the hermeneutical key and the authority of scripture gave rise to another meeting on the authority of the Bible held in Louvain in 1971.

The key question of Louvain was, to what extent is the Bible authoritative for Christian thought and action? There is no simple answer to this question. First, church traditions differ in their understanding of biblical authority. Furthermore, historical criticism has made us aware of the diversity in the biblical testimony itself and thus the question remains which of the testimonies are authoritative. Finally, the historical distance raises the question to what extent the words of the Bible can still have authority.[4]

The Louvain report points out that there are various definitions of the authority of the Bible. We may speak of the authority of the Bible as a literary work, as a cultural-historical document and as basis of the church. The authority of the Bible refers to the Bible as word of God that speaks to people. This authority of the Bible is derived ultimately from the authority of God.

Biblical authority must be understood as a relational concept, not as an aggressive power, but as a testimony that must be freely accepted. At the same time authority transcends individual human experience.[5] The relational concept of authority does not mean that authority coincides with a human value judgment of the Bible, as if human experience assigns authority to that. The biblical testimony shows its God-given authority to the one who recognizes its authority. The authority of the gospel is ultimately grounded on the Spirit.[6]

The discussion on the authority of scripture is narrowed down to the question concerning the relation between scripture and God's revelation in Jesus Christ and the relation between revelation and the diversity of interpretations. The Louvain report mentions several criteria for distinguishing between the value of various interpretations. But final judgments of the value of the various interpretations, by means of a "canon within a canon" or a "material centre" *(Sachmitte)*, are rejected. Instead, it speaks of "relational centres" *(Beziehungsmitte)*.[7] The situation "with its given elements and open problems" determines the perspective in which the text must be read and interpreted. It is only in this correlation between text and context that scripture can show its authority.[8]

The Loccum report of 1977, on the relation between the Old Testament and the New Testament, states that the authority of the Bible applies to the New Testament in the same measure as to the Old Testament.

Another important moment in the reflection on the concept of authority within Faith and Order was a study process which, after consultations in Geneva in 1976 and in Odessa in 1977, led to the publication *How Does the Church Teach Authoritatively Today?* It states that the present crisis of authority has made the notion of teaching authoritatively so controversial that churches refrain from their responsibility of exercising authoritative teaching. This is, however, not a solution to the crisis, rather a failure on the part of leadership of the churches to face complex demands of today's world.[9] "The church teaches 'authoritatively' when it claims to interpret authentically today the apostolic tradition as witnessed in the scriptures and the creeds as well as in the whole life of the church."[10]

The Odessa report discusses in detail the variety of teaching within the various traditions. To get closer in teaching it is necessary to clarify and diminish the above-mentioned divergence. In this context four issues should be raised:

1. The role of the past in teaching authoritatively:[11] Churches differ in their opinion on the question to what extent the past is authoritative, and also on the question of when and how often churches must speak with binding force.
2. The question concerning continuity in teaching:[12] All churches have different approaches to the issue of whether the doctrine of the church may be changed and adapted.
3. The question of who teaches in the church:[13] All churches agree that teaching must be rooted in the whole of the church. There are, however, different persons and groups with particular responsibilities in this respect. A distinction is made between church members with a personal credibility (such as saints, monks, church reformers, theologians), church members with a ministerial authority and, finally, a corporative teaching authority in representative church meetings (councils, synods, bishops conferences, etc.). The churches have different views on the mutual relationship between these three authorities and also on the extent of the influence of the entire congregation on the authoritative teaching.
4. The question concerning authenticity in doctrine:[14] All churches agree that church doctrine is in authentic agreement with the gospel if it is in accordance with the testimony of scripture and Tradition. In addition, church traditions reveal a great variety of criteria, which also determine whether teaching is done according to scripture and Tradition.

The Odessa report raises the following questions: first, the variety of different situations, which raises the question concerning the relation between teaching in particular situations and teaching addressed to the whole church; second, how far structures of church authority form a mirror of structures of authority in society; third, the significance of newly emerging models of credibility for church teaching.[15] The report also stresses the need for participation in decision-making and reception processes; participation and reception are a way to express *sensus fidei fidelium*.

When the Odessa report was accepted in Bangalore in 1978, it was emphasized that the church, before proceeding to acts of teaching, exists and lives through the work of the triune God. The authority of the church has its basis "in this *datum* of her being. The whole church teaches by what she is, when she is living according to the gospel."[16] At the same time an integrative approach to all constitutive elements of the revealed truth in the ecclesiastical teaching process is advocated.

> Although conflicts happen, there should be no false alternatives between the scriptures and the Tradition, the ordained ministry and the laity, the truth of the past and the truth of the present, and the faith of the corporate body of the church and of the individual person as these dimensions are constitutive elements of the revealed truth of the whole church.[17]

However, a comprehensive framework to see all the elements of the revealed truth in their inter-relation is still lacking.

This is provided by the fifth world conference of Faith and Order at Santiago de Compostela in 1993. All questions concerning ecclesiology, church structures of teaching and decision-making must be approached from the key concept of koinonia. Just as God's being is koinonia, the identity of the church is determined by koinonia as gift and calling. That is why the essence of the church, its structures of teaching and decision-making, its ministries must be relational.

The task of seeking a fuller, more relational church community presupposes the development of structures of mutual accountability, common decision-making and witness. Even if the differences of opinion are insurmountable, we must, in keeping with Acts 15, continue to seek to maintain the community within ecumenical structures.[18]

Santiago de Compostela as well as the later studies *The Nature and Purpose of the Church* and *A Treasure in Earthen Vessels* (the study on ecumenical hermeneutics) hold that the function and the ministry of *episcope* is essential for a relational basic structure of the church. Both within and among churches, *episcope* must preserve and construct the community in faith, life and witness. "The authority of *episcope* is grounded upon the authority of Christ's sacrificial love and humility" (Luke 22:25-27).[19]

Conclusion

To round off my paper, I list the main conclusions regarding explicit and implicit statements on authority in Faith and Order studies.

1. The nature and essence of the concept of authority is regarded as a relational concept; authority is a presupposed given which must be freely accepted. Authority is reality only when people experience it

as such. However, authority is not the same as the human value-judgment, as if authority is assigned by people. Authority is not assigned but acknowledged.
2. The sources of authority: The primary source of authority is God's revelation in Jesus Christ. However, this revelation of God is not freely accessible, but comes to us through scripture and church tradition. The authority of scripture and church tradition is subject to the revelation of God. *De facto*, however, God's revelation is to be found in scripture, provided it is "rightly interpreted". That makes scripture the primary norm and source of authority. Church tradition is subject to it. The criterion for the assessment of church tradition is the question as to how far koinonia has been maintained in apostolic faith, life and witness.
3. Church structures of authority, teaching and decision-making: Church structures of authority, teaching and decision-making must be determined primarily by the question of how far they further koinonia in apostolic faith, life and witness. This presupposes the development of relational structures of authority, teaching and decision-making.

To further reflection on the notion of authority I wish to make some remarks on these conclusions. So far implicit and explicit statements on authority within Faith and Order have largely been determined by the ecclesiastical context. By this I mean that it is only within an ecclesiastical context that the presupposed authority of scripture, Tradition, church and other constitutive elements of the revealed truth of God can be the point of departure. All these presupposed constitutive elements of authority have a so-called deontic authority. A deontic authority is a form of institutional authority. This authority only applies to those who recognize this institutional authority. People who do not belong to the Christian community, and consequently do not recognize the authority of scripture, Tradition and church, are *ipso facto* not affected by the claims of the deontic authority.

In order to appeal to people in a missionary context, but also in a context in which people increasingly fail to recognize the deontic authority of the Christian tradition, it appears necessary that within Faith and Order more attention is given to the development of a second view of authority: epistemic authority.[20] This authority is not dependent on a preordained authority of scripture, Tradition or church, or any institutional power or social need, but is entirely based on a free recognition of a person's authority, because that person has something to say or does something which throws a deeper light on the self-understanding of others. An authoritative appeal may also emanate from a person's mode of being, e.g. a witnessing martyr or a suffering fellow human being.[21] They confront us with a third view of authority: moral and/or existential authority. The classic example of such an epistemic and existential authority is Jesus. He acquired his authority not so much through an appeal to a presupposed authority of God's revelation, but rather through his authentic way of acting in the name of the Father, which led people to a deeper understanding of God, the world and themselves. Jesus acquired epistemic and existential authority especially through his suffering. The teaching authority of Jesus is based on an authentic combination of teaching and suffering *(mathein* and *pathein).*

The development of an epistemic authority presupposes the development of a theological hermeneutics which enters into the confrontation with the modern sense of reality in such a way that people come to a deeper understanding of themselves and of God and are so impressed by this that they freely recognize the authority of the Christian tradition. For the realization of an existential authority, it seems important that the teaching church *(ecclesia docens)* should reflect more than it has done so far on the development of structures of authority which help the church to learn *(ecclesia discens)* from suffering mankind.

NOTES

[1] P.C. Rodger and L. Vischer eds, *The Fourth World Conference on Faith and Order*, London, SCM Press, 1964, pp.51-52 §45.
[2] *Ibid.*, p.53 §51.
[3] *New Directions in Faith and Order: Bristol 1967*, WCC, 1968, pp.39,40.
[4] *Faith and Order Louvain 1971*, WCC, 1971, pp.9-12.
[5] *Ibid.*, p.14.
[6] *Ibid.*, p.20.
[7] *Ibid.*, p.17.
[8] *Ibid.*, p.18.
[9] "Faith and Order 1976 – How Does the Church Teach Authoritatively Today?", in *One in Christ*, 12, 1976, p.220.
[10] "How Does the Church Teach Authoritatively Today?", in *The Ecumenical Review*, 31, 1979, p.79.
[11] *Ibid.*, pp.79,80.
[12] *Ibid.*, pp.80,81.
[13] *Ibid.*, pp.81,82.
[14] *Ibid.*, pp.82,83
[15] *Ibid.*, pp.87,88.
[16] "Towards Common Ways of Teaching and Decision-making", in *Sharing in One Hope: Reports and Documents from the Meeting of the Faith and Order Commission, 15-30 August, 1978*, WCC, 1979, p.258.
[17] *Ibid.*
[18] Thomas F. Best and Gunther Gassmann eds, *On the Way to Fuller Koinonia: Official Report of the Fifth World Conference on Faith and Order, Santiago de Compostela 1993*, WCC Publications, 1994, p.260 §31; see also p.251 §31.

[19] *A Treasure in Earthen Vessels*, WCC, 1998, p.36 §36.
[20] The concepts deontic authority and epistemic authority are derived from J.M. Bochenski, *Was ist Autorität? Einführung in die Logik der Autorität*, Freiburg, 1974.
[21] The authoritative appeal that may emanate from the suffering other has forcefully been brought to our attention by the work of the philosopher Emmanuel Levinas. According to him the authority of the suffering of the other (the poor man, the widow, the orphan) refers to the authority of the other. *Totality and Infinity*, Duquesne UP, 1995.

Response to an Overview of Some Faith and Order Papers on Authority

DR MARY O'DRISCOLL

Dr Gert Jansen's paper gives us an overview of the topic of authority and authoritative teaching as it has been discussed, reflected on and developed in Faith and Order documents of the past forty years. The presentation is skilful, economic and insightful. Overall, I think the paper is one that the Faith and Order commission can comfortably accept as a basis for further discussion on the subject of authority. However, some points do need further teasing out and there is omission of some of the dimensions of the topic that have been developed in past Faith and Order documents. I imagine these lacunae are due to lack of time and the requirement to make his paper brief!

In taking as its starting-point the fourth world conference on Faith and Order at Montreal in 1963, particularly its famous statement, "Thus we can say that we exist as Christians by the Tradition of the gospel (the *paradosis* of the *kerygma*) testified in scripture, transmitted in and by the church through the power of the Holy Spirit", the paper immediately presents the basis of all it has to say about authority in the church, although Dr Jansen rightly shows that this statement opens up almost as many questions as it answers. One of the questions which he grapples with concerns the "right interpretation" of scripture, another the ways in which the Bible can be seen as authoritative.

I found useful the main conclusions regarding the *status quaestionis* drawn by Dr Jansen towards the end of his paper. I will spend the rest of my time focusing on these as well as on some other conclusions which I think we can come to.

The nature and essence of authority

"Relational" is a term which occurs several times throughout the paper. Towards the end, in summarizing what the nature and essence of authority is, it notes that authority is a relational concept existing only when it is acknowledged and accepted. This is true of all authority, but it would be helpful to explore what precisely this means in terms of authority in the church? Is the relationship to be one of perfect reciprocity, as in the Trinity, or is there some factor of dependence and priority between teacher and taught? Where does faith come in? What of reception? Are these both part of the relational process? Some analysis of faith in this discussion on authority would certainly seem to be necessary. The paper perhaps hints at this when it reminds us that authority is not the same as "a human value-judgment". But it would be good to mention faith more explicitly.

Faith can be seen as the correlative of authority in the church: we can therefore learn important things about authority by thinking about faith. For example, the classical analysis of faith includes discussion on its subjective side – what some traditions call the *lumen fide*. The subjective response to authority is dealt with in the present paper mainly in terms of hermeneutics, which can give the impression that it is a merely human act of interpretation (see final paragraph). The classical analysis would see the believer as someone gifted by God with a subjective light that allows him/her to perceive the divine truth in human statements or re-statements of revelation. The believer then believes in the authority of God, not in the authority of a text or of a teacher. Faith and Order paper 182, *A Treasure in Earthen Vessels*, on ecumenical hermeneutics, picks this up in stressing that it is the believing community which engages in the hermeneutical process (§23).

In reflecting on authority as a relational reality, we need too to consider the question of "reception". Is the paper referring to reception when it speaks of authority being accepted and acknowledged? But reception is more than acceptance and acknowledgment. It implies also a participation by the baptized in the determination of what is authoritative teaching in the church. While the exercise of authority is a ministry derived from the commission of Christ, and conferred on certain members of the church, all the members are involved in the process (see also Odessa report). They are gifted with what is often termed the *sensus fidei* (a faith instinct or an appreciation of the faith). When the people of God, through this faith instinct, manifest universal consent in a matter of faith (termed the *sensus* or *consensus fidelium*), they are engaged in reception and are also exercising authority. The Faith and Order paper of 1976, *How Does the Church Teach Authoritatively Today*? touches on the question of reception (see sect. 4), and could be helpful here.[1] The role of the Holy Spirit in leading both teacher and taught into the fullness of truth also needs to be discussed. The 1976 Faith and Order paper reminds us that it is only through the power of the Holy Spirit that the church's teaching becomes authoritative.

The purpose of authority

I notice that the purpose of authority in the church is not mentioned in the paper. The Odessa report, in its introduction, states that this purpose is "to make known the apostolic truth" both to the members of the church and to the world at large. The Faith and Order paper of 1976 expands on this,[2] pointing out that while the general purpose of authoritative teaching in the church is "to keep the church, under the guidance of the Holy Spirit, in the truth of the gospel as the church has received it through the apostolic witness", authority and authoritative structures are also there "to give guidance in the ambiguities of history, discerning good and evil... understanding the signs of the time... opening ways of reconciliation and healing, maintaining the unity of the church". In the context of today's world, all these functions are very necessary and important.

The sources of authority

The paper rightly sees God as the primary source of authority in the church. This is expanded to mean God's revelation in Jesus Christ which comes to us through scripture and Tradition. The question of the authority of scripture is reflected on in the paper, but it could do with more attention. Can one speak of the authority of scripture without some discussion on why the books of the Bible are the word of God in a way that other texts from the early church are not? (Here I am asking whether some attention should be given to "inspiration" and "canonicity" as it is in the ARCIC document, *The Gift of Authority*). Another observation: while there is a good explanation of the meaning to be given to "Tradition" (capital "T"), "church traditions" (lower-case "t") and "scripture" at the beginning of the paper, that explanation is not maintained later, where "church tradition" (in the singular and with lower-case "t") is said to be subject to "scripture" and where "the authority of scripture, Tradition and church" is referred to. Much good work done by Faith and Order in its various studies in recent years, on the Montreal statement regarding scripture, Tradition and traditions, could be incorporated into the discussion of this pivotal dimension of authority in the church.

Structures of authority in the church

In its conclusion, the paper refers to structures of authority in the church. However, no specific structures are mentioned. This is a pity because there is a need to move towards an acknowledgment and evaluation, as well as where possible an acceptance of one another's authoritative structures, if we are ever to arrive at an ecumenical exercise of authority in a reunited church. As we know, structures range from the highly organized and centralized approach of the Roman Catholic tradition, through the more conciliar and synodal approach of the Orthodox tradition, to the more direct reliance on "the sovereign authority of the holy scriptures" in a variety of ways, both communal and individual, in the Reformation traditions. All of these have strengths and pitfalls. These different approaches, which include "personal, collegial and communal" forms of teaching, have been considered in Faith and Order paper 181, *The Nature and Purpose of the Church*,[3] in its sections on "oversight" and "conciliarity". While each tradition tends to emphasize one or other in its understanding of authority, it was recognized, as far back as the Faith and Order conference in Lausanne in 1927, that all are important and need to be viewed as complementary rather than in opposition to one another.

In any serious ecumenical discussion on authority, the issue of primacy cannot be ignored. The official report from the fifth world conference of Faith and Order in 1993, *On the Way to Fuller Koinonia*,[4] has recommended that this issue be taken up seriously, and Pope John Paul II in *Ut Unum Sint*[5] asked for a fuller discussion of it by all churches and ecclesial bodies. The criterion suggested in the paper for accepting any specific church structure as authoritative is that it furthers koinonia in apostolic faith, life and witness. This criterion emerged significantly in the discussion on ecclesiology at the world conference in Santiago de Compostela in 1993. It has obvious and crucial merit, and is a highly recommendable criterion which Faith and Order needs to consider seriously in its evaluation of all authoritative structures in the church, including the papacy.

The conclusion of the paper makes an interesting comment regarding structures of authority in today's world. It notes that in our contemporary society there is very often a negative and dismissive attitude to any kind of institutional (deontic) authority. In view of this fact, the paper asks whether it would be helpful to consider epistemic and moral authority as forms of authority in the church, citing Jesus' authority as the classic example. The paper seems to use the term "deontic authority" in the sense in which Bochenski[6] uses it, but to use the term "epistemic authority" in a more derived sense. Maybe the point the paper is making, on the basis of Bochenski's terminology, would be better or as well debated on the basis of the distinction that is often made in ecclesiology between "institutional authority" and "charismatic authority"?

Conclusions

Finally, it would be helpful if Dr Jansen's paper could say more about the ecumenical implications and possibilities which the topic of authority and authoritative teaching opens up. It refers to a number of "suggestions to promote teaching in an ecumenical perspective" in the Odessa report. It would be interesting to revisit these in the light of where we are now in the ecumenical dialogue. We notice in this dialogue that, under the guidance of the Holy Spirit, as the churches grow in mutual understanding across confessional boundaries they are moving from identifying themselves in opposition to one another to identifying themselves in relation to one another. *A Treasure in Earthen Vessels* notes that "mutual knowledge of the criteriological principles guiding one another's authoritative teaching is an important contribution to mutual understanding". This mutual understanding hopefully will lead, in God's time, to "an ecumenical exercise of teaching authority", and maybe even to "a genuine ecumenical council witnessing to full koinonia". We may be far from that glorious reality now, but all our work in ecclesiology, including this present consultation on authority and authoritative teaching, has surely this goal in mind.

NOTES

[1] WCC, 1979, section 4.
[2] Section 1.
[3] WCC, 1998.
[4] Günther Gassmann and Thomas F. Best eds, WCC, 1994, p.243, §31.2.
[5] §89.
[6] J.M.Bochenski, *Was ist Autorität? Einführung in die Logik der Autorität*, Freiburg, 1974.

Reflections on Authority in the Roman Catholic-Lutheran Dialogue

DR TURID KARLSEN SEIM

The material

The bilateral dialogue initiated after the Second Vatican Council between the Roman Catholic Church and Lutheran churches through the Lutheran World Federation had as its first major result the so-called "Malta Report" of 1972.[1] Since then a host of reports have been published, and the dialogue is now well into its fifth round. Dialogues have taken place also at regional and national levels. These dialogues, especially in the USA and in Germany, have been influential.

Some of the texts from the international dialogue have been included in *Growth in Agreement I* and *II*[2] but they appear to be little known outside the bilaterally involved churches themselves. The level of agreement or rather convergence reached often depends on carefully phrased and balanced formulations. Thus the exact wording is essential and this creates the difficulty that any attempt at paraphrasing may fail to meet the necessary level of precision. This presentation is therefore to some extent a *florilegium*, a thematically ordered collection of citations from documents published by the Roman Catholic-Lutheran Joint Commission (since 1995 Roman Catholic-Lutheran Commission on Unity) from 1972 onwards.

Most of the reports somehow address the issue of authority, but I have found "Facing Unity" of 1984 and even more so "Church and Justification" of 1994 most illuminating for the purpose of this consultation.[3] "Facing Unity" reflects and also quotes extensively earlier documents such as "The Gospel and the Church", better known as the "Malta Report", and "The Ministry in the Church"[4] of 1981. As it spells out the way to unity step by step, its vision of a joint exercise of *episcope* went at the time too far for most Lutheran churches, and it may be right to say that this defeat in its reception left it *ad acta*. "Church and Justification" suffered undeservedly another form of oblivion. Even if it was sent to the churches, it ended up in the shadow of the grand event of the Joint Declaration on the Doctrine of Justification signed in Augsburg in 1999. The first out of three versions of this text appeared in 1995, shortly after "Church and Justification" had been issued, and the first and last of the versions went on a large-scale hearing to the churches. The joint declaration was not the work of the commission but of a separate smaller group set up for this purpose only, and it presents itself as a harvesting of many previous results from the international dialogue as well as from regional ones. It also underwent a particular and so far unique procedure of response and reception in the churches.

In addition to documents from the international dialogue, I have also included one text from the influential US dialogue, "The Word of God: Scripture and Tradition" of 1995. It is so far the most substantial yet succinct dialogue text (a German report *Verbindliches Zeugnis* is a three-volume work) specifically addressing this issue.

The present phase of the dialogue will hopefully finish its work on "The Apostolicity of the Church" in 2004. The results are therefore still pending, and it has not been possible to publish any interim reports. As we close in on some of the most difficult and divisive questions, the state of those questions *(status quaestionis)* seems to me to be well covered by the reflections here distilled from the texts mentioned above.

The outline

These questions have helped shape the outline of the documentation:
1. How is authority assumed by the dialogue itself, including the mutual recognition and accountability however limited to partners in dialogue? What is the status of previous results and the overall process of reception? How is the dialogue framed and influenced by the ecclesial authority to whom it is accountable?
2. Which sources and criteria appear as authoritative more or less implicitly in the argumentation of the dialogue texts themselves?
3. What do they see as the purpose of authority?
4. What is the location and the configuration of authority, where is it to be found and/or with whom? The terms "location" and "configuration" are carefully chosen to avoid using "source and criteria" or "structures of authority". Nor should it be taken to mean "levels of authority". The terminology is an attempt at accommodating the authoritative status of scripture and Tradition as well as a teaching office as "places" of authority and to explore how they are configured within a theological paradigm.

5. How is authority exercised? This question addresses the practice of authority, that is structures, levels, means, etc.

Even if each question is distinct, the answers often conflate them. Sometimes this is due to the brevity of the dialogue statements compressing as much as possible into each paragraph. But equally often the answer to one of them depends on the interaction with another. This is especially true of questions 4 and 5.

How is authority assumed by the dialogue itself?

The optimism of the early texts in the wake of Vatican II does not leave one untouched. The last paragraph of the "Malta Report" opens like this:

> At the conclusion of their work the members of the commission look back in joyful gratitude on the experience of this truly brotherly [sic] encounter. Even the discussion of opposing convictions and opinions led us to sense even more deeply our profound community and joint responsibility for our common Christian heritage.

The identity of the group is, however, clearly one of a scholarly study commission. They repeatedly state that although the commission had an official assignment, the report has no binding character for the churches, and they foresee a much broader process also on regional levels.

The impact of the "Malta Report" was immediate in that it created a general sense of thaw and of being on good speaking terms. Yet its effect was primarily a long-term one. It led simply to further dialogue, which in one perspective may be read as a reception process of this first report. It is a text to which later texts constantly refer, establishing a pattern of intertextual markers.

In "Facing Unity" there is a summary statement (§§53,54) of how the two traditions have changed or renewed themselves in ways that may lead towards the other. This is also a description of new patterns of authority or criteriology. The Roman Catholic situation is characterized by a new openness to other churches, the introduction of the hermeneutical principle of a "hierarchy of truths", and acknowledgments of its need of "continual reformation". The Lutherans on their side have a renewed appreciation of an ecclesial continuity beyond the time of the Reformation, and have reached a deepened understanding of church, ecclesial ministry and the sacramental dimension of worship as well as the significance of transmission, to use their term.

Although some of the dialogue reports may have been important in attesting to a change of climate and in their theological efforts and achievements, their authoritative status in the churches have at best remained unclear. They may have elicited responses, but fruit of the dialogue has not been effectively received. In this regard the first significant product was harvested when the Joint Declaration was officially received by the Vatican and the LWF and signed in Augsburg in 1999. It was thereby lifted to a higher level of authority than any previous dialogue result, and is now included in the Denzinger reference collection of documents.[5] However, the process towards the signing of the "Joint Declaration" may also amply illustrate the authoritative framework of the dialogue. It goes almost without saying that a process of formal reception must be carried out according to the established structures of authority in each church, and that their procedures may be different. But it still requires some degree of recognition of the ecclesial authority at work in the other church(es).

In the June 1998 (i.e. the first) "Response of the Catholic Church to the Joint Declaration of the Catholic Church and the Lutheran World Federation on the Doctrine of Justification", an imbalance between the signatories in terms of ecclesial authority was critically addressed as doubt was cast on the "real authority" of the *magnus consensus* of the synods in the life and doctrine of the Lutheran community (§6). This caused reactions on the Lutheran side as it threatened the sense of equal partnership in the dialogue process. In the so-called annex to the statement, which eventually made the signing possible in 1999, paragraph 4 readdresses the issue of ecclesial authority. Without explicitly withdrawing the former statement, it is interpreted in a "palimpsest-manner" that implies a correction. The different patterns of defining and exercising authority are not made an obstacle and the dialogue is affirmed as taking place between partners of equal rights, and that "each partner respects the other partner's ordered process of reaching doctrinal decisions", notwithstanding different conceptions of authority. It is interesting to note that the term "respect" is used rather than the term "recognize".

Not even a year later the declaration *Dominus Iesus* was issued by the Congregation for the Doctrine of the Faith. At the same time a letter was sent by the same congregation to the presidents of the Roman Catholic bishops conferences including a "Note on the Expression 'Sister Churches'" reminding the bishops that the word "church" should not be used when addressing Protestants. They remain merely "ecclesial communities" as they have not preserved the valid episcopate and the genuine and integral substance of the eucharistic mystery. In its response the Lutheran World Federation recognized that this was nothing new but expressed disappointment that thirty-five years of ecumenical dialogue seemed not to have been considered and "that the impact of these statements is the more painful because they reflect a different spirit than that which we encounter in many other Lutheran-Roman Catholic relationships".

Intermezzos or over-rulings such as these have been harsh reminders of the wider framework of authoritative structures within which the dialogue takes place and upon which it in the end depends. They have not been helpful to the dialogue but have created an ambience of uncertainty concerning the mandate and promoted caution rather than courage.

Connected with these tensions concerning ecclesial status and recognition of authority is the difference in theological paradigms between Lutherans and Roman Catholics. This means that even if one agrees on a specific doctrinal topic *(locus)*, its value or location (in German *Stellenwert*) within the total doctrinal configuration may differ. This is not just a matter of contextualization or contextual awareness. It means that an agreement may have a different effect on other issues or practices according to the partner's expectation of what ought to follow and whether it can be achieved or not.

In the case of the Joint Declaration this became utterly clear. A differentiated consensus on the article of faith that in Lutheran teaching is the one with which the church stands and falls, still had no ecclesiological consequences. The result was significant, but limited in terms of ecclesial recognition and practices. This was one of the critical points raised by Lutheran professors in Germany in their refutation of the declaration and a concern shared also by many who approved of it. The much-discussed paragraph 18 in the declaration explains how this is possible and as it speaks of "criteria", it refers to a process of authoritative discernment:

> Therefore the doctrine of justification... is more than just one part of Christian doctrine. It stands in an essential relation to all truths of faith, which are to be seen as internally related to each other. It is an indispensable criterion that constantly serves to orient all the teaching and practice of our churches to Christ. When Lutherans emphasize the unique significance of this criterion, they do not deny the inter-relation and significance of all truths of faith. When Catholics see themselves as bound by several criteria, they do not deny the special function of the message of justification.

In other words, it is a question of the location or distribution of authority within a theological and ecclesiological configuration/paradigm. In view of this the document "Church and Justification" is particularly important. It is an attempt to explore how justification-faith as a criterion may be applied as it relates to ecclesiology, and in the introductory paragraphs a statement from the US dialogue on justification by faith sets up the agenda:

> Catholics as well as Lutherans can acknowledge the need to test the practices, structures and theologies of the church by the extent to which they help or hinder "the proclamation of God's free and merciful promises in Christ Jesus which can be rightly received only through faith". In other words: "A consensus in the doctrine of justification – even if it is nuanced – must prove itself ecclesiologically" (§2).

Criteria by which authoritative teaching is established in the dialogue documents

The dialogue reports include statements on authority. But there is also a practice of authority in the reports themselves. In this part we will briefly describe this practice by asking which authoritative criteria the dialogue documents themselves apply and which sources they draw on for their argumentation, what they rely upon to establish credibility and accountability.

There is in fact little explicit reflection to be found. But the "Malta Report" has an interesting observation about what is seen as a methodological difficulty or imbalance:

> There is a special difficulty for Lutherans in that it is often hard to give an authoritative characterization of the present Lutheran understanding of the faith. While Catholics can point to recent magisterial statements... Lutherans must always refer back to the 16th-century confessions. This makes it difficult to present authoritatively the diversity, freedom and strengths of the actual life and witness to the faith in today's Lutheran churches (§11).

This is a revealing comment as it also shows the discrepancy between the two traditions in their location and exercise of authority. But the observation is accurate, and much of the Lutheran deliberations have indeed the form of a revisiting not only of the Lutheran confessions but more broadly of what is considered to be the original or pristine Lutheran position, *in casu* "Luther himself".

A telling example of this can be found in "Church and Justification" where observations about what the Reformers thought in the past become what the Reformation requires in the present (see §§210-213). Here the hermeneutic move by which past and present almost unnoticeably merge happens by means of concepts such as "the Reformation conviction" or "a Reformation perspective". Methodologically, however, this move is not clarified.

On the whole, since the divisions occurred in the past, the times of conflict are constantly readdressed and reinterpreted. The seemingly historical approach, however, is most often not historical; it is a doctrinal exploration to support an actual position or claim in today's dialogue. There is also a search for a shared history not yet tainted by divisive conflict. Thus the "golden age" of the early church is mentioned as well as the ancient creeds and the ecumenical councils. For Lutherans this is further supported by an interpretation of the Lutheran Reformation as aiming not at a break with the early tradition but as an affirmation of it. But ancient witness is not a sufficient criterion to discern the continuous guidance of the Holy Spirit. Lutherans normally respond negatively to the Roman Catholic emphasis on "irreversibility", and insist that the authority of developments in the early church, even decisions by councils, are yet to be tested by "the abiding will of the gospel" (Augsburg Confession – ch. 28). Thus the theological evaluation of even quite early determinations, for example of ministerial orders and in the field of Mariology, tends to divide more than unite.

There are surprisingly few documents where biblical reflection has a formative impact. Some texts have a high frequency of biblical references, but this is more a manner of proof-texting and of employing biblical terminology and modes of expression. A significant exception is the Joint Declaration on Justification where biblical studies clearly played a major role in the process towards consensus. As the declaration states: "Our common way of listening to the word of God in scripture has led to such new insights" (§8).

Finally, an authoritative structure, or perhaps intertextuality, seems to develop in the dialogue process itself by an internal system of reference where the reflections of earlier texts are received by the later. There is, however, no mention of how those previous documents have been responded to by the churches – if at all. It may seem that the dialogue establishes an internal reception process, laying stone on stone, but without any explicit awareness of the external reception.

The purpose of authority

There seems to be an overall agreement on the purpose of authority. The purpose is given by the divine promise and determination that the proclamation and teaching of the church remain in the truth. The Spirit of God, promised to the church and dwelling in it, enables it to continue so and gives it the authority to distinguish truth and error in a binding way, that is, to teach.

The location of authority

The reflections on where authority is located move within a configuration of scripture, Tradition and a teaching ministry/office/magisterium in the church. In this context "Tradition" is used almost exclusively in the singular following Vatican II – and reflected also in the report of the 1963 Montreal Faith and Order world conference on "scripture, Tradition and traditions". Vatican II replaced in *Dei Verbum* the plural traditions by the singular Tradition, so that it no longer refers to traditions beyond scripture, but to the process of the living traditioning of the word of which ministry is one instrument and circumstance.

Both communities wholeheartedly affirm *solus Christus*: we are saved through faith in Jesus Christ alone, and they are one in their conviction that the Bible has a pre-eminent and irreplaceable role as the inspired word of God committed to writing once for all. The word of God as permanently given in scripture is to be proclaimed by the church, the community of faith. Given the agreement that scripture is authoritative in this pre-eminent sense, the task before us is to see how the location of authority in scripture is seen to relate to Tradition and to the magisterium.

What is the understanding of its relationship to Tradition? Already "Facing Unity" had said, in referring to the "Malta Report", "The process of growth in common witness is advanced by a new consensus regarding the relationship between holy scripture and Tradition, long the subject of controversy" (§57).

Since this is an important point where long-standing divisive positions have been overcome, I have given some place to show how a convergence is theologically sustained. The following paragraphs from "Scripture and Tradition", quoted almost *in extenso*, is one of the best – if lengthy – examples:

> 16. Justifying faith, for Luther, along with the whole Western exegetical tradition, arises from and depends upon the hearing of the Word of God *(fides ex auditu)*. The way in which the Word comes to hearers is through the oral proclamation of law and Gospel, commissioned and norms by the Scriptures. The proclamation itself, the living voice of the Gospel *(viva vox evangelii)* in word and sacrament, is, for Luther, the primary way that the incarnate Word himself now comes to believers. The oral proclamation of the Gospel is what might, for Lutherans, be called the "traditioning activity", by analogy with what Catholics call the *actus tradendi*, the handling of the Word in a given context. However, for Lutherans the relation between Scripture and such traditioning activity is viewed in a light different from the Catholic perspective. Scripture is understood not primarily from the point of view of teaching, as a source of doctrinal truth, but as a source and mandate for the continued preaching of the Gospel.
>
> 21. ... *Sola scriptura* does not mean that tradition is rejected *per se*... Tradition stands under, not over the scriptural Word and its proclamation. Scripture thus evokes a tradition that accords primacy and ultimacy to Scripture itself... The tradition is an account of what the community has heard...

22. ... Everything in the church's practice, preaching, and teaching is to be subordinate to the Word of Scripture and must be judged according to the norm of Scripture. Both the structure of transmission and the content of what is transmitted.

23 ... the Lutheran understanding of *confessio*. The biblical Word shares its unique normativeness with... post-biblical confessions only because and if that is what they are: "con-fessions" *homologia*, a same-saying, a saying back of that original scriptural Word.

29. With the dogmatic constitution *Dei Verbum* of Vatican II, convergence between Catholic and Lutheran understandings began to emerge. The Council affirmed that all divine revelation was brought to perfection in Jesus Christ and that the Gospel was written down by inspiration. Vatican II also formulated the general Catholic assumption that there cannot be a real contradiction between Scripture and what the church transmits: "Holy Tradition and Holy Scripture form the one sacred deposit of God's Word which has been entrusted to the church." At the same time, Vatican II related Scripture and tradition to the magisterium: "The task of providing an authentic interpretation of God's Word in Scripture or tradition has been entrusted only to the church's living magisterium." Yet the magisterium is "not above God's Word..." It does so in a way that "holy tradition, holy Scripture and the church's magisterium are, according to God's wise design, so interconnected and united that none can stand without the others."

41. ... Underlying this shift are two basic ideas, namely, that tradition is a Spirit-inspired process in the church rather than a set of materials, and that it is concerned with life of the community in all its dimensions, including personal example, prayer and worship, and structures, rather than with teachings only.

42. The standard Catholic teaching now holds that both Scripture and tradition derive from the same wellspring who is Christ, the source of grace and truth. Christ is witnessed to by his followers, who through their oral preaching, example and institutions handed on what they had received. They committed the message of salvation to writing, giving us the Word of God in Scripture. Whether written in Scripture or preached and lived, the saving power and presence of Christ continues in the living voice of the Gospel heard in the church through the ages.

43. ... It (the Catholic community) has clearly moved to reaffirm the irreplaceable centrality of Scripture for the preaching, teaching, and the life of the church. It has moved away from the two-source theory of revelation which ascribed independent validity to tradition as a separate source of faith. At the same time it has not explicitly affirmed *sola scriptura* in at least two important Lutheran senses.

The measure of agreement concerning scripture and Tradition is such that even if divergences still exist, it is no longer an area of divisive tension. The same cannot be said about the place and significance of a teaching ministry as the last paragraphs quoted above already indicate. It is, of course, easily admitted that both communities practise authoritative teaching and have procedures for binding decision-making. But the location and status of such practices and procedures within the theological configuration is still one of the most sensitive and difficult questions in the dialogue. Even if some progress has been made on both sides, it remains a divisive issue.

Both churches, that is also the Lutheran churches, affirm that the ordained ministry is a divine institute and that it does not contradict the gospel but serves it, yes, is in correspondence with it. It is therefore indispensable. "Church and Justification" is emphatically clear:

> 189. ... not only does the institution of the ordained ministry not contradict the gospel as it is explicated by the doctrine of justification, but corresponds to it and in the last analysis receives its character of indispensability for the church from that correspondence. The Lutheran-Roman Catholic dialogue on the church's ministry had drawn attention to this also when it stated with the Accra document of that time and with the later BEM statement that the presence of this ministry in the community "signifies the priority of divine initiative and authority in the church's existence".

More basically the differences concerning authoritative status/location of the teaching ministry are a question of what its institution by God involves in terms of *ius divinum* and *ius humanum*. Both share the conviction that the historical emergence of the ministry's structure is not simply to be traced back to human – sociological and political – factors but "has taken place with the help of the Holy Spirit". But the Catholics understand and prioritize that differently from the Lutherans when they maintain that the particular organization of the ministry as it has developed through history is a divine institution. Episcopacy and apostolic succession as orderly transmission of the ordained ministry have developed as the expression, means and criterion of the Tradition in post-apostolic times. They are therefore essential for the church as church, and so necessary and indispensable as they safeguard the apostolic Tradition and are the means by which the Spirit of God identifies the church in every historical situation with its apostolic origin and integrates the faithful in the one universal faith of the church (196).

> 197. The difference between the Catholic and Lutheran views on the theological and ecclesiological evaluation of the episcopate is thus not so radical that a Lutheran rejection or even indifference towards this ministry stand in opposition to the Catholic assertion of its ecclesial indispensability. The question is rather one of a clear gradation in the evaluation of this ministry, which can be and has been described on the Catholic side by predicates such as "necessary" or "indispensable" and on the Lutheran side as "important", "meaningful", and thus "desirable".

Ultimately this reveals different constellations of salvation and church.

"Scripture and Tradition" mentions another factor often overlooked, namely the role of liturgy in the shaping and testing of doctrine, "... the church has from ancient times recognised the intimate connection between liturgy and belief, between the *lex orandi* and the *lex credendi*. In both traditions the *lex orandi-lex credendi* is cited, but there are different views regarding the relative priority" (§52). There is every reason to support the view that this deserves a fuller exploration than has yet been given to it by Lutherans and Catholics in dialogue.

"Scripture and Tradition" concludes by noting that a further dimension to the authority of a teaching is the concordant reception by the faithful (see §62).

The sign and criterion of true doctrine, which depends on the consent of the faithful, provides an appropriate transition to the last set of questions about the exercise of authority.

The exercise of authority

As indicated earlier in this paper, the location of authority should be distinguished from the levels at which and the ways in which this authority is exercised. But the distinction does not mean that these are separate issues. Indeed, there is a considerable overlap and what is being said about the exercise of authority also pertains to the need every church has for its teaching to remain sound or *recte,* for decision-making and maintaining structures to facilitate the decision-making.

"Facing Unity" describes the differences, yet with an emphasis of what are seen as "important parallels in achieving authoritative teaching" (§60). In the Roman Catholic Church the function of authoritative teaching is in a special manner the task of the bishops, who discharge this task "in a many-sided exchange regarding faith with believers, priests and theologians". Doctrinal decisions of the church are ultimately binding when "the bishops interpret the revealed faith in universal agreement with each other and in communion with the bishop of Rome". In the Lutheran interpretation, too, "the holders of the episcopal office are... entrusted in a special manner with the task of watching over the purity of the gospel." But in most Lutheran churches authoritative teaching is effected more in a process of consensus-building in which church leaders or bishops, teachers of theology, pastors and non-ordained members of the congregation participate with basically equal rights. Usually this process has synodal forms. When "Facing Unity" envisioned the path towards unity as a stepwise establishment of a joint *episcope*, this was at best premature and meant that the Lutheran reception of the document was on the whole critical. Also "Facing Unity" holds that authoritative teaching in both churches is subject to the norm of the gospel and is oriented to past doctrinal decisions recognized as binding. In both churches doctrinal decisions, if they are to become fruitful and develop their full situational force, depend on far-reaching reception in the consciousness and life of the local churches, congregations and believers. Thus authority must ultimately be exercised in some form of interdependence.

"Scripture and Tradition" notes,

> 60. In both the Lutheran and the Catholic traditions, great importance is attached to the process of assuring sound doctrine. The structures for authenticating doctrine, however, are not the same. According to Catholic doctrine the college of bishops, together with the Pope as its head, succeeding respectively to the college of apostles and to Peter, received from Christ the duty of teaching the faith with divine authority. Assisted by the Holy Spirit, these office-holders can on occasion make irrevocable determinations of faith, binding on the whole church. Such decisions, while they embody or protect the Word of God, are not regarded as being themselves the Word of God. They depend upon God's Word given in Scripture and tradition.

In "Church and Justification" a full chapter (4.5.3.3) deals with "Binding Church Doctrine and the Teaching Function of the Ministry", where agreement is again noted (with the significant characterization of the ministry as a temporal instrument) before the differences are explored as follows:

> 206. The commission to continue in the truth, like the promise to bring this about, holds good for the church as a whole. Our churches agree on this. We also agree that it is primarily the Spirit of God, promised to the church and dwelling in it, who enables it so to continue and gives it the authority to distinguish truth and error in a binding way, that is, to teach. Finally, we agree that for his activity God in the Holy Spirit makes use of temporal instruments and circumstances which he himself has bestowed upon the church as a temporal and creaturely entity; and that the ministry is one of these instruments and circumstances.
>
> 208. The difference between our churches only begins to surface where the issue is *how* [my italics] the church's responsibility for teaching is exercised. When the Roman Catholic Church attributes a special responsibility and authority for teaching to the ministry and in particular to the episcopate, this in itself does not imply any essential difference from the Lutheran view and practice. For in the Lutheran view too the ministry, along with its mission and

authority to preach the gospel and inseparably from them, is given a responsibility for the "purity" of the proclaimed gospel and the "right" administration of the sacraments "according to the gospel". It was also axiomatic for the Reformation that there are ordered ministries in the church such as the teaching office of theologians and faculties.

> 209. ... Nor was it contested on the Reformation side that a special responsibility for teaching belongs to the bishops... The episcopal structure was however not preserved in most churches of the Reformation... an alternative system for supra-parish doctrinal oversight by creating superintendents, visitors or visitations commissions.

> 213. For the sake of the gospel, the Reformation... requires that the church's ministry and its decisions should as a matter of principle be open to examination by the whole people of God... Otherwise it seems doubtful from a Reformation perspective that the teaching ministry serves the word of God and is not above it.

> 214. The binding nature of church teaching is not cancelled out by this, but is made subject to a reservation.

> 217. While it is possible for the individual bishop to fall away from the continuity of the apostolic faith... Catholic tradition holds that the episcopate as a whole is nevertheless kept firm in the truth of the gospel.

(We see here how one deals with personal mistakes, failures and misuse in the exercise of authority. There is an inevitable acknowledgment that this happens, but when it occurs, it is an individual problem and not a structural one. It does not affect "the episcopate as a whole". Here the recent occurrences in some dioceses in the US might provide interesting test cases.)

The document then conducts a rare deliberation more specifically on jurisdiction, that is authority as exercised by means of legal measures:

> 224. Catholics and Lutherans together say that God, who establishes institutional entities in his grace and faithfulness, and who uses them to preserve the church in the truth of the Gospel, also uses law and legal ordinances for this purpose.

In paragraph 227 some common basic convictions are listed, among them that even where, in line with the traditional view and terminology, the character of "divine law", *ius divinum*, is attributed to church legislation, it has a historical shape and form, and it is therefore both possible and necessary to renew and reshape it.

> 228. These basic convictions show that church law, notwithstanding its claim to be binding, is by its nature and by definition subject to a reservation as to its binding nature... No church legislation can claim to be binding in such a manner that it is necessary for salvation, thus equalling the ultimate binding nature of the gospel which is itself the binding nature of grace.

Concluding remarks

It is not easy to summarize a *florilegium* as the texts quoted should be left to speak for themselves. Nor is it easy to point at possible ways forward without pre-empting the still pending results of the present difficult round of dialogue. An exploration of "The Apostolicity of the Church" will have to address the still divisive issues concerning apostolic succession, episcopacy and primacy but within a wider approach comprising several characteristics by which the apostolic tradition may be recognized.[6] This has proved to be rewarding in Lutheran-Anglican relations, but it may be less successful in relation to the Roman Catholics partly because of their claims concerning the Petrine ministry. An agreement about the various components of apostolicity is not insignificant, and here one has already gained some results. But it still leaves unresolved the configuration of these components and the *Stellenwert* (location and status) assigned to each of them within the configuration especially the location of the teaching ministry. Related to this is the question whether the teaching ministry *(magisterium)* can be judged by the gospel, that is, whether it is subject to a reservation or not. These questions are at the core of the present discord. Nor should one underestimate the fact that power structures are not easily challenged or changed. Even if for the time being it may be wise not to insist on the ordination of women as an issue in the dialogue with the Romans Catholics, it will eventually have to be addressed when one speaks of patterns and exercise of authority in the church.

Several areas where further exploration might be profitable or which have been only scantily touched upon are:
- the significance of the authority assigned to the *sensus fidelium*;
- the role of worship and liturgy in establishing and maintaining authority;
- the theological status and role of church legislation.

More generally, there is a rather urgent need of a more direct and systematic reflection on hermeneutics and the question of hermeneutical keys (criteriology). It does come up not infrequently, but only when the subject matter itself obviously includes or requires it – such as "scripture and Tradition" or the way in which the doctrine of justification by faith is a criterion. An explicit and deepened hermeneutical awareness might also mean that insights from biblical interpretation will have to play a more compelling role beyond a traditional claim to proof-texts and the terminological convenience of the biblical language as a shared one.

NOTES

[1] In *Growth in Agreement: Reports and Agreed Statements of Ecumenical Conversations on a World Level*, Harding Meyer and Lukas Vischer eds, WCC, 1984, 168-89.
[2] See note 1, and *Growth in Agreement II: Reports and Agreed Statements of Ecumenical Conversations on a World Level, 1982-1998*, Jeffrey Gros, Harding Meyer and William G. Rusch eds, WCC Publications, 2000.
[3] See *Growth in Agreement II*, pp.443-84 and 485-565.
[4] See *Growth in Agreement*, pp.248-75.
[5] *Enchiridion Symbolorum*, Freiburg, Herder, 1st ed. 1937.
[6] Cf. *Baptism, Eucharist and Ministry*, WCC, 1982, M34.

Reflections on Authority and Authoritative Teaching in Light of ARCIC II

REV. DR WILLIAM HENN

I believe that the following statement from the beginning of ARCIC II's *The Gift of Authority* provides a good point of departure for a Catholic reflection on the theme of the present consultation:

> There is an extensive debate about the nature and exercise of authority both in the churches and in wider society. Anglicans and Roman Catholics want to witness, both to the churches and to the world, that authority rightly exercised is a gift of God to bring reconciliation and peace to humankind.[1]

Unless authority is viewed in a positive light, it is unlikely that Christian communities separated from each other will be able to agree about its nature and exercise within the church. Of course, this need not and must not blind us to negative experiences of the exercise of authority in the past. My own private opinion is that Christian divisions themselves are mainly the result of the failures of "those in authority". While it does not seem to me possible to give a completely satisfactory description of the Catholic understanding of authority in a few pages, some important elements can be listed, which I propose to do under the following four headings: (1) authority in the church in general; (2) authoritative teaching; (3) the exercise of teaching at local and universal levels; and (4) some recent developments and proposals.

Authority in the church in general: some basic principles

First of all, authority is of God, the author of human life and of all creation, the One who has chosen a people to be especially God's own. Jesus Christ is the head of the church, his body, which is one. The Holy Spirit, the Consoler, was sent by the Risen Lord to guide the Christian community into all truth and to distribute manifold gifts and charisms for building up the body of Christ into unity and maturity. The Father wills the church to be guided by God's own gracious authority, which is active in the saving missions of the Son and the Holy Spirit. Matthew's gospel closes with those inspiring and consoling words of Jesus:

> All authority in heaven and on earth has been given to me. Go therefore and make disciples of all nations, baptizing them in the name of the Father and of the Son and of the Holy Spirit, teaching them to observe all that I have commanded you; and lo, I am with you always, to the close of the age (Matt. 28:18-20).

Second, the authority of God governs what may be called the three essential activities which comprise the nature and the mission of the church: witness *(marturia)* and proclamation of the word of God which, under the power of the Holy Spirit, arouses faith in those who hear that witness; celebration *(leiturgia)* of the mysteries, the sacramental rites through which the community enters by grace into the communion of intimate union with God and, as a consequence, also into unity with one another; and service *(diakonia)*, which fosters the internal growth of the community into maturity in Christ as well as the external missionary outreach that invites others to a life of faith, worship and service.[2] If these may be considered as essential elements of the life of the Christian community and if God is the ultimate authority guiding the community, then God's authority should be understood as guiding each of these three areas: faith, worship and service.

A third principle concerns the sacramental nature of the church. After referring to some of the biblical passages about the body of Christ which one finds in Romans, 1 Corinthians, Ephesians and Colossians, the bishops at Vatican II taught that the church can be correctly understood only within the incarnational economy of salvation. The community of faith, hope and charity is also a visible organization through which Christ communicates grace and truth to all people.

> But, the society structured with hierarchical organs and the mystical body of Christ, the visible society and the spiritual community, the earthly church and the church endowed with heavenly riches, are not to be thought of as two realities. On the contrary, they form one complex reality which comes together from a human and a divine element. For this reason the church is compared, in a powerful analogy, to the mystery of the incarnate Word. As the assumed nature, inseparably united to him, serves the divine Word as a living organ of salvation, so, in a somewhat similar way, does the social structure of the church serve the Spirit of Christ who vivifies it, in the building up of the body (cf. Eph. 4:15).[3]

Fourth, these principles coalesce to provide a way of understanding how authority in the church may be related to ordained ministry. Ordained ministry is a visible, institutional means which Christ himself instituted, in a general way, both during his public life and in the period immediately after the resurrection, the further development of which was guided by the Spirit which Christ promised to send to his nascent community. Jesus is the Good Shepherd, who continues, until the end of time, to be pastor of his flock. Ordained ministers represent the Good Shepherd; they are the weak, human instruments who are consecrated in the Holy Spirit so that Christ may continue to exercise with authority his threefold office of prophet, priest and king, guiding his church in faith, in worship and in the mission of serving the Father's plan of salvation for the whole world. One of my favourite passages from Vatican II's Decree on Christian Unity seeks to express this Catholic vision which relates episcopacy to the three essential dimensions of ecclesial life:

> It is through the faithful preaching of the gospel by the apostles and their successors – the bishops with Peter's successor at their head – through their administration of the sacraments, and through their governing in love, that Jesus Christ wishes his people to increase, under the action of the Holy Spirit; and he perfects its fellowship in unity: in the confession of one faith, in the common celebration of divine worship, and in the fraternal harmony of the family of God.[4]

Authoritative teaching

In this view, then, Christ exercises his authority as Good Shepherd through the ordained ministers in the three areas of witness (proclamation of the word leading to faith), worship (sacraments), and guidance of the community (internal collaboration and missionary outreach). Because our consultation focuses in a particular way upon teaching, I will now set aside the second and third of these and concentrate on the first exercise: authority in witness, that is, in proclaiming and interpreting the word of God and guiding the community in faith.

Teaching has always been of great importance in the life of the Christian community. It would not seem exaggerated to say that this begins with Jesus himself, who was known during his earthly ministry as the teacher, one of the most frequent titles applied to him in the synoptics and John. It is difficult not to notice the joy underlying the reaction of the crowds to the teaching of Jesus at the end of the Sermon on the Mount: "They were astonished at his teaching, for he taught them as one who had authority, and not as their scribes" (Matt. 7:28-29). A text that has been treasured by Catholic theologians who have reflected upon teaching authority is that associated with the mission of the seventy, whom Jesus sent out to proclaim the nearness of the kingdom of God and to labour for an abundant harvest: "He who hears you hears me" (Luke 10:16).

Nearly 25 years ago, the respected Catholic biblical scholar Joseph Fitzmyer contributed a study to the Lutheran-Roman Catholic dialogue in the USA entitled "The Office of Teaching in the Christian

Church According to the New Testament."[5] Fitzmyer grouped the various books of the NT into seven chronological blocks (the genuine letters of Paul, doubtfully genuine letters of Paul, the synoptic gospels, Acts, the deutero-Pauline letters, James, and the Johannine literature), methodically exploring the use made by each block of the words "to teach", "teacher" and "teaching". Each level provided evidence that the function of teaching existed within the early Christian community, playing an important role in its life and development. Some New Testament sources linked teaching explicitly to leaders such as the apostles (Acts 4,42), but others also exercised the role of teacher (1 Cor. 12:28; Eph. 4:11; 1 Tim. 3:2).

In my opinion, one of the contributions of ARCIC II's *The Gift of Authority* is its attempt to situate the teaching authority of pastors within the broader life of the church as a whole. The revealed word of God is addressed to the whole community; it is not the private possession of a particular group. Laity, theologians and ordained ministers all have a responsibility to receive and hand on the word of God, each according to their specific capabilities (*Gift*, 28). Catholics will recognize immediately the affinity between this idea and *Lumen Gentium* 12, which affirms that "the holy people of God shares also in Christ's prophetic office" and that "the whole body of the faithful... have an anointing which comes from the holy one (cf. 1 John 2:20 and 27)." Within this context, *The Gift of Authority* describes the *sensus fidei* as "an active capacity for spiritual discernment, an intuition that is formed by worshipping and living in communion as a faithful member of the church" (*Gift*, 29). The discussion of the *sensus fidei*, and its correlative notion of *sensus fidelium*, seems to be one of the principal ways in which ARCIC II takes up the task requested by the official Anglican response to ARCIC I, which asked that the dialogue further explore "the role of the laity in decision-making within the church".[6] The relationship between those who exercise *episcope*, "the ministry of memory", on the one hand, and the whole people whose reception of God's word in faith may be summed up in the expression *sensus fidelium*, on the other hand, is described by means of the analogy of a symphony. Because the Holy Spirit is at work within the church, there is harmony between *episcope* and *sensus fidelium*. The "ministry exercised by the bishop, and by ordained persons under the bishop's care" is attentive and "alert to the *sensus fidelium*, in which they share... Thus the *sensus fidelium* of the people of God and the ministry of memory exist together in reciprocal relationship" (*Gift* 30).

Such harmony is one of the dominant themes of *The Gift of Authority*. This quality is apparent in the document's refusal to get caught up in false disjunctives or to oppose traits of Christian life which must in fact be held together as complementary. Thus *The Gift of Authority* rejects opposing freedom to obedience. Jesus who imparts the truth which makes one free (John 8:31) is the same one whose embrace of the Father's will may be rightly called "life-giving obedience" (*Gift* 10). Or, again, there can be no question of choosing between the faith of the individual or the faith of the church (cf. *Gift*, 11-13); they go together. Similarly, in order to discern God's will, the church is not faced with the option of consulting either scripture or Tradition, but both. The text seems to say, rightly in my view, that various similar dichotomies are false dichotomies. No adequate ecclesiology can be satisfied with a list of "either/or" oppositions such as: either the word of God or the teaching of the bishops, either the ordained ministry or the laity, either the local church or the universal church, either synodality or primacy. Disagreement about authority often derives from the mistake of opposing two realities or two values or two subjects which simply should not be opposed. The genius of *The Gift of Authority* is continually to point this out.

Exercise of teaching at local and universal levels

Perhaps no theme has had a greater impact within the life of the Catholic church since Vatican II than the relation between the local and the universal church. Many students of the history of ecclesiology point out that, after the schism between East and West, often symbolically dated as beginning with the mutual excommunications of 1054, the West increasingly gave prominence to the universal unity of the whole church under the guidance of the bishop of Rome. Actually, the development was somewhat cyclical, with the periods marked by strong papal authority being interrupted by periods or movements emphasizing the authority of the bishop (conciliarism and gallicanism being the two prominent examples).[7] Vatican I (1869-79) seemed a triumph of the emphasis on the universal unity of the church under the leadership of the pope and one of the principal aims of Vatican II (1962-65) was precisely to bring greater balance to Catholic ecclesial doctrine, by emphasizing the role of the bishop in the local church.

Universality and locality are both essential qualities of the church of Christ; they are expressions of what it means when the creed confesses that the church is "catholic". They are both values; if either were lost or weakened, the church would be hurt. Both dimensions include appropriate ministries of authority, including a ministry of authoritative teaching. At the same time, a degree of tension between the values of universality and locality seems almost unavoidable. The exercise of authority in fostering the unity of the whole seems vulnerable to devolving easily into a uniformity that stifles the legitimate diversity of the local churches. On the other hand, the variety of expressions of faith and discipleship which flourish in local churches seem capable of devolving into a particularism which threatens to divide the worldwide community. A basic principle, very congenial to Catholic ecclesiology, was expressed by ARCIC'S *The Gift of Authority* in the following way: "The mutual interdependence of all the churches is integral to the reality of the church as God wills it to be. No local church that participates in the living Tradition can regard itself as self-sufficient" (*Gift* 37).

ARCIC II tries to describe the way in which the values of universality and locality are harmonized in a series of paragraphs devoted to the theme of synodality (*Gift*, 34-40). These begin with a beautiful description of the whole church, comprised of the communion of all the local churches, as a community walking together (playing on the Greek word *synodos*) under the guidance of the Holy Spirit in fidelity to the living Word of God. Next follow the document's strongest paragraphs about bishops. Bishops need a certain pastoral authority to exercise *episcope* effectively within a local church. This means that they must be able to make and implement decisions for the sake of communion. The faithful "have a duty to receive and accept" these decisions. "The jurisdiction of bishops is one consequence of the call they have received to lead their churches...; it is not an arbitrary power given to one person over the freedom of others." There is a complementarity between bishop and community which is symbolized and expressed by the prayerful dialogue between president and people during celebration of the eucharist. These affirmations, all from *Gift* 36, succeed in harmonizing a clear and decisive episcopal authority with a sensitive respect for the faith of the individual believers who make up the community. This is the kind of authority which one naturally associates with Jesus himself, the shepherd and bishop of souls (cf. 1 Pet. 2:25).

The section continues by recalling some of the structures which facilitate synodality, pointing out that "the maintenance of communion requires that at every level there is a capacity to take decisions appropriate to that level. When those decisions raise serious questions for the wider communion of churches, synodality must find a wider expression" (*Gift* 37). In order to actualize this synodality bishops need to meet together. Consulting the faithful will also be a necessary aspect of their episcopal oversight (*Gift* 38).

Only within the context of synodality does ARCIC II take up the theme of primacy; the synodality of the church is served not only by the conciliar and collegial exercise of authority but also by primatial authority (cf. *Gift* 45-48). Both Anglicans and Roman Catholics acknowledge that various forms of primacy have been a part of the life of the church from very early. One may recall that canon 6 of the very first ecumenical council attributed a certain regional primacy to Alexandria, as was also recognized for the cities of Antioch and Rome by a very ancient custom.[8] ARCIC II affirms that the "pattern of complementary primatial and conciliar aspects of *episcope* serving the koinonia of the churches needs to be realized at the universal level" (*Gift* 46). Once again, the dominant emphasis of *The Gift of Authority* is upon compatibility: primacy need not be opposed to conciliarity or collegiality. The same can be said about the unique moments in which the minister charged with serving the unity of the whole church needs to speak out on behalf of the whole. *Gift* 47 acknowledges that the bishop of Rome "offers a specific ministry concerning the discernment of truth, as an expression of universal primacy", but adds that "every solemn definition pronounced from the chair of Peter in the church of Peter and Paul may, however, express only the faith of the church. Any such definition is pronounced within the college of those who exercise *episcope* and not outside that college." I would see a certain parallel between this way of speaking and what Vatican I says about the pope's authority when he teaches *ex cathedra*. There it is said that, in speaking *ex cathedra*, the pope, because of his ministry of primacy, "possesses, through the divine assistance promised to him in the person of Blessed Peter, the infallibility with which the divine Redeemer willed his church to be endowed in defining the doctrine concerning faith of morals."[9] Such a teaching ministry, ARCIC II asserts, must be seen as situated within the synodality which pervades the church as a whole. When it is, universal primacy should be considered not an obstacle to unity, but even "a gift to be shared" (subtitle of the final section, *Gift*, 60-63).[10]

Some recent developments and proposals

The Gift of Authority concludes with a statement about significant developments within each community and issues which each has yet to face. It seems to me that, within the Catholic church, the decades since Vatican II have seen several developments regarding teaching authority.

First of all, there seems to be more awareness of the need for collaboration between the official teachers and the rest of the church. At times, there have been tensions between individual theologians and the magisterium. At times, there seems to have been insufficient consultation of the faithful or reception by the faithful of particular teachings. The symphonic harmony described by ARCIC II has not always taken place. At least in theory, catholic ecclesiology and official doctrine advocate that kind of dialogue which promotes a full communion in faith, a dialogue eloquently proposed in Paul VI's *Ecclesiam Suam* of 1964. Surely some important steps forward have been taken, such as the role of the International Theological Commission or the Pontifical Biblical Commission in addressing questions facing the church as a whole, or the involvement of laity in international synods and in the life of the local churches at the levels of episcopal conferences, dioceses and parishes. Still, few would doubt that there is room for improvement in this area.

Furthermore, there have been important structural adjustments and innovations which are relevant to authoritative teaching. Episcopal conferences, at which the bishops of individual nations or groups of nations gather to discuss issues of shared concern, have provided a new forum for expressing the bishops' collegial care for their local churches. Several larger, sometimes continental, groupings of bishops' conferences (such as CELAM for Latin America or FABC for Asia) allow this instrument to have an even wider influence. Another interesting development is the regular holding of synods of bishops in Rome. In the 34 years between 1967 and 2001, twenty synods have been held. Usually about three hundred bishops from around the world attend these synods, along with some priest, lay and religious observers, theological experts from the Catholic church and representatives from other Christian communities. All of these people work together for an intense month to address some pastoral issue relevant to the whole church. But the synod experience is not limited to that month or to only those participants; rather, it entails a process of several years, beginning with initial consultations, upon the basis of which are written a series of texts (*Lineamenta* and *Instrumentum Laboris*), which in turn provide the point of departure for the interventions and discussions during the actual month-long synod. These lead to the drafting and approval of propositions which form a significant source for an "apostolic exhortation", written after the synod by the bishop of Rome. These exhortations are a rather unique literary form, in that they have come to quote extensively from the propositions which had been written by the bishops. Then begins the process of the reception of the fruits of the synod.

Finally, within the context of recent discussions of the primatial exercise of authority sparked by Pope John Paul II's invitation to dialogue about his own ministry, M. Buckley has suggested distinguishing between the "habitual" and "substitutional" functions of the primacy, to guard against undue intervention by the primate, while H. Pottmeyer has suggested the multiplication of patriarchates in the West so as to move towards "a triadic form of church structure": diocesan, regional and universal.[11]

These developments and proposals show that change can and does take place in the exercise of teaching authority, all the while maintaining fidelity to those essential principles which, in the Roman Catholic view, derive from the will of God. This is a hopeful sign that still greater ecumenical agreement about authority is possible.

NOTES

[1] Published in pamphlet form as *The Gift of Authority*, London, Anglican Book Centre, 1999, §5. Hereafter any references to this document will appear as follows: *Gift*, paragraph number. This report is also printed in *The Pontifical Council for Promoting Christian Unity: Information Service*, 100/1, 1999, pp.17-29, followed by a commentary written by the author of the present essay.

[2] The use of these three Greek words to describe the essential dimensions of the church is taken from a reflection by the International Theological Commission of the Catholic church published in 1997 and entitled "Christianity and the World Religions", *Origin*, 27, 149, 1997, pp.151-66, at II.C. §§75-77.

[3] *Lumen Gentium* 8.

[4] *Unitatis Redintegratio* 2.

[5] *Teaching Authority and Infallibility in the Church*, "Lutherans and Catholics in Dialogue VI", Minneapolis, Augsburg, 1978, pp.186-212.

[6] *The Truth Shall Make You Free*, Lambeth Conference 1988, London, 1988, p.211.

[7] I have sketched out this pattern in "Historical-theological Synthesis of the Relation between Primacy and Episcopacy during the Second Millennium", in AA.VV. *Il Primato del successore di Pietro*, Vatican City, 1998, 222-273.

[8] G. Alberigo et al. eds, *Conciliorum Oecumenicorum Decreta*, Bologna, Dehoniane, 1991, pp.8-9.

[9] H. Denzinger and P. Hünermann eds, *Enchiridion Symbolorum: Definitionum et Declarationum de Rebus Fidei et Morum*, 37th ed., Bologna, 1996, §3074; English from J. Neuner and J. Dupuis eds, *The Christian Faith*, 7th rev. ed., Bangalore, HarperCollins, 2001, p.321, §839.

[10] To these comments about primacy, one could add what is stated in a text by the Congregation for the Doctrine of the Faith, "Reflections on the Primacy of Peter", in *Origins*, 28, 1998-99, pp.560-63. These reflections were the result of a study undertaken in response to John Paul II's desire "to find a way of exercising the primacy which, while in no way renouncing what is essential to its mission, is nonetheless open to a new situation" (*Ut Unum Sint* 95), an invitation in part inspired by the report of section II, §31, #2, of Faith and Order's fifth world conference (cf. *Ut Unum Sint* 89).

[11] M. Buckley, *Papal Primacy and the Episcopate*, New York, Crossroad, 1998, pp.62-74, and H. Pottmeyer, *Towards a Papacy in Communion*, New York, Herder & Herder, 1998, pp.132-35. The series to which these books belong also includes Archbishop J. Quinn, *The Reform of the Papacy*, New York, Crossroad, 1999; and W. Henn, "The Honor of My Brothers: A Brief History of the Relationship Between the Pope and the Bishops", in *Ut Unum Sint: Studies on Papal Primacy*, Herder & Herder, 2000.

Authority in Context: Methodist Bilateral Conversations and Councils of Churches

REV. DR HERMEN SHASTRI

I see my task in this presentation as being twofold. The first is to offer a survey of the recent theological discourse on the question of the teaching authority of the church, within the framework of the bilateral report of the joint commission of the Roman Catholic Church and the World Methodist Council. The second task is to locate the issue of "authority" as it is experienced in the context of ecumenical relations in the life of a national council, in this case that of Malaysia.

The fourth report of the international Catholic-Methodist dialogue (1997-2001), *Speaking the Truth in Love: Teaching Authority among Catholics and Methodists*, is the seventh in a five-year series of studies. The present report builds upon the earlier reports which have taken up themes such as towards a statement on the church (1982-86); the apostolic Tradition (1986-91); and the word of life (1992-96).

Speaking the Truth in Love as a whole reflects a rich harvesting of theological insights tending towards affirming commonalities, and reveals a growing maturity as it begins to take up one of the thornier issues of ecclesiology. A strong pneumatological emphasis undergirds the report: "The themes of the Holy Spirit and the church, studied in previous phases of this dialogue, have now led to the more precise question of how the faith which comes from the apostles is transmitted from generation to generation in such a way that all the faithful continue to adhere to the revelation that has come in Jesus Christ" (see introduction §1).

If "authority" is about how the church teaches, acts and reaches doctrinal decisions in faithfulness to the gospel, then the question of the instruments of authority within the church become crucial, and the report takes up the core ecclesiological issues of the respective bilateral partners.

The report is divided into two parts: the first explores the theological convergences and differences between the two traditions in a comparative and systematic way; the second is more descriptive, seeking to explore "the current understandings and practices internal to Methodism and Catholicism respectively, though in a style intended to be more readily intelligible by the partner and by others" (2). The report ends with a summary conclusion of "recognizable commonalities" and "outstanding differences", providing hints for the direction of future theological exchanges.

Survey of discussion of part one

The report begins by focusing on the Pauline passage of Ephesians 4:1-16, a popular ecumenical text, which uplifts unity in the one faith and one body and envisions the various ministries given to the church by the ascended Christ as instruments to build up the body of Christ. So, although the passage recognizes a diversity of gifts enlivened by the one spirit, the exercise of such gifts has a teaching dimension in so far as it promotes unity in faith with the consequence that "matters of faith" and the "ability to distinguish between right and wrong teachings" (5) are maintained.

Catholics and Methodists are able to affirm together "the core of Christian doctrine" that revolves around the revelation of God's saving love in Christ and which finds expression in the visible koinonia (communion, community) of Christ's disciples, the church (7). Even how part one of the report is titled indicates the growing convergence:
1) the church as communion in love and truth;
2) God's prophetic community, anointed with the Spirit of truth;
3) the means of grace, servants of Christ and his church.

Important in the report is the recognition and status of the historic dogmas, the Apostles and the Nicene-Constantinopolitan Creeds, in the church's liturgies of both the traditions. The creeds not only "function as a rule of faith *(regula fidei)*", but are also "normative for conciliar and other official teaching"(8).

But the question that arises is how the church decides between divergent traditions and conflicting interpretations of the gospel, and it is here that the report explores the teaching authority presented by the two traditions. While the Catholics maintain that since apostolic times a decision-making process was present, "[when] at the local level pastoral care was entrusted to a college of presbyters under the presidency of a bishop, with the bishops themselves forming a college at the universal level, in which the Roman see presided 'in clarity'"(19). When bishops gather in council and give accent to the same doctrinal decrees, they exercise "a magisterial responsibility on behalf of the universal church" (19).

The Methodists, on the other hand, identify the Conference, an annual gathering of clergy and laity, with its bishops (in the UMC tradition and presidents in the British tradition) who exercise spiritual oversight "whereby the supervision of teaching is exercised by the Conference and the superintendent ministers acting in its name"(19).

The Catholics would assert the "charism of unfailing truth and faith" (20) given to the bishops and attribute the doctrine of "infallibility" exercised by the pope in union with the bishops (First Vatican Council), in order to guard over matters of doctrine and sacred tradition.

The Methodists maintain that the Conferences may formulate doctrinal statements as needed, but these Conferences "do not ascribe to them guaranteed freedom from error" (21). Methodists understand themselves to be under an obligation to accept as authoritative what can clearly be shown to be in agreement with scriptures.[1]

It is also interesting to note that in the paragraph on teaching the Truth, though both traditions accept scriptures, the creeds and the doctrinal decrees of the early ecumenical councils, there are differences in how doctrine is received by the people. The question needs to be asked as to how far decisions made at the Methodist Conferences hold final authority in the interpretation of doctrine. Throughout its history Methodism has shown itself to be vulnerable to schisms, and much of this was related to rejection of decisions of Conferences. Though the report maintains that "refinement and reformation of teaching is part of an ongoing process through conferences" (24), the issue of divergence cannot be adequately met by returning only to the standard doctrinal text of Methodism, that is, the sermons of John Wesley, his explanatory notes on the New Testament, and the 21 articles of religion. On the Catholic side, the accumulation of decrees and pronouncements by episcopal synods and the pope inform the Catholic church, constantly ensuring that the unity of the church is served.

Drawing upon the language of *Lumen Gentium* and Wesleyan hymnody, section II of part one, "God's Prophetic Community, Anointed with the Spirit of Truth", highlights the point that it is the entire church, ordained and lay, that is involved in discerning the truth, with the Holy Spirit empowering the whole people of God in the work of the church. Both traditions affirm, "The whole body of believers, lay and ordained together, is called to the task of proclamation of the gospel. It is the whole church which remains rooted in a communion of faith and life with the apostles themselves, faithful to their teaching and mission" (35).

A very insightful theme taken up in this section is the importance of the *sensus fidei* for the church's abiding in the truth. Each believer through the guidance of the Holy Spirit is made able "to recognize and respond to the word of God, to discern truth from falsehood in the matters of faith and morals, to gain deeper insights into what they believe and to apply that belief to daily life" (37). The fact is that individuals and groups "can fall away from the truth and from holiness of life". The report emphasizes that the individual act of faith, "I believe", must always participate in the communal act of the church, "We believe" (37). The report, however, refers only to the *sensus fidei*, not to the *sensus fidelium*.[2] The reason perhaps is the focus on the believer's participation in discernment, "All believers together are 'co-workers with the truth', with a co-responsibility for discerning and proclaiming the truth of the gospel, always under the leading power of the Spirit of the Truth. Authoritative discernment and proclamation can never be understood properly in isolation from the anointing by the Spirit of all the baptized, individually and together" (43).

In section III of part one, "The Means of Grace, Servants of Christ and His Church", the nature of the teaching office is taken up in each tradition. The term "means of grace" signals a convergence, where both traditions agree that, "The whole church is called to be a channel of God's grace to the world; within the church individuals and institutions become agents of the Lord and thus servants of their brothers and sisters" (49).

Catholics see in the term "means of grace" notions of sacraments and sacramentals. In the report, however, the two traditions continue to register their theological differences over sacraments, two against seven (58). Differences are not denied and questions are left open for further exploration in the future dialogues (61).

On the question of the ordained ministry, both traditions agree that by ordination a person is irrevocably called and set apart by God for special service in the community of believers. Catholics understand ordination as a "sacrament singling out men within the church to be living signs and instruments of the continuing pastoral oversight and leadership of Christ himself" (65).

Methodists understand ordination as a gift from God, "In it men and women who are called... are accepted by the Conference after examination"(66). They are ordained by the bishop or the president of the Conference, by the laying-on of hands, and given charge to preach, administer the sacraments and uphold the order in the church. "While Methodists do not understand ordination as a sacrament, it is a liturgical action involving the community's prayer for the gift of the Holy Spirit appropriate to the particular form of ministry" (66). The unresolved issue remains; "Catholics ask Methodists whether they might not use sacramental language, such as has been used of the church itself, of ordained ministry in the church, and of its authoritative discernment of the truth of the gospel. Methodists ask Catholics why, given human weakness and fallibility, they understand ordained ministry not only as a sign but also as a guarantee of the active presence of Christ by the power of the Holy Spirit, especially in particular acts of authoritative discernment and proclamation" (68).

On the question of apostolic oversight, both traditions recognize the ministry of the *episcope*. There is agreement that bishops "guard, transmit, teach and proclaim, corporately and individually, the apostolic faith as it is expressed in scripture and Tradition..." (75). But differences remain on the nature of corporate *episcope*, and the extent to which the laity are included in the exercise of this ministry.

Catholic exercise of corporate *episcope* operates at the level of diocese where diocesan synods assist the bishop in his ministry of oversight and teaching. At the same time the communion of bishops worldwide in union with the pope guard and transmit the apostolic teaching of the church in unity with scripture and Tradition. Methodists exercise corporate *episcope* only within the parameters of the Conference while Catholics understand the gift of apostolicity as belonging to the whole church, "this is served and guaranteed by the apostolic ministry of the bishops" (75). The question remains, is the corporate exercise of *episcope* as in a Methodist Conference equivalent to the apostolic ministry of bishops understood in the Catholic church?

With regard to the role of the laity, the report reflects both traditions affirming their participation in authoritative teaching. While in the Methodist Conference lay participation is guaranteed and recognized, the Catholics locate authoritative teaching to the college of bishops with the bishop of Rome at its head. So, there is still no complete agreement of the extent of lay participation in matters of authoritative discernment and teaching. "A significant point of divergence is the idea of a guaranteed or 'covenanted' means of grace, and the grounding this gives to the Roman Catholic understanding of the teaching authority of the college of bishops united with the pope. Methodists wonder whether a doctrine of a guaranteed indefectibility of teaching takes full account of human frailty and sinfulness,... Catholics wonder how, without such a 'covenanted' understanding, Methodists can be sure that their preaching and teaching is truly that of Christ and his church" (82).

Amid the mutual affirmation that "all forms of ministry are communal and collegial", there still remains a lack of agreement on the degree of certainty that preaching and teaching are truly that of Christ and his church.

Survey of discussion of part two

The second part of the document does not introduce new themes; instead it provides the historical context of both traditions, making it helpful in understanding the theologies and polity that have developed in each tradition. In fact, for the general reader, it may be more practical to read this section first before going into the weightier concerns of part one.

"Methodist Understanding and Practice" makes the following points (86-98):

- That John Wesley believed that "the people called Methodist were raised up by God in a particular situation for a particular task, that is, 'to reform the nation', particularly the church, and to spread scriptural holiness over the land".
- Doctrinally, the early Methodists followed the Anglican doctrinal formularies, specifically the thirty-nine Articles of Religion, the Homilies, and the Book of Common Prayer, under the guidance of John Wesley.
- The early Methodists understood their movement as a revival of genuine Christianity. Theirs was a prophetic ministry, proclaiming salvation, both individual and social, to 18th-century England. The goal was to spread scriptural holiness, and this mission led to the recruitment of lay and ordained preachers. The preachers met in Conference for the first time in 1744 for the purpose of guiding the revival.
- The Conference had several functions. It determined the practical doctrine of Methodist preachers, the nurture and discipleship of converts and the supervision of the mission by the deployment of ministers in different circuits, and lastly the Conference was an occasion for holding the preachers accountable for what they preached and how they lived.
- In America, in the light of the political independence, Wesley took steps to provide for American Methodism a liturgy, an ordained ministry and a general superintendency.

"Catholic Understanding and Practice" makes the following points (99-116):

- The Catholic church is a communion of Eastern and Latin churches, in each of which the church of Christ is truly present.
- Catholic unity involves holding in common all the doctrines of the church. There is space for diversity of theological insight and expression, plurality of liturgical rites and canonical discipline.
- Among the various ministries exercised in the church from the earliest times, the primary service from the beginning is that of the

bishop. Catholics understand the college of bishops as continuing the care of the apostles for all the churches.
- The church's teaching office *(magisterium)* is not above God's word, but serves the word.
- The authority of a bishop as chief pastor and teacher of a diocese is both territorial and personal.
- The pope's ministry to all his brother bishops and their churches is a pastoral service of the universal church's unity in love and truth. At an ecumenical council, the bishops, in communion with the bishop of Rome, proclaim by a definite act a doctrine pertaining to faith or morals. It is also believed that bishops are preserved from error by the Holy Spirit and this is what is meant by the "infallibility" of their proclamation of doctrine.

In the conclusion, the document provides a brief summary of the key differences which require further exploration. The similarities point to the authoritative teaching of the church resting on the Catholic side of the special ministry of the bishop of Rome in proclaiming the faith of all bishops, and on the Methodist side the Conference as the final authority of the interpretation of doctrine with the qualification that the latter is not "guaranteed freedom from error".

Differences include the lack of complete agreement on "the essential components of the gospel" (118), the role of the laity as compared with the ordained ministry (119), and the relationship between ordination (and its sacramentality), authoritative teaching and the sure guidance of the Holy Spirit (120). *Speaking the Truth in Love* is clearly a step forward in the ecumenical relations between Catholics and Methodists and it continues to strive for "full communion in faith, mission and sacramental life".

Issues of authority in the context of the council of churches

Since its inception in 1948, the Council of Churches of Malaysia has brought together 16 member churches representing the mainline Protestant churches and eight national Christian organizations. Among its six objectives in its constitution the first reflects the Lund principle, namely, "to offer itself as an instrument or agency to the churches in Malaysia whereby they can more and more do together everything except what irreconcilable differences of sincere conviction compel them to do separately" (art. 5.1).

In practice, the council brings together the episcopal heads and presidents of the various churches for regular consultation on matters of Christian teaching and witness and larger concerns of the nation. The decisions made by the heads of churches are respected but the

Council holds no legislative power to influence or determine decisions made by the various member churches as autonomous bodies.

When it comes to the issue of authoritative teaching, the agenda of meetings of the heads is often filled with matters dealing with the spread of doctrines that threaten unity among churches and the recognition of "new" churches and movements that operate beyond the ecumenical mandate of member churches.

As is the case in many parts of the non-Western world, Malaysia is faced with the problem of schisms in doctrine and authoritative leadership within the churches. There is a general tendency of the laity to flock to "appealing" churches or "conventions" which purportedly promise "renewal" or "revival" and offer contemporary and modern expressions of Christian worship. The leaders of such "churches" are a power unto themselves and exercise their authority with little reference to the other existing churches in the country.

In the light of such a situation, the Council constantly appeals to its members to commit themselves to mutual accountability. This means that member churches make a commitment to seek to implement within the life and witness of one's own church the decisions reached by the heads of the various churches.

In the recent years more efforts are being made to acquaint the churches with documents of the Faith and Order commission so that interests in matters of doctrine, its teaching and practice within and between the churches could be better explored and through conciliar agreements be implemented and made binding among the member churches.

NOTES

[1] Even the representative body of the World Methodist Council does not and cannot legislate for the churches, but seeks to reflect their mind and, when it is agreed, to represent them.

[2] In the ARCIC II's report on *The Gift of Authority*, the *sensus fidei* is presented as a subjective "active capacity for spiritual discernment", which contributes to the formation of the *sensus fidelium* through which the church as a whole remains faithful to Christ.

Authority in Contemporary Ecclesiology
Some Reflections
REV. DR MARTYN PERCY

I am tempted to say, from the very beginning, that only the church could pose such a question to itself: How can we teach with authority? The premise seems to be that what the church mainly lacks in its engagement with contemporary society is *authority*; that without this, the church cannot be heard, is not given its due respect, and can be ignored. A body – of belief or believers – that is not regarded by the public and is ignored by the masses has a dubious claim on being an authority. It can preside over and proscribe for its followers, but to outsiders, the grammar of assent simply looks like a quaint curiosity – or, perhaps worse, something between a hobby with too many rules through to a totalitarian regime.

So, how can we teach with authority? It is a simple enough, six-word question. And yet to answer it requires some genuine honesty about the premises that fund such an enquiry. We might begin by asking: Who is asking the question? Who is the "we" of this question?[1] Is this a concern of bishops, theologians, pastors, priests and educators? And if so, is there any evidence that the laity cry out with the same voice?

First, where is the issue of authority in the ecumenical movement today, and in contemporary ecclesiology? What are the pressure points in bilateral agreements, and in other forms of ecumenical conversation? Second, given the enormously wide range of hermeneutical habits within the churches, how is it possible to teach with authority when there is apparently so little agreement on interpretation? Third, how can the issue of authority in contemporary ecclesial theology be properly assessed and understood? Fourth, how do the creeds and scriptures function authoritatively in the churches and in theology?

The tension between the authentic and authority is, in my view, one of the most important (but relatively unexplored) keys to understanding the apparent crisis in contemporary ecclesial identity. Put simply, people's perception of the authentic can question the authority they are placed under, just as much as an authority can interrogate the prevailing establishment. This leads to a debate about the author of a particular aspect of authority – does the dogma under question come from the Creator or the created (*opus Dei* or *opus hominum*)? Equally, is the authentic given by the Author (i.e., part of the created order), or called into a new existence by the *authority* that is above it? (Of course I am well aware that this antinomy is fundamentally false, since inspiration and revelation all comes *through* the agency of created order. Nevertheless, the division between the authentic and authority will serve our purposes well here, in establishing the contours for the debate).

Reflections on authority and teaching

I am more than conscious that this paper may appear to have spun off from its original concern: authority in contemporary ecclesial theology. However, there is method in my atypical approach, which will become apparent as the discussion proceeds. The relationship between authority and authenticity remains a fundamental concern of mine and, in turn, it has a direct impact on establishing a theology that articulates the nature and purpose of authority and, therefore, of education and formation. In my recent commentary on the final ARCIC document,[2] I take issue with the assumption that reaching this kind of top-level theological consensus (i.e., agreements between very senior ecclesiastical and theological persons) constitutes a proper way of setting about the business of doing theology.

I make several criticisms of the ARCIC document, although you should know that broadly I am supportive of its findings. The first criticism is that the report pays no attention to the significant doctrinal and liturgical differences between Roman Catholics and Anglicans. In ignoring these (presumably because they are deemed to be either too contentious or peripheral), the report assumes that an agreed statement makes for an agreement. It does not. By ignoring the genuine differences (and social histories), the nature of the report, although clearly authoritative, lacks a dimension that would give it more authenticity.

Second, the absence of local grass-roots conversations, dialogues and exchanges constitutes an impoverished kind of theology. If the report were a more extensive kind of research, it would have listened to the genuine and lived experience of those on the ground, who are practising their faith in Anglican-Roman Catholic ecumenical projects on a day-to-day basis.

Third, there is an assumption that cherished cultural particularities (and they inevitably have theological significance) can be swept aside by a form of ecumenism that seems to presuppose its own authority. For example, the nature and purpose of the Church of England invests something in the monarch being its supreme governor, which in turn, partly characterizes the ambivalent and open nature of English religion. At the same time, the pope is a head of state, as well as presiding over an ecclesial system where the nature and practice of authority "feels" rather more proscribed to that which might be encountered in Anglicanism. Yet the ARCIC document mentions none of these matters as an impediment to full and visible unity, as though five hundred years of political history and cultural conditioning were somehow irrelevant. Again, in not dealing with authentic differences, the authority of the report looks thin. If people's genuine grass-roots concerns have not been taken into account, exactly how does the report carry weight?

The ARCIC report, *The Gift of Authority*: The failure of the authors to consult widely means that certain issues and realities are overlooked. I must also add a further concern. In what sense can "authority" be truly a "gift"? Only, it seems to me, if it is asked for, wholly offered (i.e., not imposed) or appreciated for what it gives of itself. But to be a true gift, in any conventional sense, it no longer becomes the property of the donor, since it becomes part of the economy of exchange – it can be received with thanks, or rejected as unsuitable. Authority, as a "gift", implies a covenant relationship, in which obedience cannot be commanded as of right.

To sum up, *The Gift of Authority*, though laudable in so many ways, *lacks* ultimate authority because of its insufficiency in grounded authenticity, and is therefore part of the problem (not the solution) to the crisis of authority in ecclesiology and ecumenism. If such reports do not deal in "real" issues and do not consult with "real" Christians and their churches, it will not gain the authentification of the masses of the laity that it needs, which will ultimately deprive it of any authority – the very thing it presupposes it has. It is simply theological double-speak to say that a document still has authority even when no one pays attention to it or believes in it.

First, it must be remembered that there are various types of knowledge that constitute the Christian communities of which we are part, and which form the basis of ecclesial authority or the personal fundaments that construct the Christian lives of individuals. There is considerable plurality amongst the churches. For example, those that are liturgically or doctrinally formed (i.e., through tradition) may struggle to relate to those churches where certain experiences (e.g., speaking in tongues) validate membership and give grounds for authority. For some, the authority of orders will be pre-eminent. For others, the validation of authority rests on charismata, experiences of the numinous and the ability to reify the life of the Holy Spirit within the midst of the congregation. Within this matrix, the weight of authority given to scripture, tradition, reason and culture will vary enormously. In other words, Christian "knowledge" (and therefore authority) is a deeply contested concept.[3]

Second, knowledge, and therefore the authority that proceeds from it, is not an inert corpus of material lying "out there" in some ethereal world,[4] but is rather part of the dynamic discourses that constitute communities. That is not to say, of course, that knowledge is only a social construction of reality, to parody Berger and Luckmann.[5] It is, rather, to own the fact that knowledge requires commitment in order to assume an authority, and this must be an ongoing dynamic process which is open to constant renewal. Furthermore, knowledge has different competencies that are related to its purposes. Practical knowledge has a different authority to that of academic knowledge.[6] A knowledge that ceases to have value or meaning for a community inevitably loses some of its authority. Knowledge and authority must therefore be continually rediscovered in the ordinary processes of dynamic sociality; it can never assume a right to privilege without the sacrifice of engagement and debate.

Third, and following the previous two points, we might ask how authority functions in the church as a learning community? To what extent are ecclesial communities equipped with the resources to become communities of critical reflection, or exploration, and of distinctiveness? This question goes to the heart of the knowledge-authority axis, and makes further demands upon the assumptions about the kinds of knowledge that underpin authority. We might say that in a modernist mindset, the contours of authority are well articulated, and the purposes of knowledge attainment clear and precise. But in a more post-modern climate, there is an almost in-built sense of indecision, indeterminacy, and openness.[7] The ends that may be perceived turn out to be only beginnings; rule books become guide books; the pillar of flame a beacon to guide rather than being a light to follow. The shaping of ecclesial communities becomes a process of development rather than a comparatively static correspondence to a finite body of knowledge.

Authority and discipleship

To turn, finally, to the crisis of authority in ecclesial authority. At this point, it would be right to recognize that many will still be fearful for the fate of Faith and Order if the question of unity is de-coupled from that of authority. But this is where the burden of this paper starts to emerge. I am advocating for more open and faithful disagreement (celebrating the diversity of discipleship) as a part of ecumenical dialogue and truth seeking, which in turn is to be seen as a truer pathway to the churches owning a more authentic teaching authority. But how can I be sure that such a programme will be faithful to tradition? To answer this, I turn to an area of research that was my first love: Christian fundamentalism.

Even in fundamentalistic communities, there is considerable divergence on what constitutes an inerrant Bible. And bearing in mind that for such communities, authority flows from the inerrancy of scripture (which is to say that ecclesial and ministerial authority is regarded as being under the Word), the patterns of authority and teaching in such communities will vary widely. Where there are similarities between them, they may be morphological rather than doctrinal (style, not substance). Of course, a review of the authority of the Bible in different denominations would reveal a similarly significant range of diversity. Some treat the sacred text as a rule book (instructions to be followed, carefully), others as a guidebook (a few rules, many recommendations, warnings, suggestions, etc). Most denominations employ a combination of the two approaches. (But is it not the case that the parabolic tradition of Jesus gives the church precisely this permission to act so fluidly?). We may have agreement on what the fundaments of tradition are – but not on how to understand them, what weight to place on different aspects of faith and order, nor how to be Christian in the contemporary world. Ecclesial communities are unavoidably hermeneutical rather than (vapidly) receptive. They are within the (ultimate) parable of Jesus Christ – experiencing God's story of incarnation, redemption and resurrection as it continues to unfold within them and around them, the Word made flesh.[8]

It seems to me that that the authority of the church and its teaching rests not, primarily, on what the church says, and with what clarity, but on the quality of its discipleship. The authority of the churches – at least in public life, but surely also in ecumenical dialogue? – is constituted in the calibre, character and depth of its discipleship. If this at once sounds too slippery, we would do well to remember that the New Testament offers remarkably little by way of definition as to what a Christian actually is. Christians are known by what they do (activity and vocation), some words that they say (confess), and by what they have (the Spirit of God). But the New Testament does not give the churches a credal definition of what, precisely, a Christian must (or must not) believe in order to count themselves amongst the saints. To be sure, creeds are important, if not vital, for maintaining unity and identifying authority, both internally and externally. But the authority of the church depends primarily on an authentic discipleship that manifests the love of God for the human race and for the whole of the created order. We are known by our fruits, not our seeds.

The stress on discipleship as the fundamental basis for teaching authority takes us back to the commencement of this paper, and the insistence on the need for parity between authenticity and authority. This was partly grounded in the work of Nicholas Healy,[9] who rightly emphasizes Christian life and discipleship as the "concrete" ground (no less a place for the *theodrama* than a high-powered synod) that can counter-moderate the idealist traits of blueprint ecclesiologies. An emphasis on discipleship also indicates why, on certain occasions, the church fails to be received as an authority by the world, since it lacks authenticity and characterful discipleship. Put more strongly, I would argue that the teaching authority of the church rests not on dogma, but on discipleship. And this is surely why, in the (so-called) great commission of Matthew 28, there is an explicit link between authority, teaching and the making of disciples. It reminds me of some words usually attributed to St. Francis: "Go and make disciples of all nations. And if absolutely necessary, use words."

So, can the church afford the risk of truly teaching, rather than indoctrinating? Perhaps. And perhaps we need to take it, remembering that there is, like it or not, an intrinsic relationship between adherence and authority, that rests on authenticity, and is, in turn, continually transformed by the grace of our Lord Jesus Christ, the love of God and the fellowship of the Holy Spirit in the life of all Christian disciples. Ecclesial authority rests not, I venture, on faith being ordered or the church being managed; it is located in inspiration and commitment. Theologians should learn to lead by example. Or, as Merton once put it:

> The purpose of education is to show a person how to define themselves authentically and spontaneously in relation to their world – not to impose a prefabricated definition of the world, still less an arbitrary definition of the individual themselves...[10]

In educating, and with authority, have we the courage to offer true liberation to our brothers and sisters in Christ? Can we let go of control, and still hold fast to Christ? Only time will tell, as the authentic and the authoritative wrestle and weave together in the life of the church.

NOTES

[1] The question is explored in some depth in Visser 't Hooft's *Teachers and the Teaching Authorities*, WCC, 2000, where a helpful distinction is drawn between the *magistri* and the *magisterium*.

[2] *The Gift of Authority*, London, Anglican Book Centre, 1999.

[3] I think of my own work as a priest, and recall, as a curate, visiting Jimmy and Lily. They were both devout Anglo-Catholics, and their house was filled with religious memorabilia. They were almost literalistic in their beliefs, trusting entirely in the dogmas and authority of the church. Yet when Jimmy died of cancer, the certainties of Lily's "vernacular spirituality" constituted an authoritative base for her bereavement. For Lily, Jimmy was "always present" and "had not left". She would cite instances of seeing him in the home or garden. For her, it was inconceivable that he had left her for heaven. There are two kinds of "knowledge" here: dogmatic and intuitive/personal – but they are held together, without difficulty, in the life of an "ordinary" Christian on a Bedford housing estate, even though one type of knowledge undermines the authority of another.

[4] R. Barnett, "Witchcraft, Astrology and Knowledge Politics", in R. Barnett ed., *The Idea of Higher Education*, Buckingham, UK, Open UP, 1990, p.43.

[5] P. Berger and T. Luckmann, *The Social Construction of Reality*, New York, Doubleday, 1966.

[6] R. Barnett, *The Limits of Competence*, London, OUP/SRHE, 1994, p.160.

[7] W. Doll, "Foundations for a Post-Modern Curriculum", *Curriculum Studies*, vol. 21, no. 3, 1989, p.250.

[8] S. McFague, *Speaking in Parables*, London, SCM Press, 1975.

[9] N. Healy, *Church, World and Christian Life*, Cambridge, Cambridge UP, 2000.

[10] T. Merton, *Love and Living*, London, Sheldon, 1979, p.3.

Authority in Contemporary *Ecclesio* Theology

MRS SARAH S. KAULULE

In order to respond to the question of authority in contemporary ecclesial theology, it is crucial to begin by defining the term "authority". However, authority can only be properly understood and applied within a given context and environment; otherwise, the basis and application of that authority becomes difficult to accept, or to appreciate later on. Hence, a brief background and understanding of the history of the union in the United Church of Zambia (UCZ) will be used as the context within which this response is made.

The United Church of Zambia's union is interesting because churches with different traditions came together. The UCZ united different tribes, races and missionaries into one church. It not only has an evangelical and social outreach in the nation, but most of all it has a rich diverse background, which enables the church to move on ecumenically.

Ecclesio authority

The question of authority is undoubtedly at the centre of tensions in the churches today because various confessional traditions differ greatly in their ways and modes of teaching. This is so especially if authority is placed in human wisdom or cultural experience. Unless it is understood in and located as an "incommensurable divine revelation that intrudes unto our world from beyond [and as] a word personally addressed to us calling us to repentance and obedience", these tensions are bound to continue.

From the biblical perspective, the word "authority" means "right" or "power" (Matt. 7:29; Acts 1:7; Rom. 13:1; Rev. 12:10). The Latin word for authority originally referred to "moral weightiness based on prestige, age or wisdom". In my own understanding, the word "authority" indicates the right to exercise power in a given sphere. Therefore, authority may mean power and the right to determining what is true or valid. It carries the connotation of both a binding force and liberating power. In other words authority does not only direct and control us, but it also sets us free for creative service.[1] The only authority over our spiritual life must itself be spiritual. Thus only a religion taught by the Holy Spirit has the right to exercise authority.

The religion of authority and the religion of the Spirit are synonymous. This is evident in the church, which Jesus Christ founded. In fact, it was to this church and to this church only that the Holy Spirit came with power (Acts 1:8, 2:4). This is the authority that Christ refers to when Christ says to his disciples, "Go ye therefore, and teach all nations, baptizing them in the name of the Father, and of the Son, and of the Holy Ghost... And lo I am with you always, even unto the end of the world" (Matt. 28:19,20). He further says, "Where two or three are gathered in my name, there am I in the midst of them" (Matt. 28:20). Our Lord Jesus Christ gives his presence in the holy communion and in the union made in baptism between himself and the believer. Furthermore, He does so in government and discipline. He says, "Whatsoever ye shall bind on earth shall be bound in heaven" (Matt. 28:18); and he says to the apostles, "As my Father hath sent me, even so I send you" (John 20:21). In 1 Corinthians 12:5-6 we are reminded of "the way in which authority is conceived and practised in the service of the one authority of Jesus Christ and the various forms" which are always dependant on historical developments, different gifts, ministries and capabilities which have their goal in the one spirit, the Lord, the one God who inspires them. These are the bases on which spiritual authority in the church is granted.

Social scientists' understanding of authority

A social scientist understanding of authority is important since *ecclesio* authority is exercised on, and by, individuals within a social set-up. Max Weber's theory of bureaucracy, first published in the early 1900s, was influential in forging a basic understanding of the social structures in organizations. Weber saw the idea of bureaucracy as an alternative to the organizational practices that were dominant during an earlier period of history. It therefore becomes natural to think of organizations in terms of hierarchy because it is a common feature of most modern organizations and continuing belief by many managers that every member of an organization should report only to one person.

In Weber's view, a church or religious congregation is an organization. Mary Jo Hatch argues that in organizations tasks are too large for individual persons to perform by themselves. It is for this reason that different people with different skills and abilities will need to work as a team in order for them to achieve the vision of an organization. But to achieve the set purpose, differentiated tasks and workers must be well integrated so that the differences in the activities being performed are well coordinated. In this way, each member could have a clear path through the hierarchy stretching from themselves to their boss and all the way to the top person. In this hierarchy, levels of authority and responsibility and formal channels of communication are linked to each other. This kind of hierarchy is called "the unity-of-command principle".[2] Ultimately, organizational behaviour can be influenced by "the cultures, set values... norms and beliefs reflected in the different structures and systems"[3] of the people who work there, and in the case of a church, people who worship there.

Authority in the United Church of Zambia

It is not the purpose of this paper to go into details of the tensions in the churches but to simply present what is pertaining today in the United Church of Zambia as far as authority and authoritative teaching is concerned.

The UCZ is a church that was born out of the coming together of:
- the church of Barotseland established by the Paris Evangelical Missionary Society of France;
- the Zambia district of the Methodist church established by the Methodist Missionary Society;
- the United Church of Central Africa in Rhodesia working in Northern, Luapula and Copperbelt Provinces.

Such a union is a testimony that Christians from different Christian traditions can come together as one in Christ, but of course this calls for a great deal of understanding and acceptance of one another. It calls for considerable teaching to keep the ecumenism alive each time the church is threatened with a split or has its authority questioned by some of its members. Such has not spared the UCZ, but as I have said earlier I will not discuss this issue in any detail.

The United Church of Zambia embraces, among others, the Reformed tradition. The reformers always regard the Bible as an instrument of the Spirit; a tool used by the spirit to bring the truth of the gospel to the hearts of men and women. In this tradition, the Bible is the matrix of the church because it is a source of revelation. Further, the reformers perceive biblical authority as having a higher place than church authority because it is based on the primary witnesses to the revelation of the Holy Spirit. H.-H. Esser agrees with this fact when he says "the sole authority over and in the reformed doctrine is Jesus Christ himself".[4]

The United Church of Zambia today

In order to enforce the authority of the church, the United Church of Zambia has put in place a synodical structure with the mandate:
a) to articulate the argument for those decisions, which are important for the orientation of the doctrine and life in terms of the holy scriptures to the call of the triune God in the contemporary situations;
b) to maximize unanimity in the formulation of such synodal decisions (Rom. 15:6);
c) to publicize the voting figures and the views of the majority.

All issues are dealt with collectively within the church. All matters needing further clarification are passed on from the congregation to presbyteries, which in turn report to the synod. Once confirmed and accepted, the issues acquire the basis of truth and authority, which is generally binding for the whole church.

Although the church has authority in so far as it submits to the higher authority of the revealed word of God, Jesus Christ is the head and goal. The Bible is the original witness to the mighty acts of God who is the ultimate or eternal source of this revelation. As the UCZ constitution, rules and regulations (CRR, 1994 p.3) states, "The church has authority to interpret its doctrine but always in agreement with the word of God." Therefore, Jesus Christ himself is the sole authority and the head of the church.[5]

The United Church of Zambia is a contemporary church and the basis of its teaching is the Bible and hence the upholding of the biblical authority. Generally, the church is a royal priesthood of all believers, which means that all its members can approach God through Christ and can therefore share in the calling and authority of the whole church. Through the Holy Spirit all its members have all the privileges and duties of a priesthood of believers offering to God in and with the Son the sacrifice of themselves and all their powers. It is the duty of the whole church and every member to spread the good news of the kingdom and the message of salvation through Christ. "The ministry of the church... in its priestly, pastoral and prophetic aspects is derived from the risen and ascended Lord who is at once the Great High Priest, the Chief Shepherd of Souls and the Eternal Word of God" (CRR p.10).

Because the church is conscious of using all gifts that God has given to humankind, both the clergy and the laity are embraced and have a role to play to exercise this authority in terms of teaching and leading in the church. As the CRR states,

> It is the duty and privilege of every believer to share in the ministry of the church so that the many gifts are used to the full e.g. life and witness of all Christians in the world, spiritual care, growth and governance of the church,

teaching, youth work, lay preaching, church fellowship and social services (p.10).

Acknowledging the priesthood of all believers that God invests in both the clergy and the laity, the clergy are ordained by the laying-on of hands as ministers of both the word and sacrament. In ordination, God in answer to the prayers of the church gives and guarantees the calling of these men and women whom God calls for the ministry. The ordained ministry of the United Church derives from Christ as continued by his apostles and continues to receive its authority from Christ through the Holy Spirit.

The church affirms that the ministry is given to the church as a task of the whole body and therefore the ordained ministers work as part of the body of Christ and his task. The laity in their spiritual assignments complement the ordained ministers. Even though the church recognizes the special role of the ordained ministers, Christ is recognized as the head of the church from whom the ordained derive the authority to lead and give guidance in the church.

Cultural and traditional influence

The different traditions within Zambia have had an influence in the understanding of the authority and authoritative teaching in the United Church of Zambia. Although "authority" is conceived and practised in the service of the one authority of Jesus Christ, historical developments, cultural differences, tribal traditions, community settings and customs have impacted greatly on the understanding and practice of the ecclesiastical authority within the church. Much as it is appreciated that UCZ comes from a rich and diverse background, the diverse traditions sometimes affects the ecclesial authority. For instance, the role of the male and female has a culture implication which specifies who does what. Women may tend to take up a low profile during debate and decision-making and leave decision-making to the men. In such instances the ecclesial authority is compromised and decision-making is not inclusive.

As far as youth is concerned, most African traditions may not allow youth to participate actively among the elderly and even in cases where they will, like in the United Church of Zambia, where the constitution allows such participation, the traditional dictates impinge on the freedom of expression. Although the power in authority is ultimately shared within the constitution of committees composed of the clergy and the laity, both women and men, discrimination becomes automatic because of the cultural and social set-up. Nevertheless, there

Authority in Contemporary Ecclesio Theology 153

has been much advocacy concerning the issue of inclusive leadership. Deliberate efforts have been made to include a woman and a youth in meetings and conferences and even in local church leadership. This is crucial since women still play a submissive role and the youth are the future generation. But the environment is still suppressive and impinges on their right to exercise authority. It can only be hoped that with time, the authority of the Bible will be accepted and over-rule such cultural tendencies that disadvantage the women and the youth.

With this basic thesis, the doctrine of the authority of the church marks itself off from both a hierarchical and a democratic view of anarchy and arbitrariness in the church. The church is understood in hope on the ever-renewed grace of the triune God. Because authority is conceived and practised in the service of the one authority of Jesus Christ, for the United Church of Zambia the non-theologians in particular assume a particular active responsibility for acceptance and implementation of decisions in whose drafting they have themselves played an active part, making it easier for church members to make a spiritual appraisal of synodal decisions arrived at in a spiritual manner.

NOTES

[1] See Pullan Leighton, *The Authority of the Church*, Oxford, 1923.
[2] Mary Jo Hatch, *Organisation Theory: Modern, Symbolic and Postmodern Perspectives*, London, Oxford UP, 1997, p.165.
[3] Charles Handy, *Understanding Organisations*, London, 1985, p.185.
[4] Hans-Helmut Esser, *The Authority of the Church and Authority in the Church According to the Reformed Tradition,* Faith and Order study, Geneva, WCC, 1976, p.51.
[5] *Ibid.*, p.52.

Response to "Authority in Contemporary Ecclesiology: Some Reflections"

DR NICHOLAS CONSTAS

It shall not be so among you (Matt. 20:26)

"Authority in Contemporary Ecclesiology: Some Reflections" offers a number of pointed challenges to the ethos and organization of the churches. Drawing attention to the gap between "authority" and "authenticity" (a decoupling, as it were, of theory and practice), Percy calls for a "contextual theology" that would attend more responsibly to the actual social, cultural and personal experiences of the faithful. Teaching which seeks simply to reproduce or reassert the ideological claims of a particular institution may perhaps be "authoritative", but to the extent that it is insufficiently engaged with critical social factors (including the actual values which inform ecclesial structures and polity), it suffers a loss of credibility (or "authenticity"). Ultimately, the process is self-defeating, inasmuch as authority without authenticity has at best a dubious hold on its own power. Rhetoric without reality, in other words, is like a "blueprint" (to use one of Percy's images) without an actual corresponding structure; a soul without a body clinging to existence (like the hungry ghosts of Tibetan Buddhism) through coercion, oppression and violence.

Percy calls for the churches to be fully engaged with culture and society. Rather than dictate from above, or from without, the church (in an activity modelled on the incarnation) must enter deeply into the spirit and substance of the issues that it seeks to address. The church, of course, is already situated within society, of which it is a constituent part, including those societies which are ostensibly secularized, although the simple fact of location in or contiguity with society does not guarantee robust social engagement.

Percy's paper contains more themes than I am able to cover in my brief response. I trust that I have at least touched upon some of his central concerns and described them with reasonable accuracy. At this point I would like to adopt a more analytical approach to the paper, and for a moment attend closely to its rhetoric, for I was struck by the degree to which the argument is advanced through the use of various oppositions; in particular, the master binary which informs the entire document: authority/authenticity.

To a certain extent, binary thinking is a basic modality of human thought and is a process which appears to be deeply rooted within the physiology of the brain, itself composed of left and right hemispheres. On the other hand, such thinking is construed differently by different cultures, and binary oppositions deeply inform Western philosophy and consciousness, and thus non-Western Christians (who on this point may find themselves in greater sympathy with the religions of Asia) may feel uncomfortable with these sharp separations. Where some posit real, ontological disjunctions, others understand conceptual distinctions generated by a certain perspective of thought. Such conceptualizations, far from being mere abstractions, are important in shaping our interpretation of reality.[1] Consider, for example, the traditional analogy that God and the world stand in relation to each other as "author" and "book"; whatever value such an analogy might have, "author" and "book" are two entities that can be rather easily separated from each other with negative consequences for a theology of creation, the sacraments, natural theology, religious art; and not least, of course, the environment itself. If, however, we understand the relationship of God and the world in terms of a "text" and its "meaning", we find that it is much more difficult to disentangle meaning and understanding from its instantiation within a particular medium or form.

With this in mind, we can turn to the relationship between "authority" and "authenticity". As if it were a kind of Japanese *koan*, we might perhaps begin by asking if the words "authority" and "authenticity" form one idea or two separate ideas (with the sinister word "authority" somewhere off in the left-hand position, and the word "authenticity" concerned with what is right)? Do we conceptualize two sides, or do we express both in a single action? Should we see a problem with no logical solution, or a limitation of logic which needs to be broken through by a change of mind (metanoia)? What is the truth or reality to which these terms refer? Whatever that reality might be, it can only be, as Percy argues, that of our own experience. "When Jesus had finished these sayings, the crowds were astonished at his teaching, for he taught them as one who had authority *(exousia)*, and not as their scribes" (Matt. 7:28-29). Here, authority and authenticity (ratified by "the crowds") are one. Jesus is authoritative because he is authentic, and authentic because he is authoritative. Perhaps we are best served by holding these values in tension, by seeing "authority" as antinomic, having both a positive and a negative value, for authority is a category predicated both of the demonic (cf. 1 Cor. 15:24; Eph. 6:12) and of God (Rom. 13:1-2).

Of course, I am aware that by reinscribing the categories of East and West I am engaging in a kind of reverse Orientalism, and have thereby constructed precisely the sort of binary opposition that I claim to detect in Percy's paper. But as I have tried to suggest, the response to this *aporia* lies not in rejecting one term in favour of the other, but in struggling to know them together. Here, Percy's reference to the theology of the incarnation as a paradigm for the life of the church provides us with an important lead. Through the hypostatic union of two natures in Christ, God introduces a bond within the structure of the world that is able to unite all polarities, including that between absolute and relative being, a coincidence of opposites reconciling human beings to God and each other.[2] Surely the best example of this differentiated unity in the patristic period is found in the theology of Maximus the Confessor. Cultivating the grain of a suggestion dropped in Galatians 3:28, Maximus produces a series of five polarities (i.e., male/female, paradise/earth, earth/heaven, intelligible/sensible, God/creation), all of which are overcome and united in the person of Christ.[3]

With the help of an architectural metaphor in Percy's paper, we can approach the same problematic from yet another point of view. Blueprints and buildings normally exist in conjunction with each other, even if the plan is nothing more than an idea in the mind of the architect. The tabernacle of ancient Israel, for instance, was based on a heavenly archetype, a microcosm of creation revealed to Moses on the summit of Mt Sinai. And though the language of "archetype" and "copy" is frequently dismissed as "dualistic", when properly understood it is in fact the priestly view of the world and cannot be readily dismissed (as "mystification", "idealism", etc.) without a fundamental loss of Christian understanding and experience. To continue the architectural metaphor, among the glories of Romanian Orthodoxy are its magnificent churches that are painted on both the "inside" and the "outside", a programmatic device which effectively (and beauteously) subverts those very categories. The church is in the world but, in virtue of its painted exterior, the world becomes the church, with the church building serving as a kind of *iconostasis*, a threshold affording movement between two worlds, a conjunctive centre where heaven and earth are united.

In the same way that a "threshold" is not a "door", however, a union of opposites does not provide closure, but on the contrary opens the human person up to new and creative vistas. The unfolding of meaning is a process in which one problem solved discloses another. Every new synthesis becomes a thesis for its opposite, and Percy is right to remind us that "we live by hope". Along these lines I would like to explore an alternative line of thought regarding the question of "authority" using the insights of theological anthropology and apophatic theology. In patristic anthropology, "authority" *(exousia)* is one of the attributes often identified with the *imago Dei*, and thus is not only a characteristic of an institution, but rather a quality which lies close to the heart of what it means to be human. As an aspect of the *imago Dei*, "authority" in many respects remains a mystery, for like life itself the living icon of God in creation cannot be exhaustively defined by a system of concepts, a conclusion which many researchers in the cognitive sciences are increasingly coming to recognize.[4]

What is true of individual human beings can perhaps be reasonably asserted of communities of human beings. Many patristic writers, for example, believed that the plenitude of the *imago* did not reside in any particular individual, but within humanity as a whole, including those past, present, and yet to be born. Classical political thought similarly moved with relative ease from the individual to the collective and proposed that the state was simply the soul writ large. We may wonder if the same transparencies are not manifest in the church, recalling that "church" and "soul" are interchangeable as images of the bride in patristic and medieval commentaries on the Song of Songs. Like the individual human body, the corporate body of the church is woven together from many elements: liturgy, scripture, Tradition, the faithful, clergy, sacraments, icons and councils (to mention only a few), all of them authoritative and all of them authentic. However, none of these elements can be singled out as having, on its own, authority over all the rest, for if one of them could, what would be the use of the others?

Of course, if the church is "merely" an institution like any other, then these analogies will appear naive and nonsensical, and instead of deluding ourselves with theology we would be better served by principles of corporate management and models of institutional behaviour. However, a great deal is made to hang on the word "merely", a sleight of hand, as it were, for what is in fact a wager on debasement that would render the *Pietà* "merely" a block of marble, or Bach's *Mass in B Minor* "merely" an effusion of sound waves, or the human person "merely" a collection of electro-chemical processes. If, however, the church is understood both as a human institution and as the living body of Christ, then the above-mentioned "metaphors" can also be taken as the height of realism. Ultimately, the disjunction of *Amt* and *Geist* rests on a misunderstanding not simply of Christianity, but of life itself, for if life is to exist and flourish, body and soul belong together, and it is to the fullness of life that Percy prophetically calls the church.

In a memorable phrase, Gregory Palamas remarked that "true theology is not found in theories and arguments, but is manifested in works and in life... every theory, it is said; contradicts another theory, but what theory can contradict life?"[5]

Authority is an enigma and a problem.[6] It is an enigma in its essence and a problem in its value. Power is both what we worship and at the same time hate. There is something divine and something demonic about it. Herein lies its terrible mystique. In response to this dilemma, authority must be both affirmed and negated, embraced and renounced, confessed and repudiated.

The sinfulness of power is, on the one hand, a theme which runs through the Bible from the first book of Kings down to the apocalypse. Samuel knows that to "set up a king" means to "reject God". He warns the people of tyranny, and announces their coming enslavement by the very power which they seek to establish (1 Sam. 8:10-22). In the gospels this thought is carried much further, indeed, to a kind of radical extreme:

> The princes of the earth exercise dominion over them, and their great men exercise authority *(katexousiazein)* over them. But it shall not be so among you; but whoever would be great among you must be your servant, and whoever would be first among you must be your slave (Matt. 20:25-28; Luke 22:25-27; Mark 10:42-44).

It should be stressed that these words are reproduced with striking insistence and exactitude in all three synoptic gospels. The fourth gospel embodies their meaning in the narrative of the washing of the feet. The path of Christian ministry, therefore, is opposed to earthly greatness and power, and Christ refuses the power to rule, which is offered to him twice, once in the desert and once in Jerusalem, as a temptation of the devil. And he was betrayed by Judas, slandered by the high priests, and abandoned by the people in part because he was not a messiah who exercised earthly power, and because he did not come down from the cross.

Thus there is something demonic about power, for it is from the devil. "And the devil said to him, 'To you I will give all this power *(exousia)*, and their glory (i.e., the kingdoms of the world); for it has been delivered to me, and I give it to whom I will.'" The condition for obtaining this power is to fall down and worship the devil (Luke 4:5-8; Matt. 4:8-9). This is perhaps the most forceful thing said against the very principle of authority and yet it is amplified by the apocalypse, which testifies that the demonism of power will grow throughout history. Unprecedented authority over all the nations will be given to the

Beast and Antichrist, and they will receive that authority from the dragon (the devil) precisely because the condition for obtaining authority will have been fulfilled: all the earth will fall down and worship the devil (cf. Rev. 13).

But this is to tell only half the story, and it would be a mistake to derive a kind of radical Christian anarchy from the anti-authoritarian passages cited above. In virtue of the antinomy character of authority, the Bible also proclaims that "there is no authority *(exousia)* but of God, and those that exist have been instituted by God. Whosoever therefore resists authority resists the ordinance of God" (Rom. 13:1-2). Paul's words, moreover, are supported by those of Christ: "You would have no power *(exousia)* at all against me unless it had been given you from above" (John 19:11). And the phrase "render unto Caesar the things that are Caesar's, and to God the things that are God's" (Matt. 22:21) requires us to carry out the legitimate demands of power, reminding us that Christ came not to destroy the law but to fulfil it. Perhaps even more direct than these is the fact that God is always called the heavenly and earthly king, the "ruler over all" *(Pantokrator)*, and the divinization and transfiguration of the world is always designated as the "kingdom of God".

Authority, as these various passages suggest, is a condition and activity with both positive and negative values, being both from God and from the devil. Obviously we cannot impute the demonic aspects of power to the kingdom of God, and thus the antinomy of power must be a phenomenon of our experience of life in the world. Indeed, it is the power of the world which is antinomic, tragically split into thesis and antithesis, requiring affirmation and denial. The kingdom of God is not itself an antinomy, but rather resolves the antinomy. Thus to sacralize power, to identify the authority of God with any earthly authority, and to argue that "what God is in heaven, the ruler is on earth", is blatantly anti-Christian and anti-biblical, resting on a confusion of the absolute "kingdom" with earthly power, and on a total incomprehension of the words, "my kingdom is not of this world" (John 18:36). And history demonstrates that the greatest evil necessarily assumes the form of power, while the greatest good never does so.

Authority has taken on two different meanings, and reminiscent of Augustine's distinction in the *De doctrina christiana* (i.e., of "use" and "enjoyment"), they can perhaps best be conveyed as "power for use" and "power for power's sake". The power that comes "from God" and is religiously and morally justified is "power for use" – it is power in the service of truth and justice (cf. Rom.

13:1-4, where Paul provides for these same criteria). The one in authority, therefore, is God's servant, and that person bears his or her authority strictly for the defence of good and in the struggle against those who are evil. The other meaning of power is a demonic lust for mastery, a pathology of power for power's sake, because it serves no higher principles: it serves no one and nothing. On the contrary, this kind of power forces everyone to serve it. Here, authority is not at all for the struggle against evil, but for the perpetration of evil and the intimidation of the good, that is, of those who have no desire to fall down and worship it.

That any authority is divine under any conditions whatsoever is something that Christians have never claimed. On the contrary, Christianity affirms a communal ideal based not on power but on mutual service through the fulfilment of gifts and through interaction in love and solidarity. The Christian solution to the antinomy of power is the establishment of a hierarchy of values: power has value when it serves truth and justice. Justice and the law have value when they serve and make possible the fellowship of love. Under these conditions, authority receives sanction from above. Conversely, power truly belongs to the devil whenever the hierarchy of values is perverted: when power serves no one and nothing except itself; even worse, when it uses all the means of evil, recognizing nothing higher than itself. And if evil always takes the form of power, the highest good does not concur in doing so ("it shall not be so among you"). This is perhaps because the nature of command and submission always involves a replacement of my will and freedom by the will and freedom of another; a replacement of my "I" by the "I" of another involving an obedience due to fear and not to conscience. Such a situation becomes oppressive when my own conscience does not acknowledge the command to be reasonable or just. But the stage of higher human interaction in love is not anarchy at all, but a fellowship referred to by Christ when he said, "You are no longer slaves of God the Father but friends and sons and daughters." The "way and the truth and the life" (John 14:6) which are set forth here are for the whole of humankind, and not simply for that branch of society in the world that we call the "church". Nevertheless, it is the church which has been called to lead and teach and shine forth the light, authentically and authoritatively, both by word and above all by example.

NOTES

[1] See John David Dawson, *Christian Figural Reading and the Fashioning of Identity*, Berkeley, Univ. of California Press, 2002, who argues that modern commentators have misread Paul by imposing upon his thought a binary interpretive framework which he himself did not use. "Poststructuralist conceptions of meaning, according to which the Pauline distinction between 'letter' and 'spirit' is cast as an irreconcilable conflict between what is literal and what is nonliteral, obscures Paul's efforts to preserve his Jewish identity. By consistently restating Pauline accounts of divine performances in history as claims about meanings in texts, Paul's complex formulations of discontinuity within continuity are transformed into mutually cancelling binary oppositions" (pp.19-20). It is therefore not abstract semiotic theories which explain the movement of the narrative, but concrete historical reference; Wittgenstein's "embodied performance" over and against Derrida's "presence or absence of meaning" (pp.5-6). Dawson's concern is for the impact of such misreadings on the history of relations between Christians and Jews.

[2] On which see Nicholas of Cusa, *De docta ignoranta*, tr. H.L. Bond, New York, CWS, 1997, p.206. It is worth noting that Cusanus arrived at his celebrated notion of the *coincidentia oppositorum* under the influence of Byzantine theology, culminating in a mystical experience which he underwent aboard a ship returning from Constantinople. Through his union of eastern and western theological traditions (including an essay on the contemplation of icons, *De visione Dei, ibid.*, 235-89), he embodies the very *coincidentia* of which he speaks.

[3] For a summary, see L. Thunberg, *Microcosm and Mediator*, 2nd ed., Chicago, Open Court Publ., 1995, pp.373-427. It is worth mentioning that at the council of Florence, one of the Orthodox delegates, Mark of Ephesus, recommended that Maximus's theology be used as the basis for the reunion of the churches, and not that of Gregory of Nyssa, who had, in Mark's opinion, "missed the mark". The issue at hand was the doctrine of purgatory, to which passages in Nyssa seemed to give support, although to the Orthodox it seemed but a vulgarized form of Origenism, a heresy which had likewise envisioned an end to the fires of hell; for references, see my "'To Sleep Perchance to Dream': The Middle State of Souls in Patristic and Byzantine Literature", *Dumbarton Oaks Papers*, 55, 78, 2001, p.113.

[4] For two different understandings concerning the "problem" of personal identity and the notion that human nature can be reduced so e.g., moral choice, reason, language, sociability, sentience, emotions, or consciousness, see J. Le Doux, *Synaptic Self: How Our Brains Become Who We Are*, New York, Viking Penguin, 2002; and F. Fukuyama, *Our Posthuman Future*, New York, Farrar, Straus & Giroux, 2002.

[5] Triads 1.3.13.

[6] In what follows, I use the words "authority" and "power" interchangeably in accordance with the Greek definition of *exousia* (derived from *exestin*, i.e., "ability to perform an action"); cf. LSP s.v., *exousia*: "power or authority"; "power over"; "absolute power or authority"; PGL, s.v., *exousia*: "power", "authority", "power of choice", "evil spiritual powers", etc. The word *dynamis* generally denotes "power" in the sense of intrinsic ability or potential. In the Septuagint, the words *ischys*, *kratos*, *dynamis* and *exousia* express the absolute power of God, whereas in the New Testament, the power given to Christ and the devil is generally denoted as *exousia*.

Authority and Authoritative Teaching in the Church

Report

For Christians the triune God is the ultimate authority, whether for the church or for creation as a whole. Authority is given and received in order to serve communion with God and with one another, filling life with holiness and strengthening the unity of the church. Authority is both a gift and a duty: a gift to be cultivated and shared freely with others according to the life of the Holy Trinity; a duty to be exercised in a way reflective of communion, accomplished in loving cooperation with and for others.

We can rejoice that reflection by the Christian churches in ecumenical dialogue has arrived at significant convergence regarding the written account of the story of God's love for human beings as recorded in the scriptures. The written word of God is "traditioned" in such a way that scripture and Tradition cannot be radically separated from one another; scripture is the concentration of the Tradition and Tradition is the extension of the scripture. The word of God must play a primary role in our reflections on the nature of authority and its presence and exercise in the church.

The New Testament on exercise of authority and mission

The example of Jesus Christ himself is of tremendous importance for gaining a proper perspective upon the presence and exercise of authority. His ministry was characterized by teaching with authority and healing. His good news was announced to the poor, the captives, the blind and the oppressed (cf. Luke 4:18). It was an authority which placed itself at the service of human persons. The nuances of two important New Testament words – *exousia* and *dunamis* – help us to further illustrate this. When Jesus performed deeds of power *(dunamis)*, it provided those who benefited from his actions with the occasion to recognize his authority *(exousia)* and his opponents with the opportunity to deny it. His authority was self-emptying: it included the "power to lay down his life" (John 10:17-18).

The category of "mission" is helpful in understanding how the church participates in the authority of God: "All authority in heaven and on earth has been given to me. Go therefore and make disciples of all nations, baptizing them in the name of the Father and of the Son and of the Holy Spirit, teaching them to observe all that I have commanded you; and lo, I am with you always, to the close of the age" (Matt. 28:18-20). Jesus names twelve to carry out the mission and at another place says that the mission of the church must be an outreach of love to help those most in need: "Whatever you do to one of the least of these my brethren, you do to me" (Matt. 10:1 and 25:40,45).

These Christological suggestions need to be complemented by the witness of the New Testament regarding the relation of the Holy Spirit to the church, a witness which is more forcefully conveyed in the material from Luke-Acts and John. As Jesus takes his leave of the apostles in the opening scene of Acts, he states, "It is for you to know times or seasons which the Father has fixed by his own authority. But you shall receive power when the Holy Spirit has come upon you; and you shall be my witnesses in Jerusalem and in all Judea and Samaria and to the end of the earth" (1:7-8). A parallel can be drawn between the beginning of Luke and Acts regarding the overshadowing by the power of the Holy Spirit: as the power overshadowing Mary led to the birth of her Son Jesus, so the power received by the disciples at Pentecost brings about the "birth" of the church. (cf. John 14:16-17,25-26).

Authority – church – world
In the earliest community, the apostles and their co-workers also taught and healed with power, after the example of Jesus; their authority too was recognized. How far is such teaching and healing with power still within the mission of the church in today's world?

One of the principal purposes of authority in the church is to maintain the community in knowledge of the truth by discerning the authentic interpretation of the gospel. Teaching and learning constitute a dialogical process, which means that teaching authority is fundamentally relational and actively seeks the *sensus fidelium*. At the same time the scriptures themselves play a normative role in discernment.

The church does not live in isolation from the world. The church is in the world, often tempted to be of the world. The church's members do not dwell in the church alone, for as the church they inhabit communities that embody diverse images, ideologies and institutions.

Teaching authoritatively

Teaching of the church takes place in the midst of multiple teachings from a wide variety of sources. Cultural, social, national and political institutions "teach" diverse understandings of the world, human existence and the purpose of life. These "teachings" are mediated by economic structures, political arrangements, educational institutions, and – permeating it all – the mass media.

On a different level, teaching occurs in each assembly of believers through word and sacrament, the liturgy, and various forms of catechesis. On yet another level, implicit teaching occurs in the architecture of church buildings, church organizational structures, forms of service and mission, and patterns of family life.

In virtue of its source and origin in the triune God, authority is relational and interdependent. There can be no authority unless two or more persons are in relationship. Perhaps the best way to bring into focus the relation between authority and communion is to explore the ecclesiological theme of reception. "He came to his own home, and his own people received him not. But to all who received him, who believed in his name, he gave power to become children of God" (John 1:11-12). The reception of the word in the power of the Spirit is the human response to the initiative of God in this divine-human dialogue which constitutes the mystery of salvation. The dialogue between God and his people gives rise to the communion which is the church. Therefore, the church must be always a communion in dialogue.

As the churches give and receive teaching that bears the marks of ecclesial authority, they are led by the Holy Spirit towards convergence in the truth that makes possible shared, common teaching. Such teaching will achieve levels of authoritative teaching that will be capable of overcoming the fragility and confusion that sometimes characterize the church's voice.

In the contemporary world of competing authorities, it may be more important for the church to be clear about the core of its teaching than to draw boundaries at the edges of its teaching. It makes no sense to talk of authoritative teaching – its source, purpose, location and exercise – apart from an understanding of the truth of the gospel. The church should listen as well as speak, learn as well as teach. It must always teach with "humility and gentleness" (Eph. 4:2).

> But speaking the truth in love, we must grow up in every way into him who is the head, into Christ from whom the whole body, joined and knit together by every ligament with which it is equipped, as each part is working properly, promotes the body's growth in building itself up in love (Eph. 4:15-16).

Authoritative teachers

Authority to teach is given to bishops, councils and conferences, to pastors, professors, to church school teachers, to parents. Such authorization may be formal or informal, regular or collegial. Verbal or active, yet the churches all entrust teaching to a variety of offices and persons. The authority of the communion of teachers and of each teaching office is expressed in words and deeds, explicit and implicit modes, in receiving and in giving. "There are varieties of gifts, but the same Spirit; and there are varieties of activities, but the same Lord; and there are varieties of activities, but it is the same God who activates all of them in everyone. To each is given manifestation of the Spirit for the common good" (1 Cor. 12:4-7).

Authority and freedom of choice

Freedom is a precious gift, one of the qualities by which human beings are rightly said to have been fashioned in the image of God. Thus it seems incomplete to consider authority and authoritative teaching without some reference to their relation to freedom of choice. One of the purposes of teaching the truth by Jesus himself was that "you will know the truth and the truth will make you free" (John 8:32). The exercise of authority after the example of Jesus would be characterized by a profound recognition and respect for the freedom of human person. "For freedom Christ has set us free; stand fast therefore and do not submit again to a yoke of slavery" (Gal. 5:1). The gift of freedom should not be confused with notions of human autonomy, self-sufficiency and isolation but is rather a call to mutual accountability, service and the obedience of all to the gospel of Christ.

Holiness as authority in the church

God is the source of holiness. To recognize holiness is to recognize the presence of God in human beings. The authority of Jesus is reflected in a special way in the lives of God's holy people. Their truthfulness, integrity and authenticity in living according to the gospel is seen by their fellow Christians, who spontaneously grant to them a certain recognition of their moral authority.

Holiness is so interwoven with authority that, in some traditions, any reality enjoying authority is also called "holy" – holy scripture, holy Tradition, holy synods, bearers of ecclesiastical office. The authority of the prophet or of the charismatic leader is often the authority of holiness.

3

Ministry and Ordination in the Community of Women and Men in the Church

29 November-5 December 2003
Bad Herrenalb, Germany

Ministry in Faith and Order
One Woman's Ecumenical Memory
DR MARY TANNER

The question of ministry was firmly on the agenda of Faith and Order at the first world conference in Lausanne in 1927. This is not surprising as Lausanne was, in part, the result of a response to Bishop Brent's plea at Edinburgh 1910 that credible mission requires the unity of the church, and that the unity of the church requires a ministry acknowledged (recognized) in every part of the church as possessing the sanction of the whole church. This continuing conviction that a ministry, acknowledged by all, is essential for unity has meant that ministry has been central in the work of Faith and Order for more than 75 years. Faith and Order's work on ministry falls naturally into four phases.

Lausanne 1927 to Edinburgh 1937: the classical agenda stated

We have come to associate the work of Faith and Order in this early period with the comparative method. The incredibly serious, academic papers on ministry that formed the basis of the work of section 5 on ministry at Lausanne follow that method with heavy-weights like Martin Dibelius and Sergius Bulgakov explaining ministry from the perspective of their own traditions.[1] And yet, surprisingly, the short but very readable report of the section is a model of ecumenical convergence method enumerating first five agreed propositions and then, in the light of the agreement, expounding matters of disagreement.

The agreements state that:
- ministry is a gift of God, through Christ to the church, and essential to the church;
- ministry is perpetually authorized and made effective through Christ and the Spirit;
- the purpose of ministry is to impart the benefits of Christ through pastoral service, preaching the gospel and the administration of the sacraments;
- ministry is entrusted with government and discipline of the church;

- entry into ministry is through an act of ordination, by prayer and the laying-on of hands on those gifted for the work, called by the Spirit, and accepted by the church.

Among the differences highlighted were: the nature of ministry; the nature of ordination and the grace conferred by it; the function and authority of a bishop; and the nature of apostolic succession and the subject of the ordination of women was at least spoken of. Lausanne commended as fruitful for future discussion the place of episcopacy, councils of presbyters and councils of the faithful in the life of the early church, many believing that episcopal, presbyteral and congregational dimensions of ministry, the threefold triad, must all have a place in a reunited church. This is a theme that reappears again strongly nearer our own time and is one that I, at least, think has much more to contribute to the discussion than we have yet drawn out of it.

Ten years later Faith and Order's second world conference in Edinburgh again set out what was agreed, and highlighted outstanding differences in much the same way as Lausanne. Chief among them was the issue of apostolic succession and whether it was *the* true and only guarantee of sacramental grace and right doctrine. There was something very stark in the way that the question was put. Once more Edinburgh repeated the commitment to episcopal, presbyteral and congregational systems as belonging to a reunited church.

There are some striking things about those first two world conferences with their detailed and very academic approach: the over-riding conviction that agreement on ministry was urgent for the sake of the unity of the church; the genuine willingness on the part of most to see the positive in others whose view of ministry differed; and a determination not to unchurch one another in the process of discussing even this most difficult of ecumenical issues.

Phase II: discovering a new context

Very little progress was made in developing the classical agenda set out in the first two world conferences in the following 25 years. Some attribute this impasse to a sense that it was never going to be possible to reconcile an authoritative ministry with the historical episcopate and apostolic succession, with the orders and sacraments of churches that did not possess them. The result was that the third world conference at Lund in 1952 had no separate section on ministry. The little it did say came from the section on intercommunion. What the conference concluded was that the question of ministry should not in the future be seen as an isolated issue but located within an ecclesiological framework, with an emphasis on Christology and eschatology.

Ministry in Faith and Order: One Woman's Ecumenical Memory 171

The World Council itself had not yet moved to a fully trinitarian approach to its vision of the church.

Although little was done in this second phase to develop the classical agenda on ministry, what was happening in the wider ecumenical scene was to have considerable influence on the direction of the discussion in the future, providing a much broader context. The post-war years saw an emphasis on the role of the church in a broken, war-scarred world and with that came an emphasis on the ministry of the whole people of God rather than on the ordained or "special ministry". The work of the new Laity department of the Council was where the discussion was mainly focused.

At the fourth world conference in Montreal in 1963, section 3 had as its theme "The redemptive work of Christ and the ministry of the church".[2] Among the disparate papers prepared for the section was one from the Laity department, "Christ's ministry through his whole church and its ministers", and one from the Mission and Evangelism department, "A tent-making ministry: non-professional and non-stipendiary ministry". These papers reflect very closely the interests in many of the churches in the post-war period. They provided a much broader context in which the earlier questions about the special ministry could be re-visited. Montreal also had papers on apostolic succession by Edmund Schlink, on the diaconate by Lukas Vischer, and no fewer than eight papers on the ordination of women. The verdict of the section's chairman, however, was clear. Not much progress had been made on the ministry of the church. But the conference recognized that for the sake of the growing number of union negotiations going on in different parts of the world, Faith and Order should no longer avoid the "special ministry" discussion, for this was where churches felt their problems most acutely. There was a passionate intervention from a Nigerian who said, "We are being bullied by the older churches. Vague statements are of no use to us in our unity negotiations." As a result, Montreal called for a new study on the "special ministry", echoing what the Laity department had already seen as a vital counter-balance to its own work.

Montreal is best known for its work on scripture, Tradition and traditions. This opened up a new approach for ecumenical conversations, which was not basically comparative but convergent. Advances in biblical and patristic scholarship, and the broadening of the ecumenical community with the Roman Catholic church's entry into the scene after Vatican II, provided the ingredients for an exciting new phase of work on ministry. New Delhi's emphasis on the unity we seek, with its insistence on a ministry accepted and acknowledged by all, gave added impetus to the beginning of a third phase of Faith and Order work on the ministry.

Phase III: from Montreal 1963 to Lima 1982: a quantum leap forward

After Montreal a new process began which led, nearly twenty years later, to the publication of *Baptism, Eucharist and Ministry* (BEM).[3] The work was characterized by continuity and gradual development, in an orchestrated conversation with the churches themselves. The first stage was the presentation to the commission's meeting in Louvain in 1971 of a document called "The Ordained Ministry", which had already benefited from discussion with member churches and from collaboration with other departments of the WCC.[4] It is discursive and exploratory in nature and not always easy to follow, but it was the beginning of this extraordinarily fruitful new process and progress was made on some hard issues. The preface defends Faith and Order for taking up the theme of ministry against those who believed that every effort should now go into confronting the world's problems – race, justice, peace, the environment, development. Louvain justifies its work in terms of the church's task of reconciliation in the world, the role of the ministry in carrying out Christ's ministry of reconciliation, and the absolute requirement for a ministry acceptable to all for the sake of unity.

The Louvain text was greatly influenced by recent biblical, historical and systematic studies. It recognized that the New Testament could no longer be held to prove that only the ministers of the eucharist were ordained; or that there was a single pattern of ministry everywhere in the early church. Nor was there evidence to show how the Ignatian bishop was appointed, or whether he stood in a chain going back to the apostles through ordination; or that all ministers were from the beginning ordained by a bishop; nor is there evidence in the primitive church for a distinction between valid and illicit ordination.

Among the important new emphases that appear in Louvain are:
- the necessity of understanding the different cultural and social contexts which call for constant renewal and changing patterns of ministry: the tradition has to develop in order to be relevant;
- apostolic continuity is provided by the whole people of God and the laying-on of hands in ordination is a sign of continuity;
- episcopal succession is not the same as apostolic succession;
- the relation between the minister and the community is crucial;
- under the subject of who is to be ordained, there is a surprisingly long section on the ordination of women that begins to open up the issue and asks the churches to confront it forthrightly: "The question must be faced and the time to face it is now"! Bold words.

The final section on mutual recognition sums up the differences that remain: whether the threefold ministry is divinely given; the necessity, or otherwise, for bishops in apostolic succession; and the relation of ministerial priesthood to the priesthood of Christ and to the priesthood of the whole church.

It is easy to criticize Louvain for its wordiness and slightly muddled text. But it was building on the insights of recent academic scholarship and breaking new ground. It took seriously the new world and the new ecumenical context post-Vatican II. It opened up the way for advances to be made in the understanding of apostolicity and succession, ordination and sacramentality, and the priesthood of the ordained ministry. And it remained faithful in insisting that a mutually recognized ministry was essential for the unity of the church.

The next great advance was made at the commission meeting in Accra in 1974, with the publication of *One Baptism, One Eucharist and a Mutually Recognized Ministry.*[5] (This was my first Faith and Order meeting, which was to have a profound influence on the direction of my own life and career.) The section on ministry is much more coherent and readable, though still not the tight convergence document that was to come out of Lima seven years later. Among its important features are:

- The ordained ministry is anchored in, with and among the community. There is interdependence and reciprocity between the two. The whole community is apostolic.
- The different patterns of ministry are examined in the context of the changing world situations. While the threefold pattern predominates, the text does not exclude those who do not follow that pattern. Whatever the pattern, the essential elements that must be found are *episcope,* presbyteral function, and diakonia. There is no attempt to suggest that any one pattern should be adopted.
- There is a wonderfully balanced section on the priesthood of the ordained ministry, linking it both to the priesthood of Christ and the priesthood of the baptized community. The minister participates in both and fulfils a particular priestly service in and for the community.
- There is a quite remarkable section on apostolic succession. The primary form is found in the life of the church as a whole. The orderly transmission of ministry is a visible sign of continuity of the whole church. In the early church the succession of bishops was only one way in which apostolicity was expressed. The text wisely puts questions both to those who have and those who do not have bishops. It challenges those who do to recognize an apostolic continuity in those who do not have bishops, and those who do have bishops to recognize that they may not always have been faithful to apostolic continuity. There is no space here for the idea that historic episcopal

succession guarantees faithfulness. Indeed, many churches have come to regard it as an effective sign and not a guarantee.
- There is a lengthy section on the meaning, the act and the conditions for ordination. The section refers to the Hebrew, Greek and Latin words connected to ordination and claims that there is no warrant for building any particular theory – whether Catholic or Protestant – on the New Testament evidence alone (43). It uses sacramental language to talk of ordination (44).
- There is again a surprisingly long section on the ordination of women which ends, "Ecumenical considerations, therefore, should encourage, not restrain, the full, frank facing of this question."

The final section of the text is very important, "Towards the recognition and reconciliation of ministries", though strangely the text makes nothing of the distinction in the title between recognition and reconciliation, suggesting that at least at this stage the two were synonymous. It does, however, distinguish between recognition and full mutual recognition and introduces the notion of recognition as a step-by-step process. Recognition requires that a church is able to recognize in another the intention to transfer apostolic ministry of word and sacrament and the rite of ordination must include *episcope* and the laying-on of hands – safeguarding the "sacramentality" of ordination.

Accra was followed by a period of consultation with the churches in which further areas of study were called for. Two important consultations contributed to the next stage, the first on *episcope* and episcopacy.[6] The small pamphlet on that consultation is one of Faith and Order's most important documents on ministry. It contains seminal papers by Raymond Brown on the New Testament evidence, and John Zizioulas on the early church. The memorandum of the meeting includes, among its seven points, a suggestive passage on the three dimensions of *episcope,* now called the personal, the collegial and the communal, agreeing that these are all necessary for the life of the church and conceding that the threefold ministry does not always reflect faithfully these dimensions. The implication once more is that churches with different polities have things to learn from each other. "The ecumenical movement can be described [the report says] as the effort to restore the balance." What was being picked up here was the important reflection made at Lausanne but not developed until now. The second consultation was on the ordination of women, sponsored by the Community of Women and Men, a joint study process with the Women's department, led by Brigalia Bam, but firmly lodged in Faith and Order, with Constance Parvey directing it and nurturing it and Melanie May joining as a staff person.[7] In addition to influencing the discussions on the ordination of women, the study programme was to change forever the language in which the ministry text was written. Until this point documents used exclusive language. From now on they were inclusive. Compare the Accra text with the BEM text. The difference is striking. This simple change we take for granted now but then it had a profound impact on the discussion about ministry, the ministry of the whole people of God and the ordained ministry.

It is hard to describe how important an achievement the publication of *Baptism, Eucharist and Ministry* (BEM) was after the commission's meeting in Lima in 1982. It brought to a stage of maturity the work on ministry called for at Montreal. It marked the publication of a new *genre* of ecumenical text, the convergence text with its tightly, economically worded agreement in the main column and commentaries recording breakthroughs and outstanding issues of difference in parallel columns. It provided the churches with what that Nigerian had called for at Montreal, material that was useable in unity negotiations. Without BEM and its breakthroughs, it is doubtful whether some new partnerships of full communion, or steps on the way to full communion, would have been taken in the late 1980s and 1990s. The BEM text took in the advances of Accra on apostolicity and succession, on the priesthood of the ordained ministry. It went further on the threefold ministry, suggesting that it may be a way to unity and an expression of unity. Building on the results of the *episcope* consultation it included a crucial paragraph on the threefold dimension of personal, collegial and communal, at every level of the church's life. It included an important statement about ordination, continuing to use sacramental language about ordination. Its final section on "Towards a mutual recognition of ordained ministries" contained an important challenge to churches which have bishops as well as to those who do not. And it suggested that, on the issue of women's ordination, "openness to each other holds out the possibility that the Spirit may well speak to one church through the insights of another" (54).

The impact of BEM was totally unforeseen. It elicited over 180 official responses from churches and involved thousands of people in the study process. The six volumes of responses provided evidence of where the churches were in their understanding of ministry. There was much endorsement for the convergences in BEM. But not all churches were comfortable with all of it. There were criticisms that not enough attention was given to the ministry of the whole people of God and the necessary relation between that and the ordained ministry. Some were nervous about the endorsement of a threefold ministry as the pattern for a united church. Some were disappointed that after so much attention to the ordination of women in Louvain and Accra so little was said in this text and the accompanying commentary was criticized as an unfair statement of the position both of churches for as well as those against women's ordination. Some questioned whether episcopal succession was merely a sign of intention to be faithful to the teaching and mission of the apostles and not rather a guarantee. Others wanted more on collegiality and synodality and regretted that there was nothing on a ministry of primacy and universal primacy. There were more general issues: the use of scripture; the understanding of sacrament and sacramentality and how ordination was to be understood as a sacrament; and some asked whether there was an integrated ecclesiology behind the text that brought together Catholic and Protestant ecclesiologies.

But for all the questions and requests for further work, it was clear that the attitudes to the ordained ministry had shifted significantly since Lausanne, the language of the debate had developed, there was greater understanding of one another's traditions, a more open way of putting questions to those on both sides of an issue, and there was a degree of consensus on some issues and a definite convergence on others.

Phase IV: beyond Lima, ministry seen in an ecclesiological perspective

The immediate task of Faith and Order, following the publication of BEM, was nurturing the conversation with the churches and responding to their questions in a series of clarifications. These were important yet they are hardly ever referred to now.[8]

The main response to the Lima process came in a rather different way in the fifth world conference on Faith and Order in Santiago de Compostela in 1993. I have often struggled with the thought that the commission, the standing commission and the officers, moved too swiftly away from the itemized agenda of BEM towards ecclesiology with its theme, "Towards Koinonia in Faith, Life and Witness", and that the world conference should have been an opportunity rather to present to the churches the responses to BEM and the clarifications. The conference could have had the effect of holding up a mirror to the churches leading to a challenge to them to move on the convergences by reforming their own lives and deepening their relations with others, in other words challenging the churches to be accountable for the work done in their names since Lausanne. It would also have provided an opportunity to introduce the next study on the apostolic faith in a direct and challenging way. We might then have been able to draw out the enormous potential of that study and its challenges to the confession

Ministry in Faith and Order: One Woman's Ecumenical Memory 177

of faith in a world that presents so many questions to the faith and life of Christians.

The theme of Santiago was intended to present all of the work of the commission, including that on ministry, in an ecclesiological perspective. In doing this it was to some extent responding to one of the demands of the churches themselves for an ecclesiological context for BEM. This meant setting the work in the context of the theme of koinonia which was already understood, not as a model or image of the church, but referring to the mystery of the church, its very nature, grounded in and bestowed by the life of the trinitarian God. In the theme of Santiago, the commission was thus stating its vision of the church as a communion in faith, sacramental life and ministry, witnessing together in the world.

Santiago made little contribution to the ministry agenda itself though it did provide some suggestions for future work: the question of whether ordination can be said to be sacramental; presidency at the eucharist; the ordination of women; episcopal succession; and primatial ministry. But one paper on the theme did have very important suggestions, that of John Zizioulas.[9] Its emphasis on the church's identity as relational worked out and applied to structures, including the ministry, had the power to open up the old hard questions of ministry in a fresh way. His emphasis on synodality as a mode of the life of the whole church focused episodically in synods, and the need for primacy, a ministry of unity at the local and wider levels of the church's life to serve the diversity of the whole, could lead in new directions. There were fresh thoughts too in what he had to say about apostolicity and succession in relation to the koinonia of the church.

Faith and Order's work after Santiago was based on a conspectus of studies drawn up in light of the requests of the conference. The programme was formulated around the major study on ecclesiology to which other studies and collaborative work would contribute. There was to be a study on ministry and authority and on the church as koinonia of women and men. The ecclesiology study was described as "reflection on how the essential nature of the church is to be expressed in visible structures and forms". Clearly ministry was to be a part.

The fruits of this fourth phase in relation to ministry can be seen first in a consultation on *episcope* and episcopacy which produced an interesting enough report with some useful work on the triad, now turned round as "communal, collegial and personal" which includes exploration on how a ministry of primacy serves unity and has some imaginative thoughts on ecumenical oversight and living in ecumenical space. But the most significant thinking on ministry comes in *The Nature and Purpose of the Church*,[10] in other words in an ecclesiological context.

It is noticeable that 14 of the 52 paragraphs, 25 percent of the text, concern ministry. There is some sign that the ecclesiological location in which ministry is set now has contributed to a common understanding of the ministry, though perhaps not as much as some of us might have hoped it would do. This may be because, strangely, the notion of koinonia, that was thought at Santiago to hold out such promise for deepening our understanding of every aspect of the church's life, is hardly any longer the controlling or undergirding theme. It is there, but not linked to the primary themes of the church as the creature of the word and the creature of the Spirit.

The link paragraph that moves the text from exploring the nature of the church talks of the gifts God gives to the church for its life and mission to preserve the koinonia of the people of God. Faith, baptism and eucharist are mentioned but, oddly, not the gift of ministry. When the text reaches the ministry, it seems almost to be a repetition of the beginning of BEM and not a reflection controlled, or infused by, the ecclesiological context in particular, or by the notion of koinonia in particular. And this is true as the text goes on. Nevertheless, there are some advances on BEM. Not least of all, in the section on communal, personal and collegial oversight. The order of the three changed again in a more satisfactory way. The notion of synodality, *sensus fidelium*, and primacy are introduced. Primacy is a mode of personal ministry, inseparable from both the collegial and communal dimensions of the church's life. It strengthens the unity of the church and enables it to speak with one voice.

There are some new avenues opened up in the ministry discussion. But there are strange omissions. In an ecclesiology of communion we should surely expect something to be said about men and women in ministry representing and serving the koinonia. In an ecclesiology of communion we should expect to find something on apostolicity and succession, the role of ministry in keeping the church at one with the apostles' teaching and mission. In an ecclesiology of koinonia we should expect to find something on the holy gifts for the holy people, including the sacramental gift of ordination. In an ecclesiology of koinonia we should expect to find new thoughts about the ministry in maintaining koinonia and thus on the exercise of authority within the communion of the church. In an ecclesiology of koinonia we should expect more to be said about the role of the ministry in extending koinonia in the world and thus about ministry in relation to mission.

But, in spite of this, the fact that there is an ecclesiology text at all and that this is the location for developing an understanding the ministry of the people of God and within that the special ministry, is a significant move forward in Faith and Order's work and its approach to ministry. This and other consultations, and the next meeting of the commission in Kuala Lumpur, have the opportunity to deepen the work. After all BEM took from Montreal to Lima, the best part of twenty years, to reach sufficient maturity to go to the churches for their considered response. A work on ecclesiology is hardly likely to take less time.

NOTES

[1] H.N. Bate ed., *Faith and Order: Proceedings of the World Conference, Lausanne*, London, SCM Press, 1927, pp.232-83.
[2] P.C. Rodger and L. Vischer eds, *The Fourth World Conference on Faith and Order: The Report from Montreal 1963*, London, SCM Press, 1963, pp.63ff.
[3] *Baptism, Eucharist and Ministry*, Faith and Order Paper no. 111, WCC, 1982.
[4] G. Gassmann ed., *Documentary History of Faith and Order 1963-1993*, Faith and Order Paper no. 159, WCC Publications, 1993, pp.116-36.
[5] *One Baptism, One Eucharist and a Mutually Recognized Ministry*, Faith and Order Paper no. 73, WCC Publications, 1975.
[6] *Episkope and Episcopate in Ecumenical Perspective*, Faith and Order Paper no. 102, WCC Publications, 1980.
[7] Constance F. Parvey ed., *Ordination of Women in Ecumenical Perspective: Workbook for the Churches' Future*, Faith and Order Paper no. 105, 1980.
[8] *Baptism, Eucharist and Ministry 1982-1990: Report on the Process and Responses*, Faith and Order Paper no. 149, WCC Publications, 1990, pp.107-47.
[9] Thomas F. Best and Günther Gassmann eds, *On the Way to Fuller Koinonia*, Faith and Order Paper no. 166, WCC Publications, 1994, pp.103-11.
[10] *The Nature and Purpose of the Church: A Stage on the Way to a Common Statement*, Faith and Order Paper no. 181, WCC Publications, 1998.

The Holy Spirit and Ministry
A Lutheran Perspective

DR BERND OBERDORFER

What is ministry? What does ordination mean? We all know that these are matters of the greatest importance to the ecumenical dialogues in our time and age. Not only are there many differences in the practice and structure of ordained ministry between our churches, but there are also theological differences in understanding the meaning of ministry and ordination, its function and its proper place in the church. Many people think that these questions are crucial for all hopes to find a way to the visible unity of the church. And indeed it was, for example, the dissent in the understanding of ministry that made the Roman Catholic Church prohibit mutual eucharistic hospitality at the *Ökumenische Kirchentag* in Berlin in 2003. Yet it sometimes seems that the debates on that topic have come to a dead end. All attempts to overcome the gap between the Protestant focus on the ministry as being a function of the common priesthood of all Christians, and the Roman Catholic focus on the hierarchical priesthood as being a specific representation of Christ, seem to have failed. How should the *defectus ordinis* which is diagnosed by the Roman Catholic Church in the churches of the Reformation be healed if these churches, according to their ecclesiology, cannot see such a *defectus* in their doctrine of ministry and therefore do not feel any necessity for a "healing" of this kind?

In a situation like this, in my opinion it is wise to start anew by embedding the question of ministry in broader and deeper theological investigations on the nature of the church. The Faith and Order document *The Nature and Purpose of the Church* bases its reflections upon the formula that the church is *creatura Verbi et creatura Spiritus*, and that seems to me a very appropriate starting-point because it emphasizes that the church has its being only through the graceful presence of Christ and the Holy Spirit. We cannot understand the nature of the church unless we understand the meaning of this presence. To say it briefly: We have to start with God. In other words, we have to enquire as to the roots of the church in the communion and community of the triune God. In the first section of my paper, I would like to begin with some reflections on the mutuality of Christ and the Holy Spirit in the history of revelation, and then give an outline of the work of the Holy Spirit in the church in order to display the meaning of the Spirit for the life of the church. In the second part, I would like to focus on the church as a unity and community which is differentiated in itself by the many gifts and charismata. With this basis, I will deal with the specific function of the ordained ministry in my third section, before ending with some reflections on ministry and apostolicity.

The church as creatura Verbi et creatura Spiritus

1. The church as creatura gratiae redemptionis *(creature of the grace of redemption)*

The church is *creatura*. This is not a trivial claim. It does not simply mean that the church, being part of the world, is creature in the sense any other part of the world is. But the church is rather *creatura* in an eminent sense. It owes its being only and totally to the justifying and renewing grace of God. It is creature of God who has promised to make everything anew. It is *new* creature amidst the old. Although the church is an earthly reality, its existence is not at all a possibility of the natural world. Although it consists of natural persons, it is not their natural freedom of choice which brings them together into the community of the church. It emerges from nature, but it is not nature. Thus, the church is not primarily a creature of the Creator, but a creature of the Redeemer. Therefore, in order to understand what the church is, we have to ask what redemption is, and that means who the Redeemer is. This leads us to a trinitarian understanding of God.

In all Christian traditions, it is clear that the work of redemption is especially a work of the Son and the Holy Spirit (who both are sent by the Father to reveal and realize his saving grace). The question is how to understand the "and"? Obviously, there are differences in emphasis. The Lutheran tradition, for example, emphasized the church being a *creatura Verbi*. This does not mean that the Holy Spirit is irrelevant to Lutherans. But they always insisted that the Spirit comes only "through" the Word[1] and reveals itself only by revealing the Word. The Holy Spirit is the Spirit of Christ. Therefore, Lutherans tend to distrust any reflection on the Spirit and its specific work in itself as being in danger of loosening the link between the Spirit and Christ. This is an important aspect of the Lutheran position in the *filioque* debate. The Orthodox tradition, however, emphasizes the *spiritual* character of the church. The church is *creatura Spiritus* and is graced by the *pleroma* of the Holy Spirit which is present in its liturgy and life. Evidently, this is not supposed to qualify the meaning of Christ. But Orthodox theology has always stressed that Christ himself fulfilled his redeeming work "in the power of the Spirit", and so the biblical story of the transfiguration on Mount Tabor became crucial for the Orthodox understanding of Christ and of God's presence in the world. Orthodox theologians therefore tend to doubt whether the Western churches sufficiently realize this spiritual character of Christ and of the community of the church as being God's new creature. We can see this difference in emphasis already in the old debate on the use of *azyma* in the eucharist.

But I would like to point out that there is a necessary mutuality of Christ and the Spirit in the *Heilsgeschichte*, and to consider that mutuality can help us to understand better the trinitarian being of the Son and the Holy Spirit itself as well as the nature of the church as *creatura Verbi et Spiritus sancti*.

2. The mutuality of Christ and the Holy Spirit

We can see the mutuality of Christ and the Holy Spirit in Christ's life as well as in the life of the church. All biblical testimonies unanimously show that Jesus is the Christ, the Messiah, in the power of the Spirit. After his baptism, the heavens opened and the Holy Spirit came upon him, and the voice from heaven identified him as the beloved Son. It was then that his redeeming work began. According to Luke, the Spirit inspires his being from the very beginning. The angel tells Mary, "The Holy Ghost shall come upon thee, and the power of the Highest shall overshadow thee: therefore also that holy thing which shall be born of thee shall be called the Son of God" (Luke 1:35). Jesus himself says that the kingdom of God has come since he has cast out the devils "by the Spirit of God" (Matt. 12:28). Jesus is led and inspired by the Spirit, and he brings the Spirit which the prophets announced for the end of the days. So Jesus also reveals the Spirit.

This mutuality is crucial for the life of the church. "No one can say that Jesus is the Lord, but by the Holy Spirit," Paul writes (1 Cor. 12:3). But on the other hand, we have to be *told* by the word that it is the Spirit who opens up our heart for the word. This can be seen clearly in the story of Pentecost. Peter has to *explain* what had happened when the disciples started to speak in foreign tongues or rather were understood by foreigners in their talking. And Peter explains it with reference to the holy scripture, especially to Joel's prophecy of the Spirit's arrival in the final days. So we can say: Jesus sends the Spirit who makes Jesus present to us and makes us understand who Jesus is. The Spirit identifies the word (and the meaning of the word), and the word identifies the Spirit. And both of them reveal God as the caring and loving Father.

But let us have a closer look at what the Spirit's work is towards and in the church.

3. The Holy Spirit and the church

Certainly, God's will is to redeem the whole world (cf. John 3:16). But he starts realizing that aim by electing the church as a *communio sanctorum*, which means both the congregation of the saints and participation in holiness or, we can also say, participation in the Holy Spirit. The church, as Vatican II put it, is a sign of and an instrument for the unity of humankind. And, I would add, it is a sign of and instrument for the eschatological fulfilment God has promised to realize. But as such a sign, the church is already a form of the presence of that fulfilment. The church is an eschatological community amidst history. It is an eschatological community by recalling Christ's redeeming work and announcing Christ's final *parousia* in the end of the days. The church is the community in which the past and the future of salvation is present right now amidst history. This is the work of the Holy Spirit.

This work is a complex one. At least three aspects have to be named:

1. The Spirit reveals God and God's will of salvation and redemption which is realized in Jesus Christ. Thus, the Spirit leads people to know God, to be certain of and trust in his saving grace. In other words, the Spirit creates faith – which has an intellectual and an emotional dimension: faith means both understanding God's will and trusting in God.

2. The Spirit renews and revives. The Spirit does not only give a new understanding of God, the self and the world to human persons, but it really changes them. Justification does not only simply declare people as being just (that would be a misunderstanding of the *iustitia externa*), but actually makes people just. Justification is *vivification*. It gives *new* life amidst the old one. Obviously, this new life is a spiritual life. But that does not mean that it is invisible at all. It is not supposed to be hidden in the depth of the souls of the individual believers only to result in a different *world-view*, but rather tends to be shown and communicated in words of testimony and deeds of love.

3. The Spirit creates community. The Spirit not only renews the individual souls but also (and at the same time) forms a community of those who share the faith in the redeeming God. The Spirit establishes a new "people of God", and as well as Christ, as we can read in the letter to the Ephesians, "has broken down the middle wall of partition between" Jews and Gentiles (Eph. 2:14), and the Spirit unites people from all the different races and religious and cultural backgrounds. Whereas God, in order to prevent humankind from finishing the project of the tower of Babel, had to confound their language and to scatter them "upon the face of all the earth" (Gen. 11:7-8), God now reunites them in the power of the Spirit. No one is excluded from the community of God any longer due to restrictions caused in the circumstances and conditions of his or her physical or natural life. Unification, however, does not mean standardization. The church is not a homogeneous community but, on the contrary, a community in which the people are encouraged to practise their special skills and different talents and even to cultivate their individual and cultural identity in order to build the "body of Christ" and thereby unfold the richness of the Creator's gifts. Thus, by transforming the natural gifts to *charismata*, the Spirit forms the church as being a "city on the hill", a witness of the grace of God, a light that shines "upon the face of all the earth".

4. The Holy Spirit as Christ's presence

The church witnesses Christ as God's presence in the world, and by doing that the church is the continuation of Christ's incarnation. But this continuation is a spiritual one, it is realized and mediated by the Spirit. Christ sends the same Spirit, which has come upon him and made him the Christ, to the people. He transmits his own Spirit. He promises that he will be present himself in the Spirit he sends. The Spirit, thus, is the form of Christ's presence after his return to the heavenly Father.

Yet, although the continuity between Christ and the church is a spiritual one, the Spirit nevertheless is given to natural persons. The church, therefore, is – albeit spiritual – an earthly reality. "They are not from the world, but they are in the world," Jesus says according to St John (John 17:16,11). The church is an earthly reality in which heaven is mirrored. In other words, the church is an earthly community under the opened heaven.

This point seems to be trivial but is of crucial relevance to the understanding of the church and the Spirit's work in it. Because, although it is the Spirit who makes Christ present in the church, the

Spirit does not do that beyond the structures of earthly human life. The Spirit is not a spiritualist. The continuity between Christ and the church is realized by the Spirit by means of historical continuation. This was the fundamental insight of the 2nd-century church fathers. Confronted with the Montanists' claim that the *Paraclete* directly spoke to their prophets and revealed his will through them without reference to the "old traditions", the fathers understood that just as Christ was incarnated, so also the gospel of Christ is communicated in a way that is somehow carnal. We can say: they discovered apostolicity. They saw that beyond the simple claim to be inspired there must be criteria to discern right from wrong spirits, to ensure that it is really the Spirit of Christ who speaks to us in the present time. And these criteria must entail the dimension of historical verification. This was the time when the New Testament canon was formed and the idea of apostolic succession was born. These means were supposed to guarantee that the claim of having the Spirit of Christ cannot be based on private revelations only but can be proven publicly. If such a claim does not correspond to the apostolic witnesses documented in holy scripture, and if the person who claims having the Spirit does not affiliate with a congregation which represents the apostolic tradition, then it is not the Spirit of Christ speaking through that person.

The church, to summarize, is a spiritual reality which necessarily has a visible, earthly dimension. We cannot have the Spirit beyond this earthly dimension. The Spirit uses natural persons and their talents to communicate the gospel of Christ and communicates that gospel within a chain of historical continuity. In the following, I will unfold the idea of the church as the "body of Christ", i.e., as a differentiated community which as a whole witnesses to that apostolic continuity, before I ask what is the special function of the ordained ministry within that spiritual community.

The church as differentiated community: the One Spirit and the many charismata

"Endeavour to keep the unity of the Spirit in the bond of peace," we read in the letter to the Ephesians. "There is one body, and one Spirit, even as you are called in one hope of your calling; one Lord, one faith, one baptism, one God and Father of all, who is above all, and in you all" (Eph. 4:4-6). Undoubtedly, there is an emphasis on the unity of the church in the New Testament. But as we can see particularly in 1 Corinthians 12, it is a structured unity, a unity which entails, even encourages diversity and differentiation. "There are diversities of gifts, but the same Spirit," Paul writes. "And there are differences of administrations, but the same Lord. And there are diversities of operations, but it is the same God which worketh all in all" (1 Cor. 12:4-6). Although there is a basic unity of all Christians because they are all baptized, there are differences of gifts, administrations and operations. Not every member of the church is capable of every work.

Paul's intention, however, is to show that differences of function do not mean differences of hierarchy. Paul explains this by using the metaphor of the body. Every part of the body has its special function which is necessary for the well-being of the body. The members of the body are dependent on the different members doing their specific work. It would be naive if one part of the body declared itself independent of the others' existence. "The eye cannot say unto the hand, I have no need of thee: nor again the head to the feet, I have no need of thee. Nay, much more those members of the body, which seem to be more feeble, are necessary" (1 Cor. 12:21-22). But it would also be naive if the members ceased to carry out their respective task and rather started to do the work of the member which appears to be the most respected. "If the whole body were an eye, where were the hearing? If the whole were hearing, where were the smelling?... And if they were all one member, where were the body?" (1 Cor. 12:17). The body would collapse if the members did not cooperate by doing their respective work. Paul explicitly says that God "has set the members every one of them in the body, and it hath pleased him" (1 Cor. 12:18). And because every member has a function, which is necessary to the whole body, it is rather realism than moralism when Paul writes, "Whether one member suffers, all the members suffer with it; or one member be honoured, all the members rejoice with it"(1 Cor. 12:26).

But although this metaphor seems quite evident in itself, questions arise if we ask what it actually means with reference to the social reality of the church. Do the "members" of the body mean persons, or do they rather mean functions? If it means persons, then we can distinctively and exclusively ascribe one specific function to one concrete person. What is allowed to one person is not allowed to another. If it means functions, however, this strict distinction is not necessary. Then we could say that there are different functions in the congregation which must not be mixed, but need not be ascribed to one person exclusively. For example, we could say that it is necessary to preach the gospel in the congregation, but not necessary to give only one person the right to do that.

There is another question of equal importance: Are there functions which are essential to the life of the church, so that, without them, the church would not be church in full sense? Most of the churches only define one function to be necessary in a strict sense: the function of public preaching. Yet, as to the concrete description of this function, the different confessions give characteristically different answers.

The Orthodox and the Roman Catholic traditions insist that the ministry of the bishop as the successor of the apostles is essential to the church. The Lutheran church declares the *ministerium docendi evangelium et porrigendi sacramenta* to be necessary, but gives no definite answer of how to organize that *ministerium*. The *Confessio Augustana* only states that everybody who publicly preaches the gospel and celebrates the sacraments has to be *rite vocatus* (CA 14), i.e., appointed according to the rules. Apart from the fact that there has to be someone to perform that function *rite vocatus*, the organization of the ecclesiastical life belongs to the human traditions which are open to changes within history, and diversities referring to these human traditions, according to CA 7, do not endanger the unity of faith. Thus, the German Lutheran churches, during the many centuries when they had no bishops, did not hesitate to regard themselves as being church in a full sense. The Calvinist tradition, however, derived from the Bible the normative concept of a fourfold ministry of pastor, teacher, deacon and elder. But during its history, this concept was realized in quite different ways – which, by the way, shows that it is not too easy to derive from the Bible one and only one model of the structures of the church. The Reformed churches would not contest churches without that structure of ministry to be churches in the full sense.

We may ask why most of the confessional traditions do not unfold a detailed picture of the structures of the church apart from the ordained ministry. This seems to depend on the fact that the ordained ministry in a special sense takes responsibility for the task the whole church is called to fulfil: witnessing the gospel. So we have to ask: What is that "special sense", and how is it related to the general calling of the church? In other words: How are the common priesthood of all Christians and the specific function of the ordained ministry related to each other?

The Holy Spirit and ordained ministry

The church, as I have stated, is sign of and instrument for the eschatological fulfilment God has promised to realize. As being a *creatura Spiritus*, it reveals God's saving and redeeming grace which has definitely become real in the incarnation of his beloved Son Jesus Christ. In the power of the Spirit, the church as a whole is witness of that grace. Every Christian participates in the Holy Spirit by being baptized. The Spirit transforms the natural skills and talents of individuals to use them as witnesses of the divine grace. As faith implies understanding, we have to ascribe to every Christian a common knowledge of the spiritual reality the church has to confess. All Christian traditions know of that common knowledge and honour it. The Orthodox tradition speaks of the *pleroma* of the church which, for example, makes it necessary that the decisions of synods and councils are accepted by the members of the church before they become valid. The Roman Catholic tradition knows of the *sensus fidelium* which, although not binding to the church ministry in a strictly juridical sense, is of great relevance to the teaching of the official church ministry. The Lutheran tradition emphasizes the common priesthood of all Christians which is based on the one baptism. There is no need of a special priesthood to mediate between the Christians and Christ. This implies, albeit not the end, but a deep change in the understanding of the ordained ministry – a change, however, the Protestant Reformers insisted to be a return to the fundamental tradition of the early church.

Luther said, "All Christians are priests, but not all of them are pastors." All Christians participate in the Spirit which enables them to witness. But not all of them are supposed to preach publicly in the congregational service. Within the body of Christ, there is a special calling to the public preaching and teaching of the gospel and the public celebration of the holy sacraments. This is a matter of the church's order. There must be someone who takes responsibility for the public witness. This entails a special responsibility for the synchronical and diachronical unity of the church. That means that the minister's duty is to take care of the catholicity and apostolicity of the church. The minister, therefore, has to be well educated in biblical studies, the history of the church, its doctrinal traditions and its contemporary doctrine. The minister has to take care that his or her congregation does not separate from the community of the catholic and apostolic church.

This task is necessary to the church, and to perform it is a special gift of the Spirit, a *charisma*. But this charisma does not imply the idea that the pastor represents Christ and his redeeming and reconciling work in a special or even exclusive way. The minister fulfils in a special, namely public, way what in principle every Christian is capable and entitled to fulfil.

Because of that, gender is not decisive to the capability of being minister. If all Christians, male or female, are deemed worthy of witnessing Christ, then all of them, men or women, can be called into ordained ministry. Female gender does not belong to the natural factors that make it impossible to witness Christ publicly. If the minister does not represent Christ exclusively, and if every Christian represents Christ in a special way, then the fact that Jesus was male cannot be an argument against women being ordained. Also the fact that Jesus only chose twelve men to be his apostles need not necessarily be interpreted in the sense that he explicitly wanted to exclude women.

Obviously, there is a tension between this understanding of ordained ministry and the Roman Catholic as well as the Orthodox understanding of the ordained priesthood. This tension, as I would think, derives, *inter alia*, from a different understanding of the visible signs of apostolicity. Let me end my paper with some reflections on this point.

Ministry and apostolicity

The continuity between Christ and the Christians, I stated, is mediated through the Holy Spirit. Yet the Spirit works not beyond but in and with natural persons and structures. Therefore, this continuity must have an earthly, visible dimension. The apostolicity of the church, i.e., the loyalty to its apostolic origins, has to be visualized. There must be visible signs of apostolicity which display the identity of the church during all the centuries of its existence.

All Christian traditions agree that the loyalty to holy scripture is such a sign. Confessing the common faith in the words of the old creeds – as the symbol of Nicea-Constantinople or the Apostles Creed – unites contemporary Christianity with its apostolic heritage. Praying the Lord's prayer, Christianity shares the Spirit, in the power of which Christ could call God his Father. Celebrating the sacrament of the Lord's supper in the way Jesus introduced it on the "night in which he was betrayed" (1 Cor. 12:23) also is an act which makes the identity of the church visible.

For some relevant traditions, particularly the Roman Catholic, the Orthodox and the Anglican, the apostolic succession, i.e., the unbroken chain of bishops being ordained by bishops, beginning with the apostles, is an important and even necessary sign of the apostolic continuity. They regard the bishops as successors and representatives of the apostles. Just as Christ chose twelve apostles who had a special function among his many disciples, so the bishops have a special function, a special charisma within the community of the church, namely, according to Christ's commandment, "to feed his lambs" (John 21:15); that means, to take care of the truth of the gospel that the Christians are taught. And ordination does not only symbolize, but rather transmits, this charism, this special gift of the Spirit who is present in it. Thus, according to their conviction, without having the ministry of the bishop and without these bishops being part of that unbroken chain, a church lacks apostolic continuity.

It was one of the crucial experiences of the Reformers that the fact of having ordained bishops was not a guarantee of loyalty to the apostolic truth. The old sentence "the church is where the bishop is" lost its binding plausibility: where the bishops were, there the Reformers could not recognize the true church, and where the Reformers were, there was no bishop. Moreover, with reference to the tradition of the ancient church, the Reformers used the terms "bishop" and "pastor" or "minister" as being synonymous. Every pastor is the bishop of his congregation, and the bishop is a pastor with a specific task of leadership. So, although ordaining pastors without bishops being present, they were convinced that they remained in the apostolic continuity which is based upon loyalty to the gospel as witnessed in holy scripture. Anyway, there is no historical evidence of the chain of episcopal succession being unbroken in any of the traditions.

It can hardly be denied that the differences between the churches, referring to this point, are strong and deep. But let me try to summarize some aspects which might be helpful in opening up further discussions:

1. The Reformers agreed that there is a special charism of publicly preaching and celebrating the sacraments in the church, which is the *ratio essendi* of the ordained ministry. The church has and must have ministers.
2. The Reformers practised ordination in the sense of the *rite vocatus*. Everyone who preaches in the name of the church has to be officially called and introduced to this ministry. They were convinced that this ordination implies a special blessing by the Holy Spirit.
3. Although the Reformers did not regard the episcopal succession as being a necessary sign of apostolic continuity, they practised a kind of presbyterial succession (pastors ordained pastors). To see that might, on the one hand, help the churches with episcopal succession to acknowledge the legitimacy of the ministry in the Protestant churches in the past and present, and it might on the other hand encourage the churches of the Reformation to think about *successio apostolica* as being one (if not necessarily the only) possible sign of the Spirit's presence in church *per saecula saeculorum*.

NOTE

[1] Cf. *Confessio Augustana*, art.5.

The Holy Spirit and Ministry
Comments from a Latin American Woman
REV. ARACELI EZZATTI

My personal approach to this issue is rooted in different sources: (1) my life as a Latin American woman, a Christian, who has always been committed to be faithful to God's gospel in Christ, expressed through pastoral service to people. It has been a difficult personal pilgrimage, living in a continent which has become remote from others through dramatic social and theological changes during the last four decades; (2) my experience as an ordained minister in the Methodist church in Uruguay since 1965, facing many difficulties in accomplishing this vocation and mandate in the context of a traditional, male and authoritative society; (3) the theological reflection seeking to discern the will of God for my ministry and personal life as well, looking for the inspiration of the Holy Spirit to deal with the criticism and discrimination by other churches because of my gender; (4) the blessing of living a very rich communitarian experience within the Methodist church, in which I felt a strong commitment to exercise a pastorate in slum communities, in prisons and very poor environments; (5) the challenge through the Faith and Order commission to participate in a wider ecumenical dialogue about the ministry, a central issue from the beginnings of the ecumenical movement.

Christian church: mystery and continuous revelation of the triune God in a broken world

Though the Methodist church has developed a distinctive confessional identity, it defines its nature and mission as an expression of the universal church, founded in the self-revelation of God in Jesus Christ and sustained by the power of the Holy Spirit. It is in the Spirit of justification and sanctification, received by means of grace, that the community of believers grows up and becomes a sign of salvation for human beings and the world, granted by the authority of word and sacraments. The Methodist church's identity, grounded in the trinitarian experience of faith, is strongly founded in and inspired by Jesus

Christ's life, death and resurrection, and his ministry. As his body sharing the gifts of the Spirit, we are committed to discern the message of revelation through creation, reconciliation and consummation to announce salvation to every creature. This mission is carried out by common people called, inspired and strengthened by the power of the Holy Spirit.

The Methodist church is deeply concerned with the presence of every person as a son/daughter of God within and outside the church, as subjects of salvation. All of them are invited to be converted, to join the community of faith and to testify the kingdom, independently of differences of gender, race, nationality, economic situation. We are in favour of an inclusive community to overcome the violence of all kinds of discrimination (Luke 4:16-19).

There is no discussion within the Methodist church concerning the relationship between the local congregation and the church as a whole, articles of faith, sacramental life. However, there are some differences of organization, structure and liturgical expressions attending to the different environments, local traditions or social structures of particular significance for the identity of the people served. There are also some divergent opinions at the local or national levels regarding the issues of ministry and ministries. The process of recognition of women as fully ordained ministers has been unequal among the national Methodist churches in Latin America, depending more on sociological and cultural factors rather than theological ones. It is common to find churches which, since the 1950s, have been ordaining women as pastors and also bishops, while others are just beginning to do so. Nevertheless, ministries and ordained ministry are expressions of the general priesthood of believers and are imposed by the congregation in a process of discernment looking for the guidance of the Holy Spirit through reading of the Bible and praying. The revelation of God is given to us through us, his people, sent to live and act in a broken world (John 17:3-18). The expressions of ministry are appreciated by the members of the congregation as humble positions of faithful service to others in the name of the triune God; ministry is never seen as a privileged condition.

The Christian church: body of Christ sharing the Holy Spirit's gifts

The historic presence of the universal church is the gathering of believers not as individuals but as a body. This essentially means an integrated body of very different parts, which do not have to change their nature to be accepted and necessary, even though each part harmonizes the articulated body whose head is Christ (Rom. 12:1-8).

Leonardo Boff calls our attention to the spiritual quality of this body (1 Cor. 15:44), the body of Christ risen from death; a body free from the historic and carnal ties, free to act, present everywhere (Col. 3:11), overcoming all barriers among human beings. The empirical existence of the church includes all of us in our human diversity, weakness and sinful situation, and invites us to conversion, repentance and reconciliation, walking together to the fulfilment of the kingdom. Involved in our own context and circumstances, we are subjects of God's revelation to testify to the world, but to what world?

To envision our mission through the different ministries of the church, it is necessary to explore the relationships between church and world. What is the impact of the Christian church which proclaims love, justice and salvation in a broken and divided world, where suffering and death seem to dominate? What does it mean to talk about a community of believers, empowered by the Holy Spirit, when the reality of modern society is isolation and alienation of individuals, lack of faith and materialism? What is the image given by very rich churches which are implanted in the city, vis-à-vis very poor neighbourhoods in towns? What is the role of a deacon, a pastor, a preacher, a teacher among those living in the streets, exiled from their own land, looking for food in the rubbish areas, among those addicted to drugs and alcohol, mostly young people?

In Latin America many of the activities of a minister are carried out in the streets, outside of the sanctuaries, or in the slums, in very poor houses or refuge homes. The traditional position of the "official" priest or pastor, clearly differentiated by society, is becoming less visible. This situation raises a new question: Are the priests and pastors "spiritual" servants of God or has their role of spiritual guidance changed into the role of a social, economic or political activist? Why are the sanctuaries empty, whereas crowded outdoor religious celebrations are taking place, many times in very bad weather conditions? Fray Betto analyzed the new profile of the emerging churches and the implications of this process in the character of ministries and advised against the danger of changing the essential goal of ministry: to preach the good news of salvation. People come to the church looking for spiritual guidance, trying to cope with their painful personal and social situation. The church is the space for encounter with God. The pastor or priest is a person in communion with God who, in prayer and theological discernment, helps the people to find their way to personal conversion, to transform the structures of oppression, to re-link the broken relationship, to include the excluded of the community, to heal the damages of suffering.

Ministry and spirituality are strongly linked together, and it is necessary to explore the dimensions of a renewed spirituality which emerge from our biblical and theological discernment, our tradition, but also our embodiment and commitment to those who are suffering, and to those who are looking for justice, peace, hope and new life. But there is also the prophetic commitment towards those who are oppressing others. A renewed spirituality is possible because the power of the Holy Spirit upholds us: "... these things God has revealed to us through the Spirit. For the Spirit searches everything, even the depths of God" (1 Cor. 2:10).

Ordained ministry: a special call which radically changes one's life

The experience of receiving the gift and the call of the Holy Spirit to dedicate our life to the ministry is a mystery. It does not necessarily depend on our special skills or merits but it comes to us... It is a vocation and, as such, it is a tremendous responsibility which pushes us to conflicting decisions. There are many crucial questions: Why me? Am I sufficiently qualified? How can I relate family and ministry? It is in an attitude of prayer, humility and submission that a person can listen to, receive and respond to the call to the ministry. This process of personal and communitarian decision involves every ministry within the community of faith, but the consecration to ordained ministry is indeed a special experience. It is a source of great joy, but a costly responsibility as well.

The consecration of ordained ministry – an ecumenical issue

How the different churches interpret and fulfil the consecration of ordained ministry, in obedience to the inspiration and guidance of the Holy Spirit, is a delicate subject.

I would like to address two aspects. First, the importance of the community as the privileged space where a person receives the call is recognized, sustained, educated, consecrated, guided. A minister of the word and sacraments is a full member of his/her community and it is within the community where he/she grows and develops the pastoral action. This process of interaction (priest/pastor-community of faith) is very dynamic, not only because of the vital nature of people and societies, but mainly because the action of the Holy Spirit is dynamic, diverse, surprising, unexpected, extraordinary (Acts 2:1-13). There are divergent practices of the ordained ministry in the different Christian churches. Is this a sign of misunderstanding, theological weakness or disobedience to the word of God among some churches? Or is it a manifestation of the free action of the Holy Spirit?

Second, how does this delicate issue affect the unity of the church and the testimony of the good news of love to a divided world? How can it affect those churches whose practices are not accepted by others? In my own experience during 37 years of ministry, facing difficult dialogue with brothers and sisters of churches which do not accept the ordained ministry of women, I have felt a kind of uneasiness, not related to my vocation or my practice, but to my situation as a "stumbling stone" in the way towards the unity of the church and also the pain of disagreement with people whom I love and respect. I come back to the freedom in the action of the Holy Spirit, and I agree with Melanie May: God's call to us to make manifest the unity of the church is the call to be open to one another and to God, trusting the possibility that the Holy Spirit may speak to us through the experiences and traditions and insights of others.

There is a long way to go towards the comprehension and mutual acceptance of each other's ministries; not only when it is related to the ordination of women, but also ordination in a general sense. For example, is a Methodist pastor (male or female) fully recognized by other traditions? What about Pentecostal free churches and their understanding of ministry?

I believe that the affirmation of ministry – ordained or not – as a gift of the Holy Spirit, interpreted and lived by the churches according to the freedom given to us by the Spirit, is a good point of departure if we are to receive each other in love, to be open to the diversity of revelation. There are some questions which, perhaps, do not have only an intellectual answer:

- Is it possible to understand the designs of the Holy Spirit from our human limitations?
- Is it possible to set boundaries to the action of the Holy Spirit, even accepting that we need a dogmatics, a discipline, an organization?
- Our common journey towards looking for visible unity – can it avoid the discussion of some issues like the ordination of women? Does unity then imply silence and some exclusion?

We must, in prayer, love and mutual respect journey together, waiting in humility for the revelation of those things which we still do not accept or cannot understand. The kingdom is coming.

Reflections on "Vocation" and "Ministry"

DR DONNA GEERNAERT

A community of disciples

From the pattern of divine intervention established at the time of the exodus, it is evident that God chooses to interact with a people. God calls a people and, even in the most personal of prophetic calls, it is the good of the people that predominates. The choice of a people is continued and extended in the activity of Jesus. While scholars question the historicity of many of the events recorded in the gospels, the gathering of a group of disciples around Jesus seems an undeniable historical fact. Further, it seems evident that Jesus was prepared to include women among his followers. In fact, the inclusion of women – along with tax collectors and sinners – among the disciples seems indicative of both the world-reversing character and the nearness of the reign of God that Jesus proclaims is "at hand". While the parables present the reign of God as a world of right relationships in which compassion, mercy and forgiveness are structural realities, Jesus' interaction with the outcasts of his society so actualizes these alternate realities that the representatives of the worldly power which is being reversed sentence him to death. For the followers of Jesus, however, the resurrection again reverses this worldly condemnation so that the reign of God can be lived by anticipation in the present world.

In light of their experience of the resurrection which enables them to see the crucifixion as an event of salvation, Jesus' disciples find renewed faith and come to understand themselves as the eschatological community of God, the church (ecclesia). For the early church, the outpouring of the Spirit at Pentecost is an established fact which fulfils the ancient prophecies concerning the last days (Acts 2:16-17). Transformed by the presence of the Spirit, the community becomes the temple of God (1 Cor. 3:16), capable of proclaiming the gospel with convincing power (1 Thess. 1:5). Although they were dramatically changed by their experience of the resurrection, the disciples did not understand themselves to be taking the place of Jesus. They did not simply continue to proclaim the reign of God as they had during his life-time. Instead, the post-resurrection period is marked by a clear transition from Jesus the proclaimer of God's reign to the disciples the proclaimers of Christ. According to Edward Schillebeeckx, the very pattern of Jesus' calling of the disciples suggests the origins of a relationship consistent with this change. Specifically, he asserts that the conversion-model in the call narratives is used to show that "turning to Jesus to follow him is the metanoia (complete about-turn) demanded by the coming kingdom of God". And he writes, "In that conversion the nevertheless still-to-come rule of God becomes an already present reality." Further, the habitual practice of Jesus' close disciples of being his companions "is the pre-Easter model of what was reckoned after the Easter events to be simply 'Christian living'".[1]

In continuity with the disciples' experience of call, the Christian community after Easter sees conversion to Jesus as the condition for membership in the community of salvation. "In the New Testament the explicit message conveyed by the idea of 'following Jesus' is that fulfilment of the Law... is no longer sufficient for salvation. What now mediates salvation is one's relation to Jesus."[2] In this context, the church becomes the place of contact with Christ and his message, the place where authentic discipleship is possible. "The preaching of the gospel is not merely an account of the historical saving act of God in Christ; Christ himself is at work in the word which is preached."[3] The focus of mission and ministry in the church is to enable Christians to enter into an immediate relationship with Jesus in the Holy Spirit.

Insofar as the church's ministry is oriented towards the making of disciples, it will also be defined by the concept of discipleship. When ministry is viewed as discipleship, for example, sharp distinctions between the minister and those ministered to are avoided. Avery Dulles states, "Discipleship is the common factor uniting all Christians with one another, for no one of them is anything but a follower and a learner in relation to Jesus Christ. As disciples, all must help, using their own talents for the benefit of the rest. All are ministers and all are ministered to."[4] In a community of disciples, no one is to be called, in an absolute sense, teacher, father or master (Matt. 23:8-19). As several parables and sayings of Jesus illustrate, the exercise of leadership in the church is not to reflect secular models. "Whoever wishes to become great among you must be your servant, and whoever wishes to be first among you must be slave of all" (Mark 10:43-44, 9:33-37).

Part of the attractiveness of imaging the church as community of disciples is its relation to the pre-Easter context of Jesus with his company of chosen followers. Thus, the concept of discipleship may throw light on church structures which have developed in the post-resurrection period. While it is clear that there is no uniform order or structure in the early church, it is equally evident that every community is ordered and structured in some way. Convinced that "Jesus is Lord", members of the early Christian community saw the reign of Christ continued in the church through the charismatic gifts of the Holy Spirit. Further, since all of these gifts have their source in the Holy Spirit, there may be tension but there can be no radical opposition between charismatic and administrative ministries (Rom. 12:6-8; Eph. 4:11-12). In later theological reflection, this understanding of church structure suggests a concept of administrative office as instituted charism with the specific task of safeguarding creative fidelity to the gospel. This view of church structure highlights the mutual relatedness of all charisms within the community of disciples. Since all members of the church remain disciples together, no one's gift may be despised. All charisms are to be respected and every gift is to be judged by its contribution to the integrity of the church's life and mission.

A theology of vocation

The pastoral plan from the third continental congress on vocations held in Montreal in April 2002 offers an outline of a theology of vocations. Beginning with the call narratives of the four gospels, it states that "the notion of vocation is fundamental to the biblical understanding of the human person: in relation to God, to the community of believers, and to a mission to be accomplished in the world". Four characteristics evident in these texts are summarized as follows:
1) the life of discipleship begins with a call, coming as a free and unmerited gift: while always respectful of the freedom of its recipient, the urgent and authoritative character of the call demands a response;
2) the call is to discipleship, to holiness and intimate friendship with Jesus, hearing and putting into practice Jesus' teaching, following Jesus "on the way";
3) the call is to sharing in Christ's mission of redemption, to participate in the task of transforming the world through the renewal of the believing community, to proclaiming the reign of God through teaching, healing and reconciliation;
4) the call often demands a rupture with an earlier, more comfortable existence; to follow Jesus is to leave everything behind: boats, fields, jobs, possessions, reputation, even friends and families; this new

allegiance – to Jesus, and to the reign of God – requires a life-long conversion of heart and mind, and of life itself.

Further, the pastoral plan maintains that theological reflection on the vocational nature of human existence identifies a number of central elements which may be summarized as follows:

- Fundamentally, a vocation is not defined by doing but is primarily a matter of being, in which life is consciously embraced as God's pure gift.
- The church is *ecclesia*, God's called and gathered assembly; although its differentiation into specific ministries and functions pertains to its essential structure, all God's people are joined by a common life, calling and destiny.
- As the sacrament of God's loving presence in the world, the church reflects the trinitarian mystery of Father, Son and Spirit, an infinite dynamism of call and response, in which diversity of vocation and unity of mission exist in perfect harmony and identity.
- God calls each human individual to life through love, and invites a loving response as "the fundamental and innate vocation of every human being". This call to human and divine life is celebrated preeminently in the sacrament of baptism. Thus, every Christian vocation is rooted in the baptismal call.
- Christian vocation is inherently missionary. Its purpose is to transform the world: healing, teaching, reconciling and giving life and freedom to the children of God.
- Most vocational journeys contain a few key moments when Christ's invitation to "come, follow me" is heard as a direct and personal call to the human heart. More typically, though, this call is mediated gradually: in prayer, through major events in one's personal history, through interlocking sets of experiences.
- In the dramatic encounter between two liberties – the utterly free choice of God and the free human response it elicits – an intimate bond is sealed between God and each human person. To name and claim one's unique vocation before God is a uniquely personal act. And yet, no vocation is purely self-referential, a private agreement "between me and Jesus". A Christian vocation is necessarily an ecclesial vocation.[5]

Ministerial religious life

Sandra Schneiders, a member of the US-based Immaculate Heart of Mary congregation, is in the process of writing a three-volume work on religious life in a new millennium. Her reflections on "ministerial religious life" offer an illustration of the integral linking of ministry and vocation.[6] Schneiders begins by identifying religious life as "a charism, a gift to the church". Defining the basic charism of religious life as "the call to perpetual self-gift to Christ in consecrated celibacy for the sake of the reign of God" (or, "the exclusive, lifelong God-quest centred in a particular kind of love of Jesus which calls some people in the unique form of total and irrevocable self-gift to the exclusion of any other primary relationship, life project or cause"), she notes that this charism has been specified in various ways throughout Christian history: domestic virgins, hermits, cenobites, monastics, mendicants, missionaries, etc. Further, "just as the basic calling of the Christian can be shaped by charismatic specification in the life of apostle, teacher, administrator, healer and so on, it would seem that forms of religious life might, at least analogously, be regarded as charismatically distinguished".

After a brief historical sketch, Schneiders concludes, "The impulse to service of the neighbour as a direct and necessary expression of their quest for God and love of Christ, as intrinsic to their religious vocation, has been present among women religious from the earliest days of the church." Further, she states,

> The recognition that ministry is intrinsic to this vocation does not reduce the charism of ministerial religious life to a simple "response to a perceived social need" as some, including some religious, have suggested when they have not succeeded in finding some highly original spirituality at the origin of a particular institute. Many people, including women, throughout history have responded from religious or humanitarian motives to the needs of the suffering without becoming religious. The total commitment to Christ in lifelong consecrated celibacy lived in community and mission cannot be explained by and is not required by a desire to meet a need, however urgent that need might be. Rather, total commitment to Christ entails an equally wholehearted commitment to his members in need. Ministry for religious is neither simply the overflow of love of God nor a substitute for it. It is its expression, its body in this world. The second commandment is as important as the first and for ministerial religious the embodiment of love of God is active service to the neighbour.

In summary, "the originality of the mobile ministerial form of religious life (in contrast to the stable form specified in the monastic lifestyle) is twofold. First, it is truly religious life, which was finally recognized by papal decree... Second, it is essentially and intrinsically ministerial, which was fully recognized by Vatican II, but that ministerial identity does not flow from ordination but from religious profession and is therefore not specified by hierarchical agendas and functions but by the charism of the congregation itself."[7]

Religious profession, Schneiders maintains, is primarily a unitary and unifying act; a solemn, formal and public act, by which a person takes her whole life into her hands and freely disposes of it in self-gift to Christ and his body within the congregation. In this holistic context, the vows are seen as distinct promises bearing on particular spheres of life. But even considering the vows in their individuality, and without negating the legal obligations assumed by profession of consecrated celibacy, poverty and obedience, it is important to maintain the poetic and prophetic character of the language used. Religious life is not primarily about taking on obligations one did not have as a lay person. It is about a relationship that gives a definitive shape to one's life within an alternate life form in the church and which, like the life of Jesus, has the salvation of the world, the coming of the reign of God, as its purpose.

In religious life, she asserts, the vows have always had a *ministerial* function, although this often received less attention in early times and has tended to dominate disproportionately in post-Reformation congregations. Celibacy, until very recently, was seen as freeing the religious for a kind of selfless and unfettered service of the neighbour that was not possible for the person "burdened" with family responsibilities. Poverty, which Jesus specifically linked with freedom to preach the gospel (cf. Matt. 10:8-10), was raised to a particularly high level in the ministerial project of the mendicants in the Middle Ages but has played various roles in the ability of religious congregations to accomplish remarkable ministerial feats with the slimmest of resources. Obedience became the primary vow among ministerial religious, specifically because of its role in the deployment of religious in ministry under centralized authority. This interpretation occurred as early as the foundation of the Dominicans in the 12th century and reach its apex among the Jesuits in the 16th century. Most modern ministerial congregations have followed the lead of the post-Reformation clerical orders in seeing obedience as the central vow and virtue of religious life, particularly as it operated in the carrying out of the order's ministry.

NOTES

[1] Edward Schillebeeckx, *Jesus: An Experiment in Christology*, New York, Seabury, 1979, pp.224-29.
[2] *Ibid.*, p.226.
[3] Hans Küng, *The Church*, New York, Doubleday, 1976, p.305.
[4] Avery Dulles, *A Church to Believe In*, New York, Crossroads, 1983, p.12.

[5] The above two paragraphs are summarized from *Conversion, Discernment, Mission, Pastoral Plan of the Third Continental Congress on Vocations,* Ottawa, CCCB Pubs, 2003, pp.44-46.
[6] Sandra Schneiders, *Finding the Treasure*, New York, Paulist, 2000, pp.285-86, 298, 311, 364.
[7] *Perfectae Caritatis,* decree on the adaptation and renewal of the religious life, promulgated 28 October 1965, p.8, taken from Walter M. Abbot ed., *The Documents of Vatican II*, New York, America Press, 1966.

Ministry and Vocation

DR URS VON ARX

In modern debate, the combination of the two terms "ministry" and "vocation" seems to occur in two distinct though related contexts that are relevant for this consultation.

First, to be a minister in the church implies having a vocation for a particular ministry (in the following I have in mind the ordained ministry). Calls for taking up a ministry may come from various places and sources, arise out of various contexts and experiences. In the last resort, however, the vocation must come from God – that is why vocations are prayed for. But how can we know that a baptized member of the church is called by God to a specific ministry?

In order to find out, a process of interpersonal discernment is necessary (similar to what St Paul has in mind concerning prophetic speech in the congregation, cf. 1 Cor. 12:10 – *diakriseis pneumaton*). The process will include (1) the person confronted with a call (i.e. he or she has to find out whether he or she can respond to it and accept it), and (2) other people who may act on behalf of the church. By this I assume that God the Holy Spirit is the final source of an individual vocation and that God the Holy Spirit is given to the community of the church.

This process of discernment is especially important in cases where someone says, "I feel that I have a vocation." Whether this inner mental awareness as an expression of a possible vocation is true or not true must be ascertained; a simple assertion will not be sufficient as an authentication of the vocation, although it must be taken seriously.

It is also especially important in the case of candidates to the ordained ministry, as in principle this is widely seen to be a life-long ministry (some traditions speak of the *character indelebilis* conferred in the sacramental act of ordination). The reason for ascertaining a vocation for the ordained ministry, then, may be twofold: the ministry has its foundation in the calling of apostles by Christ and consequently this should also apply for each individual minister; moreover, such a discernment may help to protect the church and the individual candidate from the misguided idea that the ministry is simply a job separated from the sense of being a servant and friend of the Lord or from the mission and ethos of the church that becomes transparent in the life of a minister.

The ordination by laying-on of hands and prayer which is to take place in the eucharistic assembly as the prime realization of what the church is may be seen as the last phase of this process of discernment. (It may continue in churches that practise sequential ordination, e.g. from the diaconate to the priesthood/presbyterate, unless this is merely a canonical formality. What will be the case after, say, twenty years of ministry? Should a form of discernment be a life-long process?)

My own church does not know a theologically and spiritually reflected and mature way of discerning vocations (nor incidentally of evoking them). There is a tendency to restrict the process of ascertainment to make sure whether or not applicants to the priesthood (presbyterate) who are to serve as vicars in a parish have the necessary qualifications to follow an academic formation in the department of Old Catholic theology in the university of Bern, Switzerland, run by the state. Due to the lack of vocations within our own church – there are always applicants from other churches – bishop and synodical council tend to welcome anybody who qualifies in academic terms and does not show conspicuous signs of being a difficult person in communicating with others or in complying with the authority structures of the church.

– Candidates to the permanent diaconate may be asked similar questions, although their training does not lead to a university degree. However, in their case an additional recommendation of a particular parish is asked for.
– Candidates to the episcopate may undergo a sort of hearing before the members of the diocesan synod (the electing body).

Since we are a small church, they may be sufficiently known from their pastoral priestly ministry, and yet to distinguish vocation from ambition is still difficult, even though there is a provision that nobody may put down his or her name for candidacy.

The other context where the notion of vocation to the ministry nowadays plays an important role is the debate on the ordination of baptized women to the priesthood, especially in churches that claim to be in the wider catholic tradition. Here it is not so much a problem of recognizing a vocation within an institutionalized procedure of securing candidates for an unquestioned ministry, but the notion of vocation is an element in a conflictual situation. The claim to be called, to have a vocation from God, is brought forward in order to invoke God's authority against the authority of those in the church who maintain that the ordained ministry (or rather the ministry of priesthood, i.e. episcopate and presbyterate) is not open to baptized women, and therefore their claim to be called by God must be an illusion or should be directed into other forms of service and witness in the church.

Although I think – and I quote from the common statement of an Orthodox-Old Catholic consultation held in 1996 – "there are no compelling dogmatic-theological reasons for not ordaining women to the priesthood", it is no help, in my view, to use the confession "I feel called to the priesthood" as a battle cry in the debate which, of course, is nonetheless necessary. It can only be an urgent stimulus for a serious argumentation, but as such the claim is not more decisive than in the other context. An overall discernment of the nature of the ordained ministry in the church as a community of women and men that are being touched and vivified by the Holy Spirit *(pneumatophoroi)* is therefore called for.

I wonder if any help to clarify the relationship of ministry and vocation is available from scripture and the early Tradition of the church, if vocation is understood as an inner call, as a process of becoming aware of being called to a specific ministry, which then can be used as a claim.

In the Pauline tradition and in other NT epistles, to be called (by God or by Christ) is a general qualification of all those who have responded with faith to the gospel preaching and are baptized (e.g. Rom. 8:30, 9:12,24; 1 Cor. 1:9; Gal. 1:15; Phil. 3:14; 1 Thess. 2:12; cf. 2 Tim. 1:9) and are obliged to live a holy life that can be described in religious and ethical terms (Gal. 5:8; Phil. 3:14; 1 Thess. 4:7, 5:24; cf. 2 Tim. 4:7; Heb. 13:20f.; 1 Pet. 1:15, 2:21; 2 Pet. 1:10). Strictly speaking, it is not a call to a specific service within the community, although according to 1 Corinthians 12 or Romans 12 the gift of the Holy Spirit *(charis)* bestowed on the faithful is differentiated into various gifts *(charismata)* so that all these gifts or receivers of gifts can be compared to the members of a body. We do not know how these gifts were recognized in the community or how each baptized person recognized his or her gift and whether this recognition had to concur with a similar judgment of the community.

More to the point is perhaps the vocation of St Paul, because his being called by God is at the same time a commission to preach the gospel among the Gentiles (Gal. 1:15f.). The whole context of Galatians (and passages in other letters) shows that this claim has an apologetic ring and was apparently questioned within the wider Christian community. It is a conflictual context. In this respect we should note that St Paul does not confine himself to simply asserting being called to the apostolate in a sort of Christ vision (as the Twelve or other apostles, cf. 1 Cor. 15:1-11), but he adds an element of ecclesial discernment or recognition for his apostolate: he went to the Jerusalem convent to lay before them (i.e. the pillar apostles) the gospel he preached to the Gentiles, "lest somehow I should be running or had run in vain" (Gal. 2:2); and these "saw that I had been entrusted with the gospel... and was given the grace..." (Gal. 2:7,9).

According to the synoptic (mostly Markan) tradition the Twelve or members of the Twelve were called by Jesus to follow him (Mark 1:16-20, 2:14, 3:13-19; cf. the sayings 5:18f., 10:21f., 10:52; unsuccessful call stories Q/Luke 9:57-62; another type John 1:35-51). This (straightforward) vocation will eventually lead into the ministry of proclaiming the gospel of the kingdom of God and thus winning humans for it (Mark 1:17; Matt. 4:19; cf. Luke 5; John 21; further Mark 3:15; 6:7: casting out demons; Matt. 10:1: healing the sick; Luke 9:1f.: both; Matt. 28,19: baptizing). These call stories may serve as models of the relationship between Jesus the teacher and the disciples and therefore reflect the nature of discipleship in general. To the extent that the disciples thus called, especially the Twelve, serve as models for those called for the ordained ministry of episcope, the call stories may be a reminder of the dominical vocation as a requisite for the ministry. How this vocation comes about and is verified or authenticated remains open. Incidentally, the same goes for Acts 13:2ff.

On the other hand, in the single instance where the access to a specific ministry is mentioned at all (1 Tim. 3:1: "If any aspires to the office of 'bishop', he desires a noble task"), nothing is said about vocation and discernment, but a list of qualifications in order to secure personal aptitude is added (cf. Tit. 1:5-9). Correspondingly ancient commentators have never interpreted this passage in terms of an inner vocation.

The model of an inner call (by way of audition or vision) was often seen in the mode the prophets of Israel received their commission and messages (Moses, individual judges and prophets). Whether the literary genre of a prophetic vocation is open to a psychological interpretation is, however, quite another question. Modern research views these stories as reflections of a literary authentication of the specific literary prophetic tradition after the death of the persons implied (this may reflect a conflictual situation in the life of the prophet himself). In the case of prophets, then, the truth of the vocation (which incidentally does not always constitute a life-long commission) should be seen rather in terms of certain signs or the overall impression that verified the claim of speaking as a messenger of God, not the claim of having been called as such.

I am not an expert in this field at all, but I think it is difficult in the patristic literature to find many instances of someone who claims to have a vocation for the ordained ministry or to find a description of vocation in terms of an introspective nature. Cyprian, for instance, may mention several elements that are implied in the making of a bishop, e.g. the voice of the people and of the clergy of the local church, the fellow bishops, and the judgment of God *(iudicium Dei)*. But the latter cannot be isolated from the whole process or identified as a distinct element (cf. *Ep.* 3:3, 43:1, 55:8f., 67:3-5, 68:2; also *Trad. Ap.* 2-3).

G. Lampe[1] does mention various people including the baptized in general as being called by God, but a call to the ministry (unlike the call to martyrdom) is not listed in this entry.

According to L. Sempé,[2] the earliest patristic reference for sacerdotal vocation as an inner call can be found with St Ephraem (d. 373). I am not quite convinced. The suspicion that speaking of a call or vocation for the ministry (somewhat in analogy to a call for monastic life) is a relatively late phenomenon seems to be corroborated in the latest articles of substantial depth I could find (although after having read an earlier version of this paper at the consultation).[3] Hervé Legrand rightly insists on the fact that in the authentic Christian tradition a vocation by God cannot be considered to be independent from a call by the church in whatever form this comes about: "la vocation au ministère, de la part de Dieu, coïncide avec l'appel de l'Église", i.e. "l'appel par l'Église est depuis toujours le critère de la vocation aux ministères" (p.626).

I was not able to consult Joseph Lécuyer[4] or the collective study *La vocation. Appel de Dieu, phénomène de l'Eglise.*[5]

NOTES

[1] *Patristic Greek Lexicon*, Oxford, 1968, *s.v. klesis*.
[2] *Dictionnaire de théologie catholique*, vol. 15/2, Paris, 1950, p.3157.
[3] Simon Légasse, Michel Sauvage, André Godin, *Dictionnaire de spiritualité*, vol. 16, Paris, 1994, pp.1081-167, and esp. Hervé Legrand, "La théologie de la vocation aux ministères ordonnés: vocation ou appel?", in *La vie spirituelle*, 729, 1998, 621-640 (updated version: http://snv.free.fr/jv096legrand.htm).
[4] "Face au sacerdoce", in *Vocations sacerdotales et religieuses*, 218, 1962, pp.61-78 (patristic documentation).
[5] *Cahiers de Froidmont*, 20, Rixensart, 1976.

The Community of Women and Men in the Church Study
How Did It Come Into Being?
REV. DR CONSTANCE F. PARVEY

The idea for a theological study on the role of women, women's leadership in the ministries of the church and the ordination of women came into being at the 1974 Berlin consultation on "Sexism in the 70s" sponsored by the sub-unit on Women of the WCC. Sub-groups at that meeting dealt with economic, social and political issues that impede women's identity, humanity and roles in church and society; lacking was a group on theology. On the spot a theology sub-group was organized and from that group, working together over several days, came a recommendation to the consultation as a whole that a major study should be launched on a theological level regarding the changing roles of women and men in the church and the implications of this change for the ways we do theology and biblical studies. And additionally, how these impact on the church; how it both does and might understand itself when it studies what these changes might mean for its renewal; and how women's gifts to the church expand, enhance and enrich its work in leadership, service, prayer, ministry and mission.

A recommendation from Berlin was then sent to the Accra meeting of the WCC Faith and Order commission to explore this topic within the framework of the WCC commitment to the unity of the church, a centuries long journey of hope to renew the richness of unity in the body of Christ that the apostolic church enjoyed and passed on and struggled to maintain against both divisions within the church communities and struggles with other spiritual movements of the age and with the perceived and often real threat of Roman imperial power. The Accra meeting took up the study in two ways:
1) it began a new study on the Community of Men and Women in the Church; and
2) it incorporated aspects of the study into its long-term initiative on "One Baptist, One Eucharist, One Ministry" under the rubrics of "the ministry" and "ordination".

At the Nairobi fifth assembly of the WCC in 1975, recommendations came to the floor both through Faith and Order in section II under "What Unity Requires" and the sub-unit on Women in section V on "Structures of Injustice and Struggles for Liberation". Hours of debate ensued about where to locate the study: was it primarily a unity issue or one of justice?

Finally, the assembly worked out an alternative: it placed the study desk in Faith and Order to work in tandem with the sub-unit on Women. This, in itself, was an unusual move. Within Faith and Order the topics around women in ministry and the ordination of women received special attention, and in concert with the sub-unit on Women the topics were placed in a broader societal framework. In addition, the tandem relationship was a resource for identifying and bringing together a community of men and women in that Faith and Order's participants were largely men and the sub-unit's participants were largely women. The men were academic theologians and ordained church authorities while the women were unordained lay leaders; a considerable number were heads of large, nationwide women's organizations, some were academic theologians, ministers and priests. Faith and Order represented the bringing together of inherited traditions while the Women's sub-unit raised new issues coming from within the concrete experiences of women serving the church through women's ministries of advocacy, education and service in the midst of injustices in church and society. (Even the fact of working across two units was already a change in the structures, an experiment that some people thought impossible.)

In a sense what the 1975 Nairobi assembly was saying is that there is no "right place" in the steps towards Christian unity for either men or women, ordained or lay, if we simply think within the framework of the status quo. New space must be opened up to give ear and voice to the struggles of the whole human family as essential to God's call for the renewal and unity of the church.

How did it address the issues we are concerned about here: women's ministry and ordination?

In 1979, the Community study held a major consultation at Klingenthal in France on "The Ordination of Women in Ecumenical Perspective". It was the third such consultation in the history of the WCC; participants were Anglican, Lutheran, Reformed, Old Catholic, Orthodox and Roman Catholic women and men scholars, clergy and church authorities from fourteen countries. The meeting was not so much about what we can say together as it was about what must be said separately. It also included stories of women's experiences in ministry and issues posed because of gender-linked, male symbols for God, androcentric theological imagery, questions of scripture that interpreted women as subservient to or "less than" men.

A section of that report relevant to issues of this consultation dealt with the Christological issues raised by ordination. It begins by saying,

> The universal priesthood of all believers and the sacramental priesthood *both* derive from the unique priesthood. The bishop and the priest only actualize, by the grace of the Holy Spirit in time and space, the unique and eternal priesthood of the High Priest.[1]

This is then expanded more fully with the aim of encouraging more research and reflection regarding the ordained deaconate for women and women entering priestly orders. (For some this paragraph seemed too cautious; for others it offered a theological way to mutual understanding that was respectful of different traditions and of various forms of church order.)

> On the basis of biblical anthropology, men and women are different and at the same time one both in accordance with the order of creation and the order of redemption. This unity/diversity can be signified in the reconciled new creation which is beginning in the church here and now, through the presence at the altar of a man and a woman, both ordained to the ministries of equal dignity, though of different symbolic significance. Others would ask yet further, is not this truth of creation and redemption best exemplified when both women and men stand at the altar as priests?[2]

The next discussion on this paragraph took place at the Sheffield international consultation on the Community of Women and Men in the Church in 1981. Among the recommendations directed to the Faith and Order commission were that:
1) more theological work be done on the significance of the representation of Christ in the ordained ministry, with particular reference to the ordination of women;
2) more encouragement be given for the development of the ordained deaconate for women and men;
3) further explorations be done regarding "the possibilities of different churches being in communion with each other when they have different policies with regard to the ordination of women";
4) work be undertaken on the question of fundamental human rights as they relate to the calling of women and men to the ordained ministry.[3]

The discussion of these issues engendered a great deal of emotion, anger and pain at Sheffield. On one side were voices from the Anglican communion whose churches had not yet agreed to ordain women and who saw this as an issue of equality, and on the other side were voices from the Orthodox churches who felt that equality had nothing to do with the issue, that it was primarily one of the interwoven relationship: tradition, theology and liturgy.

In August 1982, the Community of Women and Men study was reported to the WCC Dresden central committee which acts on behalf of the assembly between its every-seven-year meetings. Recommendations to the central committee from Sheffield evoked a heated debate that lasted over ten hours. The stir was caused by using the word "equality" in recommendations that had to do with church structures and with the ordination of women. The intention of one recommendation on equality was to study those situations, such as in the Church of Sweden, where equal rights legislation in the government had played a role in the debate over the ordination of women. It was hoped that such a study would benefit all of the churches living in societies granting more and more equality and equal opportunity to women and men and would help them look at how their gifts in this new context can be brought into the living Tradition and traditions of the church. Whirling around the same word, equality, was a recommendation from Sheffield that 50 percent of all membership elected to sub-units and committees of the WCC be women. After arduous discussion, the central committee affirmed the principle of equal participation of women and men as a goal towards which it would move, starting with the composition of WCC decision-making and consultative bodies prior to and following the WCC's sixth assembly in Vancouver, Canada, in 1983.

To the sub-unit on Women the central committee recommended that they "collect case studies of the experiences of lay women and men as they relate to ordination and hierarchical church structures" and that they "work to build a network of women in ministry, both ordained and non-ordained ministry, so that women in all parts of the world can share their experiences" and "take seriously the burden women carry in the discussion which needs to be shared equally by men and women". Although this may sound radical, it was an echo of ecclesial discussion in Faith and Order going back to the Lausanne meeting in 1927 where, with the growth of the missionary and labour movements, it raised the question of the right place of women in the "councils of the church".

It was at the Lima Faith and Order commission meeting in January 1982 that the Community of Women and Men study gave its final report, marking the end of its location as an official study desk. This

212 *Ministry and Ordination in the Community of Women and Men*

end point was also at the time when the baptism, eucharist and ministry convergence document, worked on for decades, came before the commission for final reception and authority to send it to the churches worldwide for study and response. Roman Catholic theologian Francine Cardman, in comparing early versions of the BEM drafts with the final BEM document, states that the final text "considerably reduced its estimate of the significance of the question of the recognition and reconciliation of ministries".

After the publication of the churches' responses to BEM, 1982-1990, the American theologian Melanie May, in examining them, observed that responses to BEM reveal that "the deepest differences between the churches concerning mutual recognition of ministries relate to the issues of the ordination of women and episcopal succession".

Since the formal ending of the study in January 1982, work on issues of women in ministry and ordination of women has continued. In addition, the sub-unit on Women through the Decade on the Churches in Solidarity with Women and a new programme, "On Being Church: Women's Voices and Visions", is bringing women theologians and women in ministries from around the world to share experiences of church and envision models for ministry and ecclesial life. Since 1982, many changes have taken place in the lives of women: more women are engaged in traditional and innovating ministries, ordained and lay, across the globe; more churches, as grassroots levels, are engaged in issues of women's ministries and ordination of women; more churches have ordained women, and even consecrated women bishops without it becoming a church-dividing issue; more public attention is given to the work and status of women in the church; more women are educated in theological faculties and departments of religion at advanced levels in scholarly research and teaching in studies of theology and ministry, scripture and ecclesiology; feminist scholars have brought a new hermeneutic to biblical studies, theology and worship; women leaders in ministry, lay and ordained, are partners in decision-making regarding all aspects of church life – theology, social change, higher education, authorities in church structures, on councils, partners in shaping liturgical life and prayer, etc. The list goes on...

How do we bring our experience here, now, to this place and shape the next steps?

We are approximately thirty women and men here, about half female, half male; we represent about thirty churches from around the world, East and West, North and South, Orthodox, Roman Catholic,

Anglican, Lutheran, Reformed, Methodist, Assemblies of God, China Christian Council, Church of the Brethren, Baptist Union of Myanmar, Church of Aladura, etc. We are uniquely suited and called to participate and shape this consultation on the "Ministry and Ordination in the Community of Women and Men in the Church".

NOTES

[1] *The Ordination of Women in Ecumenical Perspective*, Constance F. Parvey ed., Faith and Order Paper no. 105, WCC, 1980, p.58.
[2] *Ibid.*
[3] *The Community of Women and Men in the Church: The Sheffield Report*, Constance F. Parvey ed., WCC, 1983, p.84.

Women's Ordination
An Extrinsic Issue
DR DIMITRA KOUKOURA

Women's service and ordination in the chrch are issues that in the past few decades have become part of the ecumenical dialogue, and have prompted in the Orthodox church a creative impulse to discover the answers for itself and then to express them in various ways within the dialogue.

The initiative of the Ecumenical Patriarchate for the historic conference of Rhodes in 1988 demonstrated the interest of the Orthodox churches in all the issues which are emerging throughout Christianity, as well as the duty of Orthodoxy to give answers which stem from the spiritual experience of a living tradition of two thousand years and the dynamic interpretation of the teachings originating in the first unified Christian millennium.

In this decisive meeting, high-ranking clerics and university professors were not the only ones who were invited to express the spiritual experience of the entire ecclesiastic community *(pleroma)*, which was the earlier practice; on the contrary, the representation of Orthodox men and women, clerics, monks and nuns, lay people, young boys and girls, as well as the balanced proportion in their numbers – to the extent that was possible – was a persuasive indication of the fact that Orthodox Christians are not indifferent to social change.

If one moves from the list of guests to the papers that were presented and especially to the discussions that took place in plenary as well as in work groups, one may come to two important realizations, which are both recorded in detail in the conclusions of the conference:
1. The social changes which offer the women of today a variety of roles in modern societies encourage us to regard an expansion of their roles in the life of every local church as something acceptable and desirable. These roles have to do with teaching, catechism, charity and administration of a parish or a diocese, where men and women of the laity must have an augmented presence. The same applies to the participation of women in holy worship, their participation in the

choir and various services in the area of the church, which are related to order and dignity. The institution of deaconesses, which flourished in the first church, is recognized unanimously and is expected to reappear wherever there is need.
2. The ordination of women is not a direct result of the establishment of human rights, social justice and equality among men and women in modern society; it depends on other theological parameters, which Orthodox theologians must codify and present now for the sake of dialogue; women's ordination is an issue which, for the moment, is not their own.

In this context several papers have been written for the acquisition of post-graduate diplomas, monographs have been published, and papers have been presented in conferences dealing with the issue from various points of view. They all conclude that women's ordination shall not be accepted here and now by the Orthodox world. The texts that accompanied the invitation to this meeting are indicative of this Orthodox spirit, as is the text of the renowned professor emeritus of systematic theology Nikolaos Matsoukas, which will be presented at this consultation.

Therefore the issue of women's ordination is not a demand of Orthodox women themselves, nor is it an intrinsic issue of Orthodox communities, and especially not an urgent priority that demands an answer in order to assure the spiritual progress of local churches in Christ and peaceful relations among their members.

Throughout the last twenty years, the rich experience acquired from the varied environments of the WCC, where women's ordination is a crucial point of discussion, indicates that the clear Orthodox message is not easily accepted and is usually seen negatively.

It is usually considered as evidence of the perceived conservatism of all Orthodox Christians, both men and women, and as a fossil, perhaps, of male domination, to which Orthodox women do not react, mainly because of their eastern cultural origins. Sometimes this is perceived as the concealment of fear among women who do not dare to rebel against the oppression of men, of the clergy or the laity, and therefore Orthodox women do not demand priesthood.

These reactions are clearly an expression of the great enthusiasm on the part of Protestant women for a definite victory, which, according to them, led to the full recognition of their dignity in their Christian community. They sometimes express sadness and disappointment because this significant status is denied to their Orthodox sisters, for the lack of boldness which, as they think, makes Orthodox women reject the possibility of their ordination. These reactions suggest a partial or complete ignorance of Orthodox teachings and worship practices, of the *lex orandi* and *lex credendi*, for which both partners in this dialogue are for various reasons responsible. This may happen because Orthodox representatives do not always adequately interpret the unbroken, two thousand-year living tradition of their church, or because their Protestant counterparts exclusively focus on their own interpretative approach.

In this discussion, what must always be taken into account is the necessary distinction between two completely different things: (a) the various roles which can be assumed by women in the life of the church, and (b) priesthood, which offers access to the altar and to the performance of the holy sacraments on the part of the entire religious community.

These roles are related to the social and cultural context and to the needs of the community in space and time. Practices and policies opposed to women caused by patriarchal oppressive mentalities have been condemned, and in the passage of time they have been recognized for their unfairness and gradually eliminated. The role of women too often has been degraded or non-existent in the life of the Christian community, as it was in other social spaces. And while women are finding their place in the judicial or diplomatic corps, in parliaments and international organizations, they are also being welcomed in the councils of the parishes and dioceses, and are taking part in decisions concerning the course of the eucharistic community in space and time.

The priesthood of women cannot come as a direct result of the progress of a state of justice, nor of the establishment of human rights and the unquestionable political rights of women. It is related to theological choices and priorities of the Orthodox communities. Priesthood is perceived as one of the various gifts offered to the members of Christian communities, which happens to involve men exclusively. Nothing more and nothing less.

Holiness, however, is the direct priority of all the members of a eucharistic community and an unquestionable right for all. It is the common calling for men and women, a common practice, a common goal and joy, a gift in the grace of God. "You shall be holy, for I am holy" (1 Pet. 1:16). No human law and no cultural environment is ever able to deprive women of their participation in the Last Supper of the Lord, of the gifts of the Holy Spirit (Gal. 5:23), of their crucifixion and resurrection in the company of Jesus.

This spiritual experience offers women a power shared with men which cannot be measured in size and potential. The power to love, to forgive and to struggle with all our strength, which depends on the created space and time afforded to us, for social witness, justice, peace and reconciliation. On this point some would defiantly argue, saying: Why should not women have both priesthood and sainthood?

On the contrary, it is the greater gift that matters, the redemption of man and woman from the curse of the law, giving both of them God's protection (Gal. 3:13) which offers them a way out of common corruption and common death. It is the sanctifying grace of the Holy Spirit which makes corruptible and mortal people participants in the resurrected presence of the Lord. From this perspective priesthood is not evaluated as one of the greater, but as one of the lesser gifts, since it is not a sufficient and necessary reason for salvation.

In the matter of women's priesthood, communicative errors are made by both partners in the discussion. The way in which Orthodox representatives reject ordination often gives the impression of a male-dominated church, rather than a community of worship where men and women praise and thank God for infinite gifts and seek to receive the medicine of immortality and the betrothal of God's kingdom. On the other hand, the attitude of the other side mostly expresses triumph over an impenetrable social fortress that has been conquered, rather than a penitent and humble service in the vineyard of the Lord.

However, for so long as people are called to express their views, the more they will come to understand them and to perceive the true reasons for choices of the other participants in the dialogue. This dialogue, when taking place in the spirit of love and respect of differences, is constructive and leads to proximity, peace and – we believe – to the spiritual upbuilding of the entire church (Rom. 14:19).

Women's Priesthood as a Theological and Ecumenical Problem

DR NIKOLAOS MATSOUKAS

In the last few decades much has been said and written about women's priesthood. My serious preoccupation with this interesting subject crystallized through my role as supervisor for Constantine Giokarinis's doctoral thesis entitled "Women's Priesthood in the Ecumenical Movement".[1] This voluminous, excellent and comprehensive thesis sheds clear light on the problem from a philological, historical, social and especially theological point of view. Furthermore, from 30 October to 7 November 1988, a special inter-Orthodox conference in Rhodes focused extensively on the issue of women's ordination. Although the holy synod of the Ecumenical Patriarchate did me the highest honour of inviting me to attend as a special counsellor, I unfortunately could not participate for personal reasons. However, I later studied the opinions and the outcome of the conference.

In this paper I do not wish to analyze extensively the various aspects of the issue, which have already been examined by several theologians with knowledge and wisdom. I would merely like to emphasize some points which, in my opinion, possibly project the most substantial aspects of this subject and constitute suggestions for an ecumenical dialogue.

The numbering of the sacraments

In the scholastic manuals of dogmatic theology it is said that priesthood is one of the seven sacraments. This numbering originates in the scholastics of the West, led by Thomas Aquinas. Since the 14th century the Orthodox church imperceptibly allowed the circulation of this view, which was later imposed mainly by academic theology. The fullest theological analyses of the sacraments are found in two works by Nikolaos Kavasilas, *About Life in Christ* and *Interpretation of the Holy Liturgy*. A numbering of the sacramental ceremonies is not even implied there. On the contrary, Kavasilas emphasizes that the entire body of the church is expressed through the sacraments. In other words, the church itself as body is sacramental life in its gathering, participating in the glory of the divine kingdom. No sacrament can be autonomous, since sacraments are members and not parts of the ecclesiastical body. Thus Kavasilas (a) by using wonderful pictorial illustrations tells us that the sacraments are like the chambers of the heart, like the branches of a tree and like vines spreading from a single root; and (b) by adopting a language of physiology he tells us that baptism is birth, chrism is movement and the eucharist is nourishment. No one can move or be fed without having been born!

Therefore the numbering of the sacraments may result in isolation or separation of the individual sacramental ceremonies, which merely participate in the body, but are not the body itself; it may convey the opinion that these are mechanical or magic ceremonies. Numbering may also result in the adoption of the unacceptable distinction between obligatory and voluntary. However, even the choice of a chaste life constitutes a marriage with the church. Thus we come to realize that the sacraments are not mechanical or magical, or symbolic rituals, because they grew and still grow in natural and historical events: in the history of divine economy, which is the continuous course of a living historical community through constant epiphanies, Christ is the master of ceremonies and high priest. In the gathering of the church body, the deacons, presbyters and bishops perform the sacraments as charismatic ministers who received the necessary grace through the ordination. In other words, there is no mediating priesthood in the Orthodox church. All the members of the church participate in all the sacraments and their participation in the gathering for the performance of a sacrament is necessary – the presence of at least two or three members is necessary. This is the meaning of royal priesthood, or of general priesthood.

The exclusion of the priesthood of women

From the very beginning of the Orthodox church until today a long-standing tradition has excluded the priesthood of women. It is worth mentioning that this exclusion was effected imperceptibly and silently, without any dogmatic enactment. In this company it is not necessary to recall the well-known social factors and the priestesses of idolatry, which excluded women from priesthood. However, there is an historical paradox. To appreciate this, one must study the history of ancient Greeks based on classical texts, which prove the existence of an absolute male dominance that almost completely eliminated women's participation in culture. On the other hand, in the culture that was cultivated by the life of the church one may easily detect signs of matriarchy. In other words, church life is permeated by a delicate aura of matriarchal civilization. In texts of the Old and New Testaments, as well as in ecclesiastical patristic texts, the female presence is often dominant. More than a few female prophets are mentioned in the Old as well as the New Testament. From Deborah of the ancient biblical song, who is called the mother of Israel (Judg. 5:7), to Jael, who pierced Sisara's head with a stake and is called blessed among women (Judg. 5:24), to the praise of Ruth, Judith, Esther, etc. and to the woman of John's Revelation who surrounds the sun with twelve stars on her head (12:1-2), the matriarchal tone is distinctive. Thus, with the Virgin Mary, who fulfilled the messianic hope of salvation, the matriarchal civilization formed deeper roots and it is poetically depicted in the Akathist. The hymns to the Virgin Mary, seen from a historical and philological perspective, are related to the Song of Songs.

One might contradict this with all the things that have been repeated many times, about the unacceptable – as some regard it – disdainful and cruel attitude of some hermit monks towards women. However, despite the occasional deviations and caricatures in the life of tradition – which should naturally be expected – there is at this point a certain amount of confusion. I fear that some interpret ascetic texts through the lens of modern Puritanism. By retreating from the world, the hermit, the landless one, the high-flying eagle does not condemn, nor by any means reject women – naturally we are referring to the male hermit – but protects himself against the conventional and hypocritical world, denying any secular dependence. In this case woman is a symbol of the temptation that can bind the hermit with the conventional and hypocritical world. Therefore it is not the woman who is filthy; it is the world of hypocrisy. Strangely the world is turned upside down when some people comment on the phrase of Tertullian, which refers to woman as "the gate of hell", while people do not notice the wonderful cooperation of St Paula with St Jerome or the intense protest of a pioneering Gregory the Theologian: "Men were the lawmakers and against women did they make laws".[2] From rosebushes one picks flowers, not thorns. Finally, I would also like to state here that as Dostoyevsky gave us the best interpretation of the Lord's temptations in the legend of the Great Inquisitor, N. Kazantzakis, speaking *ad hominem*, uttered the well-known phrase, "Christ was raised by women."

According to the theological conditions stated above and the position of women in the community and culture of the church, one must recognize two things: (1) the life of the ecclesiastic body, with Christ as master of ceremonies and high priest at its head, is expressed through a variety of gifts, and consequently through carriers of those gifts, with a total equality among members, as occurs naturally in a body; and (2) the offer of the gifts by Christ the master of ceremonies and high priest is effected according to the particular nature and the receptivity of each member, while the equality among them remains unshaken.

Therefore the long-standing tradition of the church excluded women from priesthood without, however, instituting or developing relevant theological teachings. Thus one may possibly understand the difficulty and the perplexity of newer Orthodox theologians who try theologically to support the exclusion of women from priesthood, by stating the following primary reasons:

1. Christ chose only men as his disciples and then through the apostles established the apostolic succession. But one might say that this calling and the later succession do not offer a dogmatic resolution, as clearly expressed as it should be, on such a crucial matter as women's exclusion from priesthood. Furthermore, history demonstrates that Christ, as well as the later tradition, gave women a central position. One might mention the example presented by John the Evangelist, of Christ near a well in Syhar of Samaria, explaining and revealing the highest truth about God and divine worship to a Samaritan woman laden with sin. This woman immediately becomes a preacher and apostle of this truth (John 4: 4-30). Furthermore, St Paul mentions four women who had the gift of prophecy (Acts 21:9).

2. The argument that the Virgin Mary did not have a hieratic role is also insufficient. On the one hand, according to the patristic tradition, in charismatic hierarchy the Mother of God is placed right after the Holy Trinity; on the other hand, there is no direct indication of her exclusion from priesthood. In other words, I would like to emphasize that both arguments are insufficient for two serious reasons. First, every dogmatic truth must be accurate; and second, arguments that arise *ex silentio* or *ex absentia* are historically and philologically insufficient.

3. Another argument put forth is extremely detrimental to the very nature of theology: Christ, the Word incarnate, appeared and lived as a man! This argument, apart from its inefficiency, contradicts the doctrine of Chalcedon. It was best phrased by Maximus the Confessor, who clearly states that the Word through his incarnation eliminated the difference between male and female: "First he united us in himself by removing the difference between male and female, and instead of men and women, in whom above all this manner of divi-

sion is beheld, he showed us as properly and truly to be simply human beings, thoroughly transfigured in accordance with him, and bearing his intact and completely unadulterated image, touched by no trace at all of corruption."[3]

Concluding remarks

Finally, I would like to make a suggestion to the theologians who promote these or similar theological arguments. Nothing is more powerful than the long-standing tradition and practice of the church. Consequently, wherever the church as body and community of truth is convinced that this tradition must remain unchanged, it has all the power to keep it so, without using para-theological arguments that demote women as members of the body, or pray upon the charismatic community of the ecclesiastic body. This happens because in this charismatic community the members differ in their particular characteristics and their susceptibility, but absolutely not in equality. Besides, the exclusion of women from priesthood has not diminished, nor will it diminish, the charismatic life of the church.

However, one must not be restful while such rapid and massive changes in history are taking place. In my personal opinion the Roman Catholic Church will sooner or later adopt women's priesthood. What will Orthodoxy do then? The Orthodox church must be prepared not with corrosive and harmful theological arguments, but with a flawless social structure of its life, whereby men and women will work in full equality, exhibiting the rich fruit of charismatic life and cultivating education and civilization.

NOTES

[1] Epektasi, 1995.
[2] PG 36, 289AB.
[3] Ambigua 41 in 91, 1309D-1312A; the English text is from Andrew Louth, *Maximus the Confessor*, The Early Church Fathers, London and New York, Routledge, 1996, p.160.

A Lutheran Perspective

REV. DR CHRISTINE GLOBIG

I come from Germany, where the question of the ministry of women in the church was heatedly discussed over the period 1940 to 1970. As a result, most of our churches ordain women for the ministry now.

Let me introduce you to the discussion we had in Germany, since it is still fairly recent and may be of interest for the present ecumenical dialogue. It concerned not only the ministry of women in the church in general but also the question of the calling of women as bishops. In 1992 the North Elbian Lutheran Church in Germany was the first Lutheran church worldwide to ordain a woman as bishop (Maria Jepsen). Here the debate reached a new peak: Given that a woman may be ordained as pastor, may she also be a bishop? The election of Bishop Jepsen was a signal, but it was not unchallenged, which shows how sensitive a subject the spiritual authority of women is, even today.

Meanwhile three women have been ordained as Lutheran bishops in Germany. When the second woman was elected in 1999, there were still protests, though weaker than the first time. Among others there was the argument that Margot Kässmann would not be able to accommodate her ministry with her role as a mother. This is an argument which is typical for the German situation. At the beginning, ordained women pastors were not allowed to get married to avoid this conflict. Margot Kässmann has four daughters. In 1999 she could dispel this argument easily and ironically by pointing out that her male competitor had five sons.

But what of the theological discussion about the ministry of women in the church? At the basis of the Lutheran understanding of the ministry there is the distinction between the common priesthood of all baptized Christians and the ordained ministry. In the ordained ministry, one person, who is called by Christ and commissioned by the congregation, takes responsibility. The priesthood of all believers applies to all baptized Christians. There is no fundamental differentiation in their spiritual qualification: they are all capable of discernment in spiritual questions and they all are able to follow a vocation and minister if they are called.

What, now, if a woman is called? What if the congregation needs this woman as pastor, deems her competent for the ministry and wants to appoint her? What if there are women that have received the necessary theological training? (In Germany women have been allowed to study theology since around 1910.) What if there is dire need in the congregations, because there are no pastors (as was the case in Germany during the second world war, which was also the time when women were first ordained for the ministry).

Are there any reasons to reject the ministry of a woman, only because she is a woman?

The Lutheran tradition as represented in the German context does not hold the concept of a succession from an exclusively male apostolic ministry to the ordained ministry of men today. Reading the New Testament, we find that Jesus was accompanied by a discipleship of women and men. For the early church research has pointed out that more women had official functions in the congregation than we were aware of. The historic sources say that some women were called apostles: the Easter witness Mary Magdalene, Junia, who is mentioned in the 16th chapter of the epistle to the Romans, and the disciple of Paul, Thekla.

Thus the statements of the New Testament and the early church support the notion of the priesthood of all believers. All believers were invested with spiritual authority, and there were different ministries, for which both men and women were appointed if the congregation recognized their charisma. Within this concept there is no exclusively male tradition of the ministry, even though missionary ministry and church leadership were predominantly held by men at the beginning and exclusively held by men in the course of history.

Luther's position on the question of the ministry of women was a dichotomous one.

Being baptized, women partake of the priesthood of all believers, and their principal spiritual qualification is the same as that of men. But since their duty and task is in the home, they should not be leaders in the church. This is the perspective of the 16th century, in which the female area of activity was the home only. It is important to note that Luther's primary concern was that of spiritual authority, which in his opinion is given to all baptized Christians, men and women alike. Everything else is secondary and a question of propriety and order.

Those who stand up for the ordination of women from a Lutheran perspective say that things have changed with regard to this secondary question. Women are not solely working in the home any more. They have all kinds of jobs, they take over public responsibility. Thus we have the responsibility to send women into the ministry if they are qualified.

On the other hand there is the argument – which we also heard in our Lutheran discussion and which might play a role in our discussion today – that this is an inadequate and modernistic "democratic" interpretation of the concept of the priesthood of all believers, whereas this priesthood really refers to a spiritual quality that has nothing to do with public responsibility.

Frankly speaking, I am sceptical as far as this argument is concerned. Luther clearly understood the priesthood of all believers as a calling for responsibility in the church and in society. The New Testament and the early church do not testify that the calling as Christians was limited to an inner attitude or loving relationships. Nor was this the case for women. On the contrary. From the beginning, being a Christian implied being gifted for specific tasks, which we later called "ministry". These ministries were responsible tasks and within their scope they were public tasks. If women performed baptisms, which Tertullian reports for the beginning of the 3rd century (even though he did not approve), these were public acts.

The scope of women was not restricted to tasks within the family or social tasks within the congregation; they had public tasks or ministries – until man-dominated structures pushed them back.

According to the Lutheran understanding the ministry is a public ministry, based on the appointment by the congregation. (A basic confessional document, the *Confessio Augustana*, states that no one can teach publicly in the church or administer the sacraments if he or she is not legally commissioned.) Commissioned by their congregations, women can assume this public ministry today, since their spiritual qualification has never been questioned. Paul says, "Here is neither man nor woman... you are all one in Christ."

By now our congregations hold the ministry of women in high esteem, since it is an enormous enrichment of spiritual life. Our experience with women in the ministry, which we gained over the last fifty years, is positive.

My wish for the ecumenical dialogue is that we will be able to share with others these positive experiences and our theological convictions. On the other hand we, as churches that ordain women, have to admit: our experience is young, new – compared to church history – and the arguments we had were not always easy. Therefore we may be only beginners. But so far the road is full of promise.

Ecumenical Developments in Ordination Rites

REV. DR JAMES F. PUGLISI

The latter part of the 20th century witnessed a renewal in the liturgies, rites and ways in which Christians worshipped the Lord. One of the rites most frequently revised was the liturgical office for the ordination of ministers. Many different ecclesial traditions are represented in these revisions. Some churches have a long-standing, fixed tradition of ordaining that may be traced back to their origins while others are more free in choosing elements that seem best suited to the time and circumstance.

Even though ordination rites for many churches are considered "occasional services" because they do not take place with a defined regularity or are not considered as necessary for salvation, they do, in fact, have a particular importance for the ecumenical relations between churches. This importance is due to the fact that the question of the mutual recognition of ministries is an essential element for the unity of the churches. While the ecumenical dialogues between churches have produced some astounding results, the question of the ordained ministry continues to haunt the churches. We might have any number of ecumenical agreements on baptism, eucharist, spirituality, etc. but if we do not recognize each other's ministry then these agreements have little meaning. This is also the reason why the question of ministry is linked so closely to that of ecclesiology, the structuring of the church and its institutions. Even though different values are seen in the sacramental understanding of the different rites in the diverse churches and ecclesial communities, in most cases the same morphological elements are to be observed that could lead to a common understanding of what the churches are doing when they ordain or when they baptize and so forth.

It is clear that all of the churches have had to recover the principal purpose of these rites. Hence we can speak of a liturgical renewal. However, this renewal takes different forms. For some traditions, like the Orthodox and Catholic, this renewal is a process of purifying the rites so that what was understood as the core might be understood clearly today since centuries of usage and custom had heaped up ritual actions and symbols so that the essential rite could no longer be intelligible nor understood without a long didactic explanation. Even worse, the liturgical office could be misunderstood by the faithful, as frequently was the case once the liturgy was no longer in the language of the people and the faithful became spectators and no longer the real subject of the liturgical action.[1]

On the other hand, for Protestantism the liturgical renewal, as Geoffrey Wainwright describes it, was "recapturing the fullness of a sacramental celebration in which gesture and object allowed the word to be seen – and indeed handled (1 John 1:1) and tasted (Heb. 6:4f. and 1 Pet. 2:3) – as well as heard".[2] It is in this search that all of the ecclesial traditions find themselves converging towards the same sources: the word of God in the Bible and the lived experiences of the first generations of Christians in the patristic sources and their early liturgical expressions.

The worship of the church, then, has an important place in our grasping of the reality of who we are as a people made just by the grace of God. This grace of God structures our relationships with God and with one another and the world in which we live. Hence for the Lutheran canonist, Hans Dombois, what becomes the central point in our understanding of what happens in worship is the knowledge of "how God encounters humanity and how humanity encounters God, in order to form relations in our acts of worship and, from here, in the way the members of the body of Christ comport themselves".[3] I have tried to demonstrate elsewhere that it is in the process of ordination that the church comes to see how the divine grace "orders" its life and what is the relationship of each of the members to one another and to God.[4] If we are to proceed together on the path to Christian unity, then we will need to evaluate the ecclesiality of our churches in order to discern the value of their ministry. This is a fresh way of looking at the question of the "validity" of ministry that allows the churches to get beyond a "pipeline" mentality of recognizing authenticity.

It could be useful to take note of a very interesting project that has been undertaken by the churches in the Scandinavian countries. I have been invited to take part. For the past several years now there has been a study project working on the understanding of ordained ministry with the intent of incorporating an emerging common understanding of the ordained ministry into renewal of rituals of ordination in these countries. The countries taking part are Denmark, Finland, Iceland, Norway and Sweden and the churches include the Lutheran, Catholic, Orthodox, Baptist, Pentecostal, Methodist, Reformed and Free churches. The scholars and pastors taking part have had a series of meetings dealing with the methodology and epistemology of ordination revision, as well as attempting to define what is meant by ordained ministry in theory and in practice, as well as considering what elements may be identified as necessary for inclusion in the rites of ordination. This project was concluded in October 2003. It is hoped that a book will be published with the case studies discussed and the concluding theses, and that this project could provide the basis for a common ordination service to be used in the Nordic countries. It might pave the way for similar projects in geographic regions where the churches have much in common.

Ordination as a process

What I thought would be helpful in this paper is to consider the areas of convergence in some of the revision work that has been done in recent years in the rites of ordination in some churches. A starting-point for the consideration of ordination rites is to consider that the term "ordination" itself represents one element of what can rightly be seen as a process comprising the classical continuum of *electio-ordinatio-iurisdictio*. The history of ordination is an unfortunate history of the break-up of this continuum into its component parts whose meaning becomes absolutized when taken in isolation from the ecclesial process. Theological concepts eventually found in the West, such as the separation of the power of order from the power of jurisdiction, are illustrative of the breakdown of this process.

This process may be described as *ecclesial, liturgical, juridical* and *confessional*. It is truly ecclesial since the whole church is involved (meaning of the election by the people and clergy); it is liturgical because it is composed of a symbolic network (including the imposition of hands) and involves an epiclesis or invocation of the whole assembly; it is juridical for the newly ordained are immediately inserted into their new ministry and carry out their role by functioning in the office they have received which involves a pastoral charge for the edification of the people of God. As Louis-Marie Chauvet has stated, "The ritual gestures of the church are *not simple appendages* that accompany the faith: they constitute *formative elements* of faith."[5] Hence by reflecting on this ecclesial, liturgical and juridical process we may further comprehend its confessional nature, since the process involves the recognition and confirmation of the apostolicity of the ordaining church as well as allowing us to see in its foundation a balanced trinitarian theology of ordination because Christology and pneumatology are articulated together.

What do the rites have in common?

In 1982 the ecumenical text known as the Lima document, *Baptism, Eucharist and Ministry*, was published by the Faith and Order commission of the World Council of Churches.[6] In the fifth part of the section on ministry the churches reflected on the understanding of ordination and its ritual elements. The consensus reached here proved to be important for all future revisions made by individual churches of their ordination offices. This text places an essential biblical act at the core of what the churches believe needs to be contained in ordination rites, namely, that "the church ordains certain of its members for the ministry in the name of Christ by the invocation of the Spirit and the laying-on of hands (1 Tim. 4:14; 2 Tim. 1:6)..."[7] The text furthermore states that "the act of ordination by the laying-on of hands of those appointed to do so is at one and the same time invocation of the Holy Spirit (epiclesis); sacramental sign; acknowledgment of gifts and commitment".[8] In this ecumenical consensus statement the churches have recognized some essential elements that need to be present in ordination: laying-on of hands, invocation of the Spirit with the gesture being performed by those appointed to do so. While these are precise acts there is still latitude in the definition of how these will be carried out and how the churches decide who is the appropriate person to perform these acts.

From this core of ritual action many other elements might be included to help in the conveying of what actually is taking place during the ordination ritual and to what purpose. Hence churches have traditionally conceived of different ways of imposing hands (actually touching the person to extending the hands over the head, etc.), or formulating the invocation (with a pre-determined formula which is part of a long tradition or by simple invocation, sometimes declarative) or designating who will perform these acts (an individual whose office pertains to the ordination or to the ordaining conferences as in the Methodist church).

In addition to these some churches have so-called secondary rites or symbolic gestures. Some of these include anointing, the handing-on of a sign of the office received (the *porrectio instrumentorum*), the positioning in a particular part of the church (which may have symbolic significance as in Oriental liturgies) and vesting of the individual ordained. While all the churches do not hold these to be essential, from a study of the evolution of these additions it is possible to see how the central or core elements of an ordination can be obfuscated and even the meaning of the ministry eschewed.[9] The process of revising the ordination services has taken into account this factor.

However, from the revisions made to the Latin Catholic church's ordination rites in 1990, we can see that once again there is the tendency to give more importance to secondary elements through the addition of formulas. For example, in the ordination of a bishop the eloquent gesture of the imposition of hands and imposition of the gospels on his head is becoming more and more clouded by additional rites intended to "clarify" the meaning of the bishop's ministry in the church. In the revisions of the liturgy following the Second Vatican Council, these rites were simplified and in fact the giving of the pastoral staff, mitre, ring, pectoral cross, gospels was done in silence without any formula.

However, in the second typical edition of the Pontifical (1990), which by the way has just been translated into English, all of these rites are now accompanied by a formula. What is even more curious is that while the newly ordained keeps all of the symbols of his office (ring, mitre, pectoral cross, crosier) he hands the book of the gospel received back to the deacon and then is presented to the people with all the signs of power, status, etc. *except* for the one that really counts, the gospels! Even though the formulae may be beautiful and biblical, the ordination rite has now again been cluttered by secondary elements with the giving of symbols and new formulae of conferral. In the mind of the people what is being transmitted? We might say that there is an inherent danger that is lurking beneath the signs, i.e., a mutation of sense: from that of the bishop who presides over the building-up of the people of God entrusted to him as an authentic pastor, to one that sees the bishop as a figure of status and power; this is the very process that took over in the Middle Ages.

We do not wish to speak against liturgical garb which has its place in celebration but, with the 5th-century pope who admonished the bishops of southern Gaul for trying to distinguish themselves by distinctive garb, we feel that its significance is more spiritual than material[10] and that the essential of the office is seen most clearly when the rites keep in focus the central core of the invocation with the imposition of hands. Hence a caution that other churches do not follow suit, adding more to the essential rite of ordination than is necessary for its correct understanding.

It is interesting to observe that many of the churches began ordination revision more or less around the same time, in the late 1960s and early 1970s. One is tempted to venture a guess as to why this is so. Could it be because the rites no longer spoke to people, or was there a crisis in understanding the role of the ordained ministry in the contemporary world? Most probably both of these were at the root of the reason why the churches began taking a look at what they did in the area of ordination services. To this must be added the insights coming from the work achieved at the level of ecumenical reflection and dialogue as well as biblical, patristic and liturgical studies all being carried out with an irenic spirit.

In these revisions many of the churches reconsidered the prayer of ordination as well as the symbolic or ritual dimensions of the liturgical offices. This revision is another source of convergence. For example we may see several sources which have served either as models or even as the proper texts chosen for the revisions. For the office of bishop, revisions in the Anglican communion have considered the texts from the Church of South India,[11] the Anglican Methodist Ordinal project[12] and the ordination prayer of the *Apostolic Tradition* of Hippolytus of Rome.[13] Of interest to note is the fact that, until the recent revisions, the United Methodist Church in the United States has used more or less the same texts as a basis for their revision of the consecration of bishops. For the ordination prayer for presbyters and deacons, both of these tradition rely principally on the prayers that have been used in the unity scheme between the Anglican and Methodist churches as well as the traditional source. The British Methodist service book from 1975 also used the texts from the Church of South India as well as the material prepared for the unity proposal. However in the recent revision, *The Methodist Worship Book*, the prayer is a new composition of biblical quotes but also maintains a flavour of the former prayer. In addition, we find a diaconal order of ministry for both men and women which has evolved from the Wesley deaconess order. This development is to be applauded and obviously takes seriously the challenge of the BEM document which encourages churches to consider the value in the diaconal ministry. This challenge has been taken up by other churches as well.[14] Furthermore, we can observe that the setting for the ordination offices in both the Anglican communion and the Methodist churches is the eucharist, one more element of convergence towards a common understanding of the ordained ministry.

Likewise in the Lutheran churches we find the common elements of the imposition of hands and prayer and the context of a eucharistic celebration. From the variety of Lutheran ordination services in Europe and North America, we may observe two basic traditions: one which follows closely the pattern established by Luther's revision and the other which follows the model established by Bugenhagen.[15] In many of the new Lutheran services the prayer of ordination has a fully developed epiclesis which goes in the direction of the suggestion of BEM. Frank Senn has noted that an attempt to achieve a uniformity of structure in the rites of the Evangelical Lutheran Church in America and other Lutheran churches did not meet with success since there was a lack of agreement on the doctrine of the ministry.[16] A further issue is the question of the role of bishops in the new Evangelical Lutheran Church in America. This question continues to arise in the American context especially in terms of the concordat between the Episcopal and Lutheran churches. There is considerable similarity between the offices for the ordination of pastors and the installation of deaconess in the Lutheran church and the liturgies for the ordination of priests and deacons in the American Episcopal church.[17]

What are some ecumenical implications?

The implications for ecumenism can be organized along two axes. The first concerns the dialogues between the churches, and the second has to do with the life and institutions of the churches themselves.

a) Implications for ecumenical dialogue

It is important to give pride of place to the practices of the churches regarding the ordained ministry of governance, and the process of election-ordination. By pointing up the distance that may exist between, on the one hand, the theoretical statements made by the churches in ecumenical debate and, on the other hand, the ecclesial reality found in concrete church life, we may contribute towards the understanding of the increase or the decrease of these gaps. In those instances where the theoretical (i.e., the doctrinal) is borne out of the institutions of a given church, the distance is narrowed, but in a case where the practice of a particular church does not reflect in reality its own doctrinal positions, then the distance between the two poles gapes wider, and the truth expressed on the theoretical plane is directly impugned.[18]

Already some ecumenical dialogues have chosen a method that takes into consideration the institutional practices of the churches, in particular liturgical institutions such as the sacraments of initiation, the eucharist and ordination.[19] Reflection of this kind has the advantage of determining the relationship between the *lex orandi* and the *lex credendi*,[20] as well as being able to evaluate correctly the value the individual churches attach to worship in their theological reflection. What rich sources the liturgy and the liturgical assembly represent for theology, and how much they reveal of the inherent balances or imbalances (for example, the entire process of election-ordination in the apostolic Tradition, attributed to Hippolytus of Rome, the later formulas, the loss of meaning of the formulas of consecration, absolute ordinations and vocations, etc.)! This *locus theologicus* affords the churches the opportunity to confront their theological discourse with their actual practice.

b) "The one and the many" as a dynamic to explore

The relationship between "the one" and "the many" is still a problem that needs clarification, between dialogue partners in the concrete exercise of ordained ministry and in the relationship between "local church" and "universal church" (for example, the disappearance of a ministry of unity in certain churches, the reduction of the number of ministries to a sole monolithic ministry, the supremacy of power concentrated in and exercised by one local church over all the churches, the suppression of the effective role of the faithful of a given locality in the choice of their ministers, etc.). Now, in order to restore communion among the churches, we need a correct balance and proper relationship between the two elements of the dyad, "one" and "many". This dynamic is found in the institutions of the early church and it is revelatory of the communal relationship that characterized it, as seen in the letters of communion, the synods and councils, and especially in the process of the ordination of the heads of the local churches and in their representative role within their own church and among the other churches. It is interesting to note that certain ecumenical dialogues have had recourse to a method that accords much importance both to doctrinal discussion (especially in Christology, pneumatology and ecclesiology) and to ecclesial institutions as well, that is, the institutions and structural organs of the concrete life of each church. Such a dialogue can only grow deeper, as it calls upon both theory and practice within the churches.

c) The advantage of the communal model for dialogue

We must not overlook the importance of the communal model which was at the root of the life and the thinking of the early church. The study of the apostolic tradition and the procedures of the early churches is particularly revealing.[21] The apostolic tradition, with its roots in scripture and Tradition and its long history of far-reaching influence, must really be considered the point of departure for all ecumenical discussion among the churches. It is far easier to consider the rituals of the "mainline" churches, but we should not overlook the "evangelical" – or "pentecostal" – type communities. These perspectives are all the more pertinent since they take into consideration the reality of the local church and the visible elements of its ecclesial life, which is the best approach for discussions with the Pentecostal and Evangelical churches.

d) The eschatological and sacramental aspect of ordained ministry

The reflection on the relationship between doctrine and worship also enables us to focus on the gift of unity given to the church in a broader eschatological context, as being a unity that is yet to be realized.[22] This is possible since it results from a better balance between, on the one hand, the Christological and pneumatological meaning and, on the other, the eschatological function, both of which are attributed to ordained ministry in the structuring of the church and in its administration of the various ministries, that is to say, in the role that ordained ministry has to play in the building-up of the church as the actualization of the presence of Christ in the world (Luke 10:16) and as his envoy to the whole world to bring it the good news (Acts 2) of reconciliation (2 Cor. 5). Thus understood, the church is both the place of gathering and of dispersion for the spreading of the gospel. The task of gathering the people into one place and of sending out the church is entrusted to the ordained ministers, and is realized precisely in the koinonia of the Spirit and of the community the Spirit has created.

We recall that the meaning for the church of the ordained ministry's very creation consists in the perception that the church is still being built up (it is convoked in the name of another, namely, by the word emanating from God); the church is also sent on mission (the historical dimension which links a particular community to the One who was first sent) and, through the proclamation of the gospel and the celebration of the sacraments, the church is understood according to the vision of the eschatological banquet which has already begun on earth but is not yet fully realized.[23] The eschatological perspective also draws the attention formerly given to the person of the minister back towards the ministry as a charism given to the church for its service, "to equip the saints for the work of ministry, for building up the body of Christ, until all of us come to the unity of the faith and of the knowledge of the Son of God, to maturity, to the measure of the full stature of Christ" (Eph. 4:12-13).

We need to note that, although all the churches do not use the word "sacrament" for the conferral of ordination, a sacramental dimension is expressed in the practice of the churches, for the ministry is always seen as an investiture by the Spirit who grants to the ordained a specific *exousia* (function and power) to gather together the community and preside over it in the name of Christ.[24]

The ecumenical importance of the demonstration of this fact, according to the actual practice of these churches, lies in the possibility that the doctrine *(lex credendi)* faithfully represents the practice itself of the churches (especially those churches who still hesitate to apply the concept of sacrament to the conferral of ordination). This goal will be more easily reached, too, if the proper balance between the Christological and pneumatological dimensions of ordained ministry is restored to what we find in the New Testament, where Christ is present in history and in the church through the Spirit. This balance is to be seen in the sacramental epiclesis of the prayers of ordination.

e) Based on a reflection on the practice of ordination in the churches, we may ask if there is not some sort of succession relative to the transmissible part of the apostolic ministry

One thing is clear from a careful study of the texts of ordination: each church follows in the line of continuity from the church of the apostles, and its ministries are described as a service of this continuity. According to the texts, ordination always contains a dimension that confesses the apostolic faith of the whole church. The scrutiny or examination before the people of course bears witness to the candidate's moral qualities, but even more to his apostolic faith. His acceptance by the neighbouring bishops, and their required participation at the imposition of hands and the epiclesis, acknowledge that the faith of the church concerned is in accord with that of the church of the apostles. Since the existing ministers always have a decisive role in the admission of their new colleagues into the ministry, can we not speak of a succession? At least in the concrete realities there is a secondary transmission from ministers to ministers, for God is always the principal actor.

There is a second aspect that we very likely could call apostolic. These texts always attribute an active *episcope* to the ministers: they have the responsibility of watching faithfully over the apostolic faith (i.e., preserving the teaching of Christ), and to be worthy stewards of this faith (responsible for the pastoral ministry of governance and of the building-up of the church) at the same time that they stand "facing" the church (they must inspire their brothers and sisters in their responsibility for the faith and for the apostolic mission of the church, and even exercise the power of the keys).

Of course, the minister cannot be separated from his church, and the succession is a succession *within* the church.[25] Traditionally, this succession is acceded to through the imposition of hands (by those charged with this task) and through the epiclesis, the work of the whole church.

f) The restoration of the diaconate as an ecumenical step

Following on Vatican II (for the Latin Catholic church) and the multilateral dialogue (for the Protestant churches), the revival of the diaconate, henceforth permanently established, has as a consequence restored beyond all ambiguity the tripartite character of the ordained ministry in the churches of the West. For this reason, this restoration in the ecclesial traditions of the Protestants deserves special study. When the Western churches restore the diaconate, they are renewing contact with the patristic tradition and with that of the Orthodox church, which has always preserved it. So the ordained ministry as a "triad" is an important element for the theology of today and for ecumenical dialogue.

Implications for the life and the institutions of the churches

Since the churches, in the ecumenical dialogues, are not giving enough attention to the importance of the concrete ecclesial life and institutions of each church, in this last point we would like to point out a few implications for the process of purification and conversion to the light of the gospel that each one of the churches must undergo in order to realize the full communion desired by Christ.[26]

a) The concrete processes of ordination demonstrate that ordination amounts to the full acceptance of the ministers among the participating churches.

The focusing of this theological reflection on the ecclesial processes could help the churches themselves come to a clearer recognition of where they stand, and bring them to focus more sharply on *their ecclesial reality as seen in the concrete acts, relationships, and structures that make up the life of their church.* This way of proceeding could lead to a narrowing of the gap between the discourse of a church and its actual practices. The morphological sameness that we have found in almost all the rituals could contribute to this process.

So the real question for the ecumenical movement is not only to produce declarations or agreements on principles. We certainly have no intention of denying the need for bi- and multi-lateral dialogues; on the contrary, these discussions are very important for the effort to reach consensus, in order to discover the will of God for God's people. But we need to note to what degree is the concrete life and structure of the local churches traditionally the place of acceptance of the authenticity of another church, in the recognition of its apostolicity, and the building-up of the catholicity of the unique church of Christ. So the basic issue is the restoration, at least partial, of the theological and ecclesial processes of reception. It is up to the local churches to take once again the initiative in this reception, even if it is only partial, for it will help restore communion among the local churches and in this way rebuild the unity of the *Catholica*. This means, of course, that local churches must proceed in such a way as not to harm the communion that already exists; with well thought-out acts and the consensus of all in a given locality, they can provide the impetus to use approaches that will lead to full communion.[27]

As for the "validity" of the ministries of other churches, the question should not be put in those highly restrictive terms such as "matter", "form", "intention", etc., which belong to a minimalist sacramental theology. One can re-focus the debates onto the level of "ecclesiality" and the ecclesial processes that structure each church. The ministry serves the structuring of the church through ecclesial acts that are at the same time sacramental, communal, epicletic and juridical. One can only rejoice at the declaration of the dialogue between Anglicans and Catholics in the United States that speaks of "a new context" in which the question of Anglican orders can and must be explored.[28] This context is that of a better balanced ecclesiology of the communion of the local churches.

b) Reflection on the history of the practice of the churches reveals astonishing similarities in morphological (pertaining to form) identity and in the functions of the pastoral ministry, despite differences in dogmatic expression. How may this fact help the churches find solutions to the problems that still divide them?

Moreover, reflection on the pastoral charge of governance in the churches puts the churches themselves in contact with a part of their history that they may have forgotten. We have seen that the intuitions represented by the early rituals reveal theological balances, which have not always been preserved in the rituals in use today: returning to them may help the churches to find a better balance not only in the processes of admission to the ordained ministries, but also in those institutions that structure all of Christian life. These processes, in order to be fully Christian, must be trinitarian in structure, such as we find in scripture and that were taken for granted in the life of the church during the first millennium, before the separation of the Eastern and Western churches and the sundering of the church during the Reformation. This trinitarian structure is manifest in the sacramental processes through which the church is continually built up. It is through reference to this structure that we have been able to pinpoint "deviations" in the practice of the church, but convergences as well, and it is precisely through recourse to this trinitarian structure as the basis for common reflection that the churches may be able to overcome their divisions.

With this as our goal, we must of course give some thought together to the concrete problems that must be resolved: the "lack of vocations", the push for greater participation of the faithful in the life of the church, the problems ministers must face in new social and cultural contexts, the preparation of the ministers, the matter of their morale, the question of celibacy, etc. Each tradition can contribute to the formulation of solutions. In this context, concrete and frank questions can be put to one another in the light of the gospel by the local churches in a given region; for example, what is the concrete and institutional character of the grace lived by each church in its structural reality, in the sacraments celebrated. Here we approach the intuition of Hans Dombois who thinks, "If the ancient churches knew what they were doing, and if they limited themselves to those things, and if the churches of the Reformation did what they claimed, we would be very close to the unity of Christians."[29]

As for the structuring of the churches, the type of theological reflection suggested allows us to evaluate the ecclesiality of each, on the basis of the concrete processes in which the individual church reveals how it understands its relationship to the one church of Christ and to the other churches. The rituals themselves display the relationships that exist within each church and between churches: relationships between the Christians of a particular church and the structuring of that church. In a word, as H. Dombois has written, "It is a question of knowing how God encounters man [sic!], and how man encounters God, and of perceiving the interplay of the different acts of worship, and in them, to observe the way in which the different members of the body of Christ interact."[30] It is at this juncture that the churches begin to take a good look at the way in which they integrate new members, at the way in which they structure themselves on the basis of those concrete processes,[31] and at the way each church relates to God and to the world to which it is sent to serve. To sum up: each local church will seek to understand the others through their institutional structures and therefore through the gift of the grace received (there is no conflict between grace and structure), and to understand the Christian reality of its members based on their role in those structures.[32] This then is the challenge that looking at ordination rites offers us when we do this from the point of view of a theological and ecclesiological analysis, not one that is purely liturgico-historical.

NOTES

[1] Y. Congar, "L''Ecclesia' ou communauté chrétienne, sujet intégral de l'action liturgique", in J.-P. Jossua and Y. Congar eds, *La liturgie après Vatican II. Bilans, études, prospective, Unam Sanctam, 66*, Paris, Cerf, 1967, pp.241-82.

[2] G. Wainwright, *Worship with One Accord: Where Liturgy and Ecumenism Embrace*, New York, Oxford UP, 1997, p.128.

[3] "*Es geht darum, wie hier Gott dem Menschen, der Mensch Gott begegnet, um die Relationen, die sich im gottesdienstlichen Handeln, und damit auch im Umgang der Glieder am Leibe Christi miteinander ausbilden.*" See Dombois's monumental work *Das Recht der Gnade. Ökumenisches Kirchenrecht Bd. I*, Witten, Luther Verlag, 1969, p.37.

[4] J.F. Puglisi, *The Process of Admission to Ordained Ministry: A Comparative Study*, 4 vols, Collegeville, Liturgical Press, 1996-2001. Here I have attempted to study the ecclesiological and liturgical structures of ordination in the Catholic, Lutheran, Reformed, Anglican and Methodist churches from the point of view of seeing how the church is structured by the grace of God.

[5] L.-M. Chauvet, *Du symbolique au symbole. Essai sur les sacrements*, Paris, Cerf, 1979, p.85.

[6] Published as Faith and Order Paper no. 111, WCC, 1982, hereafter cited as BEM followed by the section letter and number of paragraph. See the comments on the noted convergences as a result of this dialogue as well as others, E. Lanne, "Convergences sur le ministère ordonné", in G.R. Evans and M. Gourgues eds, *Communion et réunion: Mélanges Jean-Marie Roger Tillard, Bibliotheca Ephemeridum Theologicarum Lovaniensium, 121*, Louvain, Univ. Press, 1995, pp.351-61.

[7] BEM, §39.

[8] *Ibid.*, §41.

[9] Cf. *The Process of Admission*, vol. 1, pp.154-77.

[10] See the letter of Celestine I who declared in 428 that in Rome there was no distinction proper to a bishop except the life he is to lead! Celestine I, *Ep. IV, Ad episcopos*, I (PL 50,431).

[11] *Church of South India: The Book of Common Worship as Authorized by the Synod of 1962*, London, Oxford UP, 1963.

[12] Anglican-Methodist Unity Commission, *Anglican-Methodist Unity. I: The Ordinal*, London, SPCK, 1968.

[13] G.J. Cuming, *Hippolytus: A Text for Students*, 2nd ed. reprint, Grove Liturgical Study, 8, Bramcote, UK, Grove, 1991, as well as P.F. Bradshaw, M.E. Johnson and L.E. Philips, *The Apostolic Tradition: A Commentary*, Hermenia, Minneapolis, Fortress, 2002.

[14] For example see the work of B. Bürki, "Diaconat et doctrines des ministères", in P. Pilly et al., *De geste et parole: Vingt ans de ministère diaconal dans les Églises réformées de la Suisse romande*, Geneva, Labor et Fides, 1987, pp.67-101.

[15] *The Process of Admission*, vol. 2, pp.23-26, 38f.; R.F. Smith, *Luther, Ministry, and Ordination Rites in the Early Reformation Church*, New York, Peter Lang, 1996, and the synopsis of Lutheran ordination liturgies presented by F. Schulz, "Documentation of Ordination Liturgies", in *Roman Catholic/Lutheran Joint Commission: The Ministry in the Church*, Geneva, Lutheran World Federation, 1982, pp.35-41.

[16] F.C. Senn, "Ordination Rites as a Source of Ecclesiology", in *Dialog*, 27, 1988, pp.40-47.

[17] See the commentary of P.H. Pfatteicher, *Commentary on the Occasional Services*, Philadelphia, Fortress, 1983, pp.193f., 204-215.

[18] For example, think of the great importance given to the epiclesis in the WCC's Faith and Order document BEM, §§41f. However this "invocation to God that the new minister be given the power of the Holy Spirit..." (BEM, §42a) is not always found in the contemporary liturgies.

[19] One thinks especially of the dialogues, both international and local, between Lutherans and Catholics, and between Orthodox and Catholics.

[20] For an exegesis of this principle and its value in theological epistemology, see P. De Clerck, "'Lex orandi, lex credendi': The Original Sense and Historical Avatars of an Equivocal Adage", in *Studia Liturgica*, 24, 2, 1994, pp.178-200. The Methodist exegete and liturgist Geoffrey Wainwright has also studied the relationship between the two principles and their application to a liturgical theology by Catholics and Protestants, but with differences of opinion as to the point of departure: "They [Catholicism and Protestantism] tend to differ on the question of which of the two, doctrine or worship, should set the pace, and they differ profoundly on the question of whether either or both – the church's worship or its doctrine – may fall into error", *Doxology: The Praise of God in Worship, Doctrine and Life. A Systematic Theology*, London, Epworth/Oxford UP, 1980, p.252. This critical analysis does not prevent the writer from affirming that the churches have been able to reach common ground in the revision of their liturgies in the direction of an

authentic tradition; see id., "The Understanding of Liturgy in Light of Its History", in C. Jones, G. Wainwright and E. Yarnold eds, *The Study of Liturgy*..., 506. For the concrete application of the principle *lex orandi-lex credendi* for ordination, see P.F. Fink, "The Sacrament of Orders: Some Liturgical Reflections", in *Worship*, 56, 6, 1982, pp.482-502.

[21] See *The Process of Admission*, vol. 1, pp.10ff.

[22] For example, when Vatican Council II states that the one church of Christ "subsists" in the Catholic church without strictly identifying itself with that church *(LG* 8), it makes an eschatological affirmation that acknowledges that the mystery of the church of Christ encompasses the other churches. On the meaning of the term *subsistit in*, the Roman curia has given out two interpretations, one coming from the Congregation for Doctrine and Faith = CDF [Notification on the Book: *Church, Charisma and Power: An Essay in Militant Ecclesiology* by Fr L. Boff, OFM, *L'Osservatore romano*, n. 14, 880, 9 April 1985, pp.11f.; also published in *Origins*, 14, 42, 1985, pp.683-87; and the other interpretation coming from Cardinal Willebrands, then president of the Secretariat for Promoting Christian Unity (this was a lecture delivered at the National Workshop for Christian Unity in Atlanta on 5 May 1987: "Vatican II's Ecclesiology of Communion", in *Origins*, 17, 2, 1987, pp.27-33), and more recently taken up by Cardinal Kasper. We do not know whether Willebrands's lecture was a response to the statement of J. Ratzinger or not; however, it is certain that this statement provoked much consternation in the Protestant communities as we see in the article by the eminent Methodist observer at the Council, A. Outler, "Protestant Observer at Vatican II Surveys Ecumenism Today", in *Origins*, 16, 4, 1986, pp.253-57, with an allusion to the CDF's, "Notification" on p.257.

A last contribution to this discussion would be the two lectures delivered in Rome by F. Sullivan, SJ, former professor of ecclesiology at the Gregorian University. In these two lectures he goes into a fuller exploration of the conciliar documents, the preparatory texts *De Ecclesia* and *De Oecumenismo* and their evolution, the *relationes* and *modi*, and the documents *Mystici Corporis, Mysterium Ecclesiae* and *Notificatio* to show that the interpretation of the CDF is not that of the fathers of the council; see F.A. Sullivan, "'Substitit in': The significance of Vatican II's decision to say of the church of Christ not that it 'is' but that it 'subsists in' the Roman Catholic Church", in *One in Christ*, 22, 2, 1986, pp.115-23, reproduced in id., *The Church We Believe In: One, Holy, Catholic and Apostolic*, New York/Mahwah NJ, Paulist, 1988, pp.23-33; and id., "The Decree on Ecumenism: Presuppositions and Consequences", in *One in Christ*, 26, 1-2, 1990, pp.7-19.

[23] See *The Process of Admission*, vol. 1, pp.191ff.

[24] Note that there is an overture made in BEM §§41-44 towards the sacramentality of ordination.

[25] This is the meaning of *charisma veritatis* in St Irenaeus, who does not understand it as a personal gift but links it to the entire community. The bishop does not therefore bear personal witness, but communal witness.

[26] See the call of Vatican II: "Christ summons the church, as she goes her pilgrim way, to that continual reformation of which she always has need, insofar as she is an institution of men here on earth. Consequently, if, in various times and circumstances, there have been deficiencies in moral conduct or in church discipline, or even in the way that church teaching has been formulated – to be carefully distinguished from the deposit of the faith itself – these should be set right at the opportune moment and in the proper way" (*Unitatis Redintegratio* 6). Again at no. 7: "There can be no ecumenism worthy of the name without interior conversion." We find a similar vision expressed by a recent declaration of the Groupe des Dombes: "...we see the ecumenical movement as a great process of conversion and reconciliation of our diversities in the quest for communion among confessional identities which, once cleansed of their unevangelical or sinful elements, can receive each other, become complementary and enrich each other. Difference is legitimate in *koinonia* (communion). Thus the churches are invited to arrive at a common recognition of what distinguishes legitimate differences from separative divergences", §153, Groupe des Dombes, *For the Conversion of the Churches* (tr. J. Greig of *Pour la conversion des églises. Identité et changement dans la dynamique de communion)*, WCC, 1993, p.64.

[27] In order to avoid the imbalances that exist in the functioning of the ordained ministries in their present structuring, the churches must pursue a course of common reflection and a path of action decided upon together in a process that will result in the restoration of an apostolic ministry recognized and received *mutually* as the ministry of Christ in the Spirit. Why this insistence on the role of the individual churches? Because only the churches who live in one same region, sharing an identical culture, are capable of bringing about a

Ecumenical Developments in Ordination Rites 241

process of tradition and reception, and of pronouncing a valid judgment that cannot be pronounced by other churches situated in different cultures. The Lutheran-Catholic dialogue in "Facing Unity: Models, Forms and Phases of Catholic-Lutheran Church Fellowship" (1985), §§120ff., see *Roman Catholic/Lutheran Joint Commission. Facing Unity: Models, Forms and Phases of Catholic-Lutheran Church Fellowship*, Geneva, LWF, 1985, pp.56ff. Since the universal church only exists embodied in local churches, it is difficult to see how the *Catholica* can exist outside of the concrete communion of all the churches. This communion, this unity, is thus built up in the life of each local church, but also among them, through concrete processes.

[28] Anglican/Roman Catholic consultation in the USA, "Anglican Orders: The Dialogue's Evolving Context", in *Origins*, 20, 9, 1990, pp.136-46. The full title is "Anglican Orders: A Report on the Evolving Context of Their Evaluation in the Roman Catholic Church". This declaration is the fruit of discussions based on certain new items of information coming from the Vatican archives that permit one to see the *Apostolicae Curae* as the beginning of a process of dialogue, rather than the end of it. We should note at §10 of this document that the important change brought about by Vatican II in the position of the Latin church relative to the sacramentality of the episcopacy has contributed to the creation of this "new context". We only regret that there was not a more explicit reference to the concrete processes of reception.

[29] *"Wenn die alten Kirchen wüssten und sich auf das beschränkten, was sie eigentlich tun, und die reformatorischen Kirchen täten, was sie verkündigen, so wären wir der Einheit der Christenheit um vieles näher"*, see *Das Recht...*, p.195.

[30] *"Es geht darum, wie hier Gott dem Menschen, der Mensch Gott begegnet, um die Relationen, die sich im gottesdienstlichen Handeln, und damit auch im Umgang der Glieder am Leibe Christi miteinander ausbilden"*, ibid., p.37.

[31] For example, one can ask the following questions: what is the structure of the sacraments of initiation, what relationship does the individual have with God and with the rest of the community, what are the ministerial relations and what is the status into which an ordained minister is brought through his ordination, what are the resulting structures of apostolicity, catholicity, and unity, and are they recognized mutually by all?

[32] This is, in part, the extension of the method we used in our study of the ordained ministry and of the election-ordination.

Ordination in the Eastern Churches

REV. DR PAUL F. BRADSHAW

I must at the outset enter a caveat. Not only am I not a member of one of the Eastern churches, but I cannot even claim special expertise on their contemporary theology and practice. I am a historian of liturgy who, among other things, has made a study of the historical evolution of the ordination rites of the various Eastern churches, and so it is chiefly upon that knowledge that I propose to draw in this short presentation, although I have taken the precaution of showing what I have written to some Eastern scholars in order to avoid, so far as I can, misrepresenting the current theology and practice of those churches.

The Eastern traditions are all familiar with three principal orders of ministry – bishops, presbyters and deacons – as well as two minor orders, sub-deacon and reader. Some traditions also have rites for appointment to a variety of other offices, such as archdeacon or patriarch. In some traditions, the ancient manuscripts include formularies for deaconesses, but this office has generally fallen out of use in the course of history. Ordinations nearly always take place on a Sunday or other holy day. Bishops are usually ordained towards the beginning of a celebration of the eucharist, so that they can then preside over the entire rite, although the Maronite and Syrian Orthodox traditions defer the ordination until after the eucharistic consecration is complete so that the elements may be used in the act of ordination. Arrangements for the ordination of presbyters vary: some ordain at the beginning of the rite, others after the entry of the eucharistic gifts, so that the new presbyter may participate in the eucharistic prayer, and others after the consecration, just as in the case of some rites for bishops. A similar variety is also found in the case of the diaconate.

At the core of nearly all Eastern rites of ordination is a formula, the function of which historically was to announce the results of the appointment of the ordinand, whether by election or some other means, and then to ask the gathered community to pray for the person so chosen. It thus functioned as the "hinge", as it were, between the two central parts of the process of ordination: election and prayer, and there is evidence to suggest that an early version of it was already current in Antioch before the end of the 4th century. At one time it was probably in two parts, with the people present responding to the announcement of the appointment of the ordinand with the cry "worthy", before they were asked to pray for him, as is evidenced by the Armenian rite. In other traditions this acclamation now comes at the end of the whole rite rather than at the beginning.

This proclamation/bidding formulary is interesting for what it has to say about the nature of ordination. It varies in its form between the different churches of the East, but let us look at the oldest known form of it in the Byzantine rite. Except for the name of the particular offices, it is virtually identical for each order. For a bishop it reads as follows:

> The divine grace, which always heals that which is infirm and supplies what is lacking, appoints the presbyter N., beloved by God, as bishop. Let us pray therefore that the grace of the Holy Spirit may come upon him.

The most striking feature of this is that it asserts that the appointment of the bishop is the action of God, and not just of the people who have elected him. "The divine grace... appoints the presbyter N... as bishop." In other words, it is God who chooses, God who ordains. Thus ordination is seen as a divine action, yet at the same time also a human one. It requires both the approbation and prayer of the whole people, and not just of the clergy. God reveals his choice of the candidate through the process of human election, and bestows what is needed for ministry in response to the petition of the people. Moreover, the formula declares that God's grace will make up for any human deficiencies in the person chosen, and thus implies that the purpose of the prayer which is to follow is centred upon this request, that the grace of the Holy Spirit will come upon him to supply whatever may be lacking.

Although, as the Eastern rites developed, the "prayer" portion became more complex and in some cases more confused, underneath all these later amplifications and duplications lie clear signs of two basic constituent elements: the prayer of the people and an ordination prayer said while hands are laid on the ordinand. The original form of the prayer of the people appears to have been a litany with one or more special petitions for the ordinand, though this has been heavily truncated or has disappeared altogether in the later developments of some of the churches. The ordination prayer itself is different for each of the three orders, bishops, presbyters and deacons. While those for presbyters and deacons tend to be quite distinct in the different Eastern ecclesiastical traditions, though with signs of some borrowing from one another in certain cases, what seems to be the oldest prayer used for the ordination of a bishop shows remarkable consistency across the ecclesiastical divides. They have all developed it in distinct ways, but its core is clearly visible in nearly every tradition, suggesting great antiquity. It centres around two principal images for the episcopate: the shepherd and the teacher or guardian of the truth. Sacerdotal or cultic imagery to describe the bishop's office seems to have had no part in the oldest strata but was added at a later stage in different ways in each of the various traditions.

Prayers for the ordination of a presbyter are more varied. What appears to be the older of the two prayers now found in the Byzantine rite, with versions in some other rites, does not make use of biblical typology at all, but asks that the ordinand may be worthy to stand at the altar, to exercise the ministry of the word, to offer gifts and spiritual sacrifices, and to renew the people by baptism. The other versions tend to modify the reference to the ministry of the word, since this later ceased to be a regular function of the presbyterate, and to introduce the term "priest" or "priesthood", as this became the common designation for the presbyterial office. The independent prayers found in other traditions generally also feature the ministry of the word as the chief function of the presbyterate, with the ministry of healing, of baptizing, and of celebrating the eucharist as subordinate activities.

Like ordination prayers in the East, when it comes to the diaconate there is a reticence to say explicitly what a deacon is called to do – presumably because there was a lack of agreed understanding as to exactly what the diaconate was for. Some use the typology of St Stephen and some do not. Some indicate that his ministry was in some way connected to the eucharist, but are usually not specific even about this. What is sought in the prayers are not powers to fulfil particular functions but appropriate personal qualities.

Not surprisingly, the principal ritual gesture in all rites is the imposition of the hand. Because Eastern traditions have generally followed the rule of only ordaining one candidate to a particular office on any single occasion, they have not had to deal with the problem faced by Western traditions as to what to do about the relationship between the laying-on of hands and prayer when there are a number of candidates to be ordained at the same time. Nevertheless, this does not mean that in the East the imposition of the hand always accompanies the principal ordination prayer alone. In the course of time in many rites, as prayers and other formularies increased in number and made what had been the central prayer less obvious, there was a tendency for the imposition of the hand to begin earlier in the rite and be continued throughout many of these, and this remains the present practice.

Unlike the medieval Western tradition, which required the imposition of hands at the ordination of a bishop to be performed by all bishops present, and at the ordination of a priest by the other priests together with the bishop, in the East it is usually only the presiding bishop or archbishop who lays his hand (usually just the right hand) on the ordinand, although in some of the traditions others do associate themselves in some way with this action (e.g. by laying their hand on the ordinand's shoulders), and the presence of at least three bishops is required at the ordination of a bishop for its canonical validity.

At the ordination of a bishop there is one other significant central ritual action, and that is the use of the book of the gospels in connection with the laying- on of the hand. In the Byzantine tradition the open book is placed on the head and neck of the ordinand by the archbishop before the imposition of his hand; in the Maronite and Syrian Orthodox traditions it is held over the ordinand's head by two other bishops during the imposition of the hand; in the East Syrian tradition the ordinand's back is used as a lectern on which the book is placed for a reading and it is left there during the imposition of the hand; while the Coptic tradition reserves the ceremony exclusively for the consecration of the Alexandrian patriarch and not any other bishops, paralleling the ancient Roman practice which restricted the ceremony to the ordination of the bishop of Rome alone and not any other episcopal ordinations. The roots of these varied practices appear to go back at least to the 4th century if not before, and the earliest version seems to have involved deacons holding the book over the head of the episcopal candidate. Explanations offered by early Eastern commentators as to its meaning are diverse, and none of them seem to have the ring of authenticity. Probably the original purpose had quickly become forgotten. However, if one may hazard a guess on the basis of the limited historical evidence available, it may well have been introduced at an early date in Syria, perhaps even as early as the beginning of the 3rd century, when communities were appointing a new bishop without the involvement of bishops from other dioceses. It may have been thought inappropriate for presbyters to lay their hands on a candidate for the episcopate, and hence the gospel book was used as a substitute for that and seen as representing the hand of Christ himself ordaining a new member of the apostolic college.

The only other ceremonies of ordination that can lay claim to any great antiquity are the making of the sign of the cross on the newly ordained immediately after the imposition of the hand and the exchange of a kiss at the conclusion of the whole action between the newly ordained and all those present. Indeed, although Eastern liturgies are often thought of as being generally more elaborate than those of the Western traditions, even later additions to the ceremonies of the rites tend to be somewhat more muted than those of the medieval West. Although solemn vesting in the robes of the new office and the handing over of symbols pertaining to that order do tend to emerge in the East as in the West, the anointing of priests and bishops is not practised here as it is in the West, except in those traditions that have come under Western influence.

Ministry and Ordination in the Community of Women and Men in the Church

Aide-mémoire

The intention of the consultation on "Ministry and Ordination in the Community of Women and Men" was to explore ministry from the perspective of the church viewed as a community of women and men, and to identify issues which might helpfully be explored in the development of an ecumenical convergence on ministry in the future. The subject was approached through four themes: the Holy Spirit and ministry; ministry and vocation; the ministry of women; and liturgical rites of ordination. The following are some of the issues and perspectives that the consultation highlighted and which it would hope to find reflected in any future work on the church and its ministry. We make first some general points and then treat each of the four themes. These themes are closely related and the issues are often inseparable. This means that there is an inevitable overlap in the themes raised under each section. Finally, we make some suggestions for future work. This is not a report of the consultation but simply an *aide-mémoire* of some of the points raised in the discussion.

A remarkable feature of the meeting, noted by those who had participated in earlier discussions on ministry, was that this exploration, even on the controversial issue of women's ordination to the priesthood and the episcopate, was conducted without the tense confrontation of the past. There was a genuine attempt by those who held different positions to understand the perspectives and the experiences of others.

General comments

There was agreement that the question of ministry should be explored in "the broader and deeper theological investigation on the nature and purpose of the church". While some found helpful the stress in the recently published Faith and Order study, *The Nature and Purpose of the Church,* on the church as *creatura Verbi and creatura Spiritus,* that language was not familiar to all participants (some suggested a stress on *creatura gratiae*). It was questioned whether this twofold emphasis is sufficiently trinitarian and, therefore, adequate as a controlling theme for understanding the church and its ministry. Equal weight needs to be given to the three persons of the Trinity and each person understood to be involved in every divine act. It was agreed that the notion of koinonia most aptly describes the mystery of the triune God and has helped us to understand the nature of the church as a communion of faith, life (including ministry) and witness.

The consultation noted that the ecumenical conversation since Lausanne 1927 has emphasized that agreement on the ministry of the church is required if churches are to live in visible unity. While churches recognized considerable convergence on some issues in *Baptism, Eucharist and Ministry*, there remain outstanding areas of disagreement which need to be faced together. Some of these issues were raised in this consultation and we have been encouraged to believe that there are fresh insights which could lead us further in the convergence process.

The WCC study on the "Community of Women and Men in the Church" contributed to an understanding of what it means to be a community of women and men in the church. Moreover, the study had implications for understanding the ministry of the church – both the ministry of the whole people of God and the ordained ministry. Additional insights came from the Decade of Churches in Solidarity with Women as well as from themes currently being explored as a follow-up to the Decade. Some participants stressed that recent feminist theologies provide a radically new hermeneutic for understanding the community of women and men in the church. It was agreed that the perspective *of* the church as the community of women and men needs to influence more obviously Faith and Order's work on the church and the ministry, particularly as that is developed within the current study on ecclesiology.

Our discussions were often marked by a diversity in the terminology we use relating to ministry. We are in agreement about the ministry of the whole people of God, that every baptized person has a responsibility for ministry and is given particular gift/s for ministry. We differ, however, in the terminology we use to refer to the ordained: "pastor", "minister", "presbyter", "priest"... We also differ in whether we emphasize the unity of the ordained ministry on the one hand or the threefold ordering of bishop, presbyter and deacon on the other.

There are also inevitable ambiguities in ecumenical documents. For example, it is not always clear whether references to "church" are to an ideal or to the actual life of the church today. There are also different understandings concerning where the church is to be found. The report of the Special Commission on Orthodox Participation in the WCC helpfully identifies the "existence of two basic ecclesiological self-understandings, namely of those churches (such as the Orthodox) which identify themselves with the one, holy, catholic and apostolic church, and those which identify themselves as parts of the one, holy, catholic and apostolic church".[1] This basic difference necessarily affects the way that convergence documents on the church and its ministry are read and received.

The Holy Spirit and ministry

We all agree that the Holy Spirit is at work in the church and the world. The church is not static but on a journey. The Holy Spirit both empowers the church, and challenges the church in each generation to journey in a way that is faithful to scripture and Tradition, made relevant in different historical and cultural contexts. The whole church is involved in discerning, under the guidance of the Holy Spirit, the will of God for the church and its ministry as the church travels through history.

We all agree that the Holy Spirit is given to men and women alike in baptism, bringing each person into the life of the church, the people of God, the community of women and men. At the same time, each person is called to the ministry of the church and endowed with a charism, a gift of the Holy Spirit for ministry, for service in the church and for witness in the world. The gifts are many, but the Giver is one, and the Spirit bestows gifts as the Spirit wills. Some persons may exercise several of the gifts or may manifest different gifts at different times.

The whole people of God is called to carry on the ministry and mission of Christ. The ordained ministry is a particular charism of the Holy Spirit for a ministry of both being (symbolizing) and doing (acting) in the community. Ordained ministry is for some a sign in the community of the continuation of the ministry of Christ in and among his people. Ordination also empowers individuals for certain functions in the church. These functions hold together the ministry of word, sacrament and pastoral care. The ministry of every baptized person and the special ministry are inspired by the Holy Spirit. What requires further exploration is the nature of the relationship between the ministry of the whole people of God and the special ministry. How far is the special ministry representative of the community? If it is representative of the community, some of us question whether an all-male ministry can ever fully represent the community of women and men.

A closely related question is the understanding of ministry and priesthood. We all agree that Jesus Christ is the unique High Priest of the new covenant and that his life was offered once and for all for the salvation of all. We all agree in affirming the royal priesthood of all believers. What we are not agreed on is whether, and in what sense, the ordained minister, particularly as he/she presides at the eucharist, relates to both the priesthood of Christ and to the royal priesthood of the whole people of God.

The whole church is called to be apostolic, to carry on the teaching and mission of the apostles, empowered and guided by the Holy Spirit. Apostolicity involves both past present and future, the receiving of the faith, the life of faith and the handing on of the faith of the apostles. Some see a sign of apostolic continuity in the orderly transmission of ordained ministry, within the community of faith, by the power of the Spirit. Some see a sign of apostolicity in episcopal succession. For some orderly transmission is a sign of the intention of the church to be faithful to the teaching and mission of the apostles as well as a sign of God's promise to lead the church into all truth. The ecumenical conversation might be furthered by exploring together the criteria recognizing apostolicity in another ecclesial body and its ministry.

The developments in the different churches in patterns of ministry, both ordained and lay, including the ordination of women to the ministry in some churches, challenge us in the ecumenical movement to listen to one another in order to discover what the Spirit is saying to the churches. How can we in a new stage of the ecumenical movement share together in discerning what the Spirit is saying to the churches? "Openness to each other holds out the possibility that the Spirit may well speak to one church through the insights of another."[2] For discernment we require the fruit of the Spirit – patience, forbearance, deferring to one another in love, etc.

Ministry and vocation

Through baptism, God forms a people into a community of discipleship. Baptism may be understood as a *kind* of "ordination" to Christ's ministry through the church. The Holy Spirit bestows on the baptized a variety of gifts, thereby enabling each Christian to participate in the fulfilment of the ministry and mission of the church.

Some are called to special ministries within the church which are lay ministries. Patterns of lay ministry have been diverse and flexible and responded to the needs of particular times and situations. The call to the monastic life is a distinct call. Within the call to religious life, some forms are intrinsically and essentially ministerial, expressed in active service to the neighbour. Some churches have forms of recognizing, training and accrediting lay ministries. The ministry of deaconesses is another distinct ministry.

The whole community of believers has a responsibility to identify, draw out and nurture the gifts of ministry in the service of Christ and of Christ's mission in the world. The ordained have a special responsibility to recognize and nurture the charisms among the congregations committed to their charge.

God calls and endows some members with the particular charism for ordained ministry. God's call is experienced both directly by the individual and affirmed by the community. There is the inner and outer call. Through ordination the church recognizes the call to ministry and the charism present for ordained ministry. Vocation thus has an ecclesial context.

Those with a ministry of oversight in the church have a special responsibility for fostering and nurturing vocation to ministry. The fostering of vocations among the young is a concern for many churches today. It was suggested that in some situations thought needs to be given to the preparation of the family of the one being ordained.

Ordination to the ministry is permanent but the location of service may change over time as the community, under the guidance of the Holy Spirit, responds to its needs and to its mandate. Ordination/consecration makes a difference, giving the person authority to preach the word and administer the sacrament/s and exercise pastoral care. The one ordained is given confidence that he/she speaks and acts in the name of the church and not in their own name.

Those churches which ordain women have been led to acknowledge that, through the Holy Spirit, God also calls women to ordained ministry. The sense of vocation comes both to the individual directly and, through her, to the community of faith. Many women found it hard to speak of their call to ordained ministry when there were no role models for them in ordained ministry and when the church was not open to test the vocation of women. The same forms of discernment of vocation and training for ministry apply to women as to men in those churches which do ordain women.

Ordination of women

There is a difference both between and within some churches over the ordination of women to the ministry of word and sacrament. The consultation engaged openly with the theological and the non-theological issues presented by those who hold different positions on the issue of women's ordination.

It was recognized that the ordination of women is a relatively new development in the life of some churches. Churches which ordain women are still exploring different styles and expressions of the ministry so that women are not trapped in a pattern developed in "male" and "masculine" models. In some churches which have opened the ordained ministry to women, there remain issues of deployment. Not all opportunities are fully open to women. Churches that do ordain women experience this as making women more visible and as respecting their equal dignity. For them the ordination of women both gives expression to the biblical truth that women and men are created in the image of God and also emphasizes that the church is a community of women and men.

Those who ordain women to the ministry of word and sacrament understand it as a faithful response to the demands of the gospel in the 21st century and a requirement for the credibility of the church's mission. Some churches which have ordained women do not see it as a change in the tradition of the church but, rather, as a development. The development in the ordering of the ministry of the universal church they understand as "provisional" and up for reception in the "universal church". That is not to suggest that the orders of any woman ordained by those churches are provisional or that women are not true ministers of word and sacrament. It means that this development, like any development, has to be received by the whole church. For this reason continuing the ecumenical conversation is, for those churches, vitally important.

Those churches who do not ordain women believe that they have not the authority to change the tradition of the church. The reason for not ordaining women is not predicated primarily on the arguments that Christ only chose male apostles, nor on the fact that the Virgin Mary did not have an hieratic role, nor on the fact that Christ, the Incarnate Word, appeared and lived as a man. In order to foster greater understanding of their position, these churches may need to articulate whether the non-ordination of women is a matter of the historical circumstances of the church or of the unchanging holy Tradition. Those churches which do not ordain women value the unique and distinctive contribution of women in the church which they honour and they encourage women's participation in the life and mission of the church. They seek to expand women's contribution in the life of every local church.

The fact that there are different practices over the ordination of women does not mean that churches cannot work together and share a variety of ministries in the service and mission of the church. Nevertheless, because the difference constitutes a "grave obstacle" in the path to Christian unity, churches need to go on exploring together issues which are raised in the discussion by both sides, e.g. questions of anthropology, theology, ecclesiology, sacrament and sacramentality, as well as the meaning of Tradition. We all believe that the Spirit may speak to us through the insights and experiences of others. What is important is that each church is allowed to explain its position, the truth as it sees it and lives it, and that its position is accurately described in any report that comes from an ecumenical conversation. The qualities which we bring to the discussion – openness, attentive listening and willingness to see the issue through the eyes of the other – are important.

Ordination rites

The consultation recognized the importance of exploring issues of ministry from the perspective of the ordination rites of the churches, including those of Pentecostal and Evangelical churches. While it may seem that there is much in common from the general pattern, the details sometimes reveal the differences. A comparison might be helpful in relation to:

- The way ordination rites indicate the relation between the ordained ministry and the people of God, both the local church and the wider church: Members of the congregation are not there as passive observers, but take an active role in affirming the worthiness of the candidate and promising support for his/her future ministry. This raises the question of whether ordination can be said to be related to the ministry of the "whole church" when the churches are still divided.
- In relation to what is signified in the laying-on of hands: In all traditions the laying-on of hands by those who have had hands laid on them is a part of the rite. What does this suggest about the way apostolicity and succession is understood and what is signified about the apostolicity of the whole church when laity take part in the laying-on of hands?
- Sacrament and sacramentality: All recognize the grace of God at work in ordination. Ordination is a gift of God. What does this imply about the notion of sacramentality/sacrament even when the words are not used in a particular tradition?
- The local and universal church: How far is the participation of other presbyter/bishops in ordinations understood as a link between the local church and other local churches in the wider communion of the church?

At this stage in the ecumenical movement, the presence at one another's ordinations is a way of affirming the growing fellowship of the churches. This implies for some a degree of recognition of the ministry of another church. In some cases there may be a sharing in the act of ordination itself, indicating a particular form of fellowship, e.g. "pulpit and altar fellowship" or a relation of "full communion". Being present in the sanctuary, without taking part in the laying-on of hands, may indicate a recognition of the fruitfulness of the ministry of another church. The consultation noted that more and more there is attendance at one another's ordinations even if there is no formal part taken in the service.

In churches which have ordained women, the rite used is the same as that used for the ordination of men. This indicates that women and men are understood as being ordained to the same ministry.

Suggestions for future work

In addition to the suggestions for further work the consultation identified a number of more general topics which would repay further study:
- the understanding of Tradition and traditions in relation to ministry and ordination;
- sacrament and sacramentality in relation to ordination.

The consultation recommends that:
a) the ecclesiology study could reflect more the understanding of the church as a community of women and men;
b) any future work on ministry draw upon the insights of liturgical scholars on the ordination rites of the churches.

NOTES

[1] "The Final Report of the Special Commission on Orthodox Participation in the WCC", *The Ecumenical Review*, vol. 55, no. 1, 2003, p.7.
[2] *Baptism, Eucharist and Ministry*, WCC, 1982, p.32 (§54).

APPENDIX

Scriptural Images of the Church
An Eastern Orthodox Reflection

HIEROMONK ALEXANDER GOLITZIN

I have been asked "to reflect on the way in which the scriptural images of the church are related to the understanding of the nature of the church in the Orthodox tradition". The space allotted this reflection is surely inadequate to a tradition which spans (or claims to span) the four millennia, from the call of Abraham to the present day. What follows can therefore be little more than the merest sketch, entirely dependent moreover on my own debatable powers of selection and synthesis, and thus necessarily partial and incomplete. It will, in short, reflect my own present concerns and interests, which are those of neither a biblical specialist, nor liturgist, nor patrologist, nor systematic theologian, but of a kind of historian of ideas who is particularly at home in the first half-millennium of Eastern Christian ascetical and mystical literature.

I begin my reflection with the following thesis. For Orthodox tradition, the church is nothing more nor less than Israel in the altered circumstances of the Messiah's death, resurrection, and the eschatological outpouring of his Spirit. This "inaugurated eschaton", to borrow a phrase from the late Fr Georges Florovsky, is at the same time a "new creation" (Gal. 6:15). In Jesus of Nazareth, Mary's son and eternal Son and Word of the Father, Israel has in a sense itself been crucified, raised and changed, such as to become the "first-fruits" of the new creation (1 Cor. 15:20), the "new" or "heavenly Adam" (cf. 1 Cor. 15:45ff.; Rom. 5:12ff.), the beginning of the world to come (Col. 1:18). Yet, at least in Orthodox tradition, it would be most wrong to emphasize this change, these altered circumstances, as denoting rupture pure and simple with the Israel of the patriarchs, kings and prophets. True, far and away the majority of Israel did not accept the change, and they carry on to the present apart from the church, but I would maintain that that separation was and is not so much between church and Israel as between two separate and discrete entities, as it is a schism within Israel, a schism which, if we are to believe the apostle, God – and only God! – will heal at the end of days (see Rom. 9-11). Christian and Jewish polemics, both in the early centuries of the church and in more recent times, may have often obscured this fundamental linkage and kinship, but they could not erase it. It is built into the earliest documents of Christianity and reflected continuously thereafter in Orthodox literature and liturgy. Thus for St Paul, as I read him, the discussion at issue in epistles such as Galatians and, especially, Romans centres not on the rejection of Israel, but rather, through the Messiah, on the expansion of Israel's boundaries so as to include the nations.

For Orthodoxy, therefore, the primary matrix for consideration of the nature and purpose of the church, and the images which express the church, must always be the one, unique and indivisible revelation of God to Israel, from, as it were, the *beresit* of Genesis to the "amen" of the Apocalypse. The scriptural icons of the church are, again, those of Israel. Here I venture to suggest that not one single image of the church in the New Testament, of which Paul S. Minear counts some ninety-six,[1] is wholly independent of, or unrelated to, the Old Testamental imagery of Israel. Even the notes of "new creation" and "new Adam" are affiliated with that iconography – if not directly or obviously – through the network of associations connected with the language of Zion and Temple which, drawing on associations with the "sacred mountain" traditions common in the Ancient Near East, tie the Temple mount into the stories of creation, paradise and the eschaton. The great difference, of course, is the person of Jesus the Messiah. Like the singularities or "black holes" of modern astrophysics, the gospel of Christ crucified and risen is a new point of immense gravitational attraction which at once draws and forces the ancient images into a new configuration, pulling them into orbit around the gospel truth itself. In this reordering and consequent reformulation of Israel's patrimony by the tidal forces of the gospel, we find the roots of all Christian spirituality and theology, including that of the church.

So far I have spoken in generalities. It is time to move to a few specifics. Time and space are short, books on the subject are many, so I will confine myself by way of illustration of the scriptural images of Orthodox ecclesiology to one man, one woman, two buildings, three church fathers (with perhaps another one or two appearing as buttresses), and four mountains. The man is Jacob; the woman Mary Theotokos; the buildings the Jerusalem Temple and the typical Orthodox church; the fathers are Ephrem Syrus (d. 373), Maximus the Confessor (d. 662), and Symeon the New Theologian (d. 1022); while the mountains are Sinai, Zion, Tabor and Golgotha. The first two, the man and the woman, and three of the last four have, moreover, a double advantage. They do not appear in any of the lists of New Testament images for the church that I have seen, as in Prof. Minear's excellent book, and they offer a satisfyingly complete entrée into Orthodox ecclesiology. The ordering of my exempla are, first, the one man; second, the four mountains, focusing especially on Sinai; third, Mary Theotokos and the two buildings; and, fourth, the fathers in whom we will find the foregoing commented upon and woven into the comprehensive theological and spiritual vision which, by and large, still obtains in the Orthodox world. Permit me in advance to apologise for the sketchy quality of what follows.

The revelation of God's glory

In Genesis 32:28-30, the Patriarch Jacob wrestles with the angel of God and receives as reward for his labours a new name, Israel. Other than the note of the vision of God's face, for which Jacob names the site of his contest, itself a matter of considerable interest in later Jewish and Christian literature, the point I should like particularly to underline is the double character of Jacob's new name. It denotes both the man, Jacob, and the nation of God's election. Israel is therefore a mysterious entity, at once summed up in the person of the patriarch, and thus a single organism, and an aggregate of individuals bound to the common observance of the covenant with the "God of Jacob". This genuinely corporate nature of the people of God, that is, that the latter does in fact comprise in some sense a single being, is I think of fundamental importance for the New Testamental and peculiarly Pauline notion of the church as the "body of Christ". It also lies behind such other, organic images of the church as, for example, the single "vine" of John 15:1ff., though the latter itself draws on the Old Testamental image of Israel as the "vine" planted by God's right hand in, for example, Psalms 80:14-15, verses echoed by the bishop's blessing of the congregation at the Orthodox divine liturgy.

The note of the covenant brings me to the first of my four mountains, Sinai, for whose discussion I am much indebted to Jon D. Levenson's book, *Sinai and Zion: An Entry into the Jewish Bible*.[2] Around Sinai are grouped a cluster of themes which are reflected in the New Testament imagery of the church and are elaborated later on in Orthodox tradition. Sinai is first of all the prototypical biblical theophany, the Old Testament manifestation of God *par excellence*. The brilliance of the divine glory, the *kevod YHWH*, descends on the peak sheathed in the dark Cloud of the Presence. This image and its paradox, God at once revealed and hidden, will be in play throughout the rest of the scriptures, Old and New Testament, and subsequently throughout the spirituality of both rabbinic Judaism and Christianity. At the heart of both Israel, and of Israel's extension to the nations, which is to say, the church, is the presence of the hidden God revealed, the mystery of his simultaneous transcendence and self-communication. It is thus that we discover the presence of Sinai in my two New Testament mountains, Golgotha and Tabor, a presence signalled in Orthodox tradition by the readings from Exodus 24 and 32-33 appointed for the feast of the Transfiguration, and again from Exodus 32 at the Vespers of Good Friday. It is the same Glory that appeared to Moses on the Sinai who is revealed in overwhelming light to the apostles on Tabor, and who is hung naked and bleeding on the cross. It is also the same Glory whose radiance, according to an ancient Jewish and Christian tradition, fed Moses on the mountain when he was forty days in the Cloud, and who feeds the Christian now in the eucharist. This, too, is signalled in the Orthodox liturgy, which includes a reading from Exodus 19:10-19 at the vesperal liturgy of Maundy Thursday celebrating the institution of the sacrament. The last points thus to the "upper room", the original Christian assembly, as also a kind of Sinai, and I would read this connection as reinforced by the accounts of both the Lucan Pentecost (Acts 2) and the Johannine (John 20), that is, Sinai as the place of the eschatological gift of the Spirit or, more briefly still, Sinai as type of the church.

The covenant relationship

This leads me to my second Sinaite theme, the covenant. In the covenant formulary of the Old Testament, borrowed, as seems most likely, from the ancient suzerainty treaties of the Near East, we find embedded or assumed in a number of images essential to the church. The first is that of God as King, and of Israel as his kingdom. The very first words out of Jesus' mouth as he begins his public ministry is a recollection thus of the covenant: "Repent, for the kingdom of God is at hand" (Mark 1:14 and par.) and, indeed, as the gospels go on to make clear that kingdom or reign is ultimately to be identified with the presence and person of Jesus himself. Sinai is therefore, secondly, an icon of the *eschaton*, pointing towards the end of Israel's pilgrimage and of all human history, a note once again echoed in the opening invocation of the Orthodox divine liturgy: "Blessed is the kingdom of the Father, Son, and Holy Spirit, now and ever and to the ages of ages."

Third, however, there is the notion itself of pilgrimage. Israel in the midst of the desert, not yet in the land of the promise, pledges itself (however imperfectly) all the same to fidelity, and Sinai is also the image of the people of the Messiah *in statu via*, the icon of the pilgrim church – *he ekklesia he paroikousa*, to borrow the phrasing of Ignatius of Antioch – which in the present age "has no city which abides" (Heb. 13:14). Yet, fourth, the relationship between God and his people has been sealed in "the blood of the covenant" (Exod. 24:8; cf. Mark 14:24 and par.), and that covenant is regularly "remembered" and renewed in the eucharistic assembly, so making the King present and his kingdom with him. The church at worship is thus also – and, Christian tradition holds, more perfectly – the icon (as opposed to the "shadow", Heb. 10:1) and communication of the world to come (cf. Heb. 12:18ff.). Fifth, relatedly and at least as old as the Prophet Hosea (Hos. 2:1ff.), there is God's love affair with Israel (cf. also Deut. 7:6-8) which is understood as consummated in the "marriage" at Sinai. Here we discover the source of the several New Testament images of church and kingdom that depend on nuptial language: the bridegroom (Christ), the wedding-feast, the church as spouse (Eph. 5:22-32), the invitees to the feast, the wise and foolish virgins, and the bridal chamber (Matt. 25:1-13).

The worship of God

Sinai is finally, at least for my purposes here, the revelation of true worship. Just prior to the theophany, Israel is informed of its vocation to become "a priestly kingdom and holy nation" (Exod. 19:6), a sentiment echoed in the New Testament (1 Pet. 2:4-9) regarding the church. The end and arguably the very climax of the Sinai narrative, with Moses again in the Cloud after the theophany and gift of the covenant, is the revelation of the tabernacle: "In accordance with all that I show you concerning the pattern (Hebrew *tabnit*, Greek *paradeigma*) of the tabernacle and all its furniture, so you shall make it" (Exod. 25:9ff.). This heavenly "pattern" includes the furnishings and design of the tent, together with the vestments of its celebrants – notably of the high priest – and instructions for their consecration and ministry (see Exod. 25-30 and 36-39). The book of Exodus itself concludes with the Glory and Cloud "overshadowing" (in the LXX) the newly-constructed tabernacle and taking up residence within the holy of holies (Exod. 40:34-5). Israel is now equipped with, so to speak, its own "portable Sinai", the means whereby God will travel with the covenanted people until their entry into the Land, and which will be followed by God's choice of Zion for his "holy mountain": "The Lord came from Sinai into the holy place... the processions of my God, my King, into the sanctuary" (Ps. 68:18,24). On Zion, the heavenly "pattern" is repeated in Solomon's construction of the Temple (1 Kings 5-7), whose consecration (1 Kings 8:1-11) again mirrors the tabernacle's consecration at the conclusion of Exodus. Zion becomes thus "the place" *(hammaqom)* of theophany and of God's abiding: "This is my resting place forever; here I will reside, for I have desired it" (Ps. 132:14 and many par.).

It is thus here, on Zion and in the Temple, that Isaiah sees the heavenly paradigm and its earthly copy coalesce into one (Isa. 6:1ff.), just as Ezekiel sees the Glory departing it on the eve of the Babylonian conquest (Ezek. 9-11), and returning to it again in the perfected Jerusalem of a visionary restoration (Ezek. 43). Here Malachi sites the eschatological visitation (Mal. 3:1ff.), and from this same "pattern" John the Seer builds his picture of the world and city to come (Rev. 21-22).

Sinai and Zion, tabernacle and temple, are foundational as well for New Testament Christology, ecclesiology and soteriology. The annunciation of the Saviour's conception to Mary Theotokos echoes the entry of Cloud and Glory into the sanctuary: "The Holy Spirit shall come upon you, and the Power of the Most High shall overshadow you" (Luke 1:35, *episkiasei se*, cf. Exod. 40:34 LXX). On Tabor, Jesus is fully revealed as the Glory seen by Moses on Sinai and appearing to Elijah on Horeb (1 Kings 19), while on Golgotha the moment of his dying is signalled by the splitting of the Temple veil, denoting the new "access" opened up through the cross to the Presence. The "dividing wall" is overcome, broken down, and "the one, new man" resulting is a "new creation" (Eph. 2:15 and Gal. 6:15). Indeed, the latter is a new sanctuary, where the assembly of the baptized becomes the temple and place of God's abiding. They, the people of the Messiah, are also thus called to be priests and, certainly, by the 4th century, when Christianity is allowed for the first time to emerge fully legal into the light of day, the "pattern" of Exodus 25:9 is consciously repeated in the construction of the new church buildings, as in Eusebius of Caesarea's oration, "On the Consecration of the Church at Tyre" (*HE* 10.4.2-72), with porch (recall the *ulam* of the Temple), nave (thus the *heykal*), and altar area with episcopal throne (the *debir*).

Likewise, we can – or should – catch the equally conscious allusion to the Old Testament priestly consecration, outlined in Exodus, in the lustration, anointing and clothing in white of the baptismal liturgy celebrated by, for example, Cyril of Jerusalem in the mid-4th century, and described in some detail by the nun Egeria at century's end. In the new dispensation, all Israel is accorded "access" to the sanctuary, as was signalled, for example, by the *disciplina arcana* which, precisely, limited access to the physical nave to the baptized, "the chosen race, the royal dwelling, the priestly body (construing *basileion* and *hierateuma* as separate words), the holy nation" (cf. 1 Pet. 2:9). I suggest, then, that

Scriptural Images of the Church 261

the mystagogical sermons of such 4th- and early 5th-century fathers as Cyril of Jerusalem, Ambrose, Chrysostom, and Theodore of Mopsuestia are much less indebted to the language of the pagan mystery cults than they are to the theology and general thought-world of the Old Testament tabernacle and temple, to the imagery, precisely, of the Old Testament priesthood, which only now, in Christ, has been extended to all the "Israel of God" (Gal. 6:16). In short, I think that they – together with the ascetico-mystical literature of both the 4th century and thereafter, which builds essentially on the very same imagery – are bringing into the open and elaborating on currents of Christian thought and practice that were present from the beginnings of Christianity, and that we find at the least adumbrated in the New Testament.

In the Orthodox liturgical year, quite the most dense concentration of images and scriptures touching on the nature of the church occurs in the feasts dedicated to Mary Theotokos. She is herself the outstanding type or icon of the church. Hence, as noted above, the implicit parallel in Luke between her and the tabernacle of Exodus, a parallel that is made explicit, and at considerable length, in the 2nd-century apocryphon, the *Protevangelium of James*, which, *inter alia*, portrays the young Virgin weaving the temple veil, surely an allusion to the "veil" of Christ's flesh (cf. Heb. 10:20) which will later be "woven" in her womb. The feast of the Entry of the Theotokos, 21 November, thus deploys three of the texts I noted above in connection with the entry of the Glory into the sanctuary: Exodus 40, 1 Kings 8, and Ezekiel 43. Two other Marian feasts, the annunciation and the nativity of the Theotokos, add respectively Exodus 3:1-8 (the burning bush), and Proverbs 9:1-11 (the house of Wisdom) together with Genesis 28:10-17 (the ladder of Jacob and the Beth-el, "house of God"). Of the many images applied to her in the hymnography, most of them from the Temple cultus, almost all carry the sense of something that either contains or holds, hence: candlestand (i.e., *menorah*), vessel or jar (of manna), chariot (cf. Ezek. 1), throne, ark, mercy seat (*kapporet*), holy mountain (cf. Sinai/Zion, and Dan. 2:45), holy of holies, tabernacle, temple, palace, house, meeting-place, paradise containing the Tree of Life, bridal chamber of light, gate of heaven, ladder, golden censer, incense altar, holy table (of the shewbread), living heaven, living pavillion of the Glory, and living city (cf. again Rev. 21-22). All of these are as well types of the church. All or nearly all of them have their original locus in the divinely-ordained cult and all are, again, equally types not just of the Virgin but of the Christian.

Here I touch, though most briefly, on the soteriological dimension of the cluster of images around the tabernacle and temple. Christ himself is pre-eminently the tabernacle and temple (cf. John 1:14 and 2:19-21), the "tabernacling" of the Glory or *Sekinah* among us, the "Lord of Glory" (1 Cor. 2:8), the Immanuel. The church, as his risen body into which the believers are incorporated in baptism (or with which they are "clothed", cf. Gal. 3:27, Col. 3:10), and which is made present in the worshipping assembly, is also temple (cf., e.g., Eph. 2:21-22). Third, however, the baptized Christian is temple as well (cf. 1 Cor. 6:19-20), for whom Mary Theotokos is, again, exemplar *par excellence*. It is in this imagery of the indwelling Glory, based on the Sinai and Zion traditions, that we find in fact the scriptural foundations of the Orthodox soteriology of *theosis*, deification. In the subsequent literature of the Eastern church, particularly in the writers of the ascetico-mystical tradition (i.e., after the 4th century, essentially the monks), we discover this parallelism and interweaving of the "three temples" or "three churches", to use an expression in the fourth *Liber Graduum*, continuously the subject of meditation and reflection to the end of the Byzantine era. At the heart of these reflections is faith in the participation in God – "partakers of the divine nature" (2 Pet. 1:4) – offered the believer in Christ through his church, and discovered in the inner reaches of the heart. That discovery, moreover, is not merely or even primarily an affair of the emotions (though emotion has its part to play), so much as personal experience of the transfiguring Lord, the as it were subjective validation of the truth of the dogmas and of the "real presence" of the sacraments.

Ephrem Syrus

We arrive at last at my three patristic exemplars, beginning with Ephrem Syrus. In what is arguably the *chef d'oeuvre* in a large body of writings, his *Hymns on Paradise*, he provides us with a masterful tapestry incorporating many of the traditions and images I have touched on above. Drawing on the ancient tradition of Eden as itself a mountain (cf. Ezek. 28:14), Ephrem superimposes onto the Paradise Mountain three of the other four scriptural mountains that we have been discussing: Sinai, Zion (via references to the Temple), and Golgotha, together with more than a hint of the fourth, Tabor. All four (or five) are in turn coordinated with the church and with the Christian. Looking at the mountain with Ephrem we have a series of levels or steps, while looking as it were "downwards" we are presented in effect with a set of concentric circles. Each level, each circle, represents in turn: (1) a different degree of beatitude corresponding to the church's divisions into "penitents" (and catechumens), "the just" (i.e., the baptized and virtuous), and "the victorious" (for Ephrem, the sainted ascetics); (2) one of the three components of the human being, that is, body, soul, and created spirit (Ephrem's equivalent to the biblical "heart" or the Greek *nous*); (3) stages of the ascent up Sinai as portrayed in Exodus 19 and 24, with the Presence (Ephrem deploys here, in *Hymn* 2.11, the Aramaic term, *sekinta*, equivalent to the Hebrew *sekinah*) at the summit, Moses on the heights, Aaron and the priests on the slopes, and the people gathered at the mountain's base; (4) at least the implication of the "geography" of the church building through the *Hymns*' allusions to the structure of the tabernacle and temple, thus, for example, Ephrem's echo of Exodus 25:9ff. in the following:

> The symbol of paradise was depicted by Moses who made the two sanctuaries, the sanctuary and the holy of holies; in the outer one entrance was permitted [to the priests], but into the inner one only once a year [to the high priest, cf. Lev 16]. So, too, with paradise: God closed off the inner part, but he opened up the outer, wherein Adam might gaze. (*Par. Hymn* 3.17)

In this schema, the innermost shrine of paradise (equivalent to the summit of Sinai, and the church's altar), the Tree of Life, corresponds to the Temple *debir*, while the Tree of Knowledge answers to the Temple veil dividing the *debir* from the holy place, the *heykal* (equivalent to the church nave). I would venture to add that, by implication, one could thus read the middle and lower slopes of Ephrem's mountain as corresponding, respectively, to the nave as the place of the just, and to the narthex or church porch as reserved for the penitents and those not yet baptized. In addition, and most importantly, the Glory on the peak of the mountain, the *sekinta* within the *debir* denotes the presence of Christ. It is Christ's cross (the Tree of Life) and his Glory (the actuality of the world to come) that inform both the church and the individual Christian. As with the Greek fathers, though entirely in his own Semitic idiom, Ephrem understands the purpose of Christ's advent, and of the whole economy of Israel, as our eventual deification: "At the end the body will put on the beauty of the soul; the soul will put on that of spirit; and the spirit will put on the very likeness of God's majesty" (*Par Hymn* 9.11); or, more briefly: "He gave us divinity, we gave him humanity" (*Hymns on Faith* 5.17).

These several levels or circles may be said to meet and coalesce for Ephrem in the eucharistic presence. "The body was the veil of your Glory," he writes elsewhere (echoing Heb. 10:20), "and the bread is the veil of the fire that indwells it" (*On Faith* 19.2-3). Holy communion is the (potential) moment of our recognition of the divine indwelling. As Ephrem writes in the *Paradise Hymns*, here referring to the disciples' meal with the risen Christ at Emmaus (Luke 24): "Bread...

was the key whereby their eyes were opened to recognize the Omniscient One" (15:4). It is the bread of communion, he notes elsewhere, which "tears the veil" between the believers and their perception of the Lord who is within them (*On Virginity* 36.21), and with whom they had all along been "clothed" from the moment of baptism. This is the awareness of the saints, who have "adorned themselves with the very likeness of Paradise" and in whom "is depicted the beauties of the Garden" (*Par Hymn* 6.14). The Christian saint, which is no more than to say the complete Christian, is thus the presence of paradise in a perishing world, the very assurance of the *eschaton*, the "place" of divine Presence, the manifestation of Christ, the actualization of the church and its sacraments, Sinai and Zion as more than merely "portable", but as living, breathing and speaking. This is the universal vocation of the Christian, the substance of his or her calling and gift in Christ, and the very mark of *verus Israel*.

Maximus and Symeon

My two other patristic witnesses do little more, at least for purposes of this paper, than add corroboration to what we find sketched at length in Ephrem, and we can therefore deal with them much more briefly. Maximus the Confessor's brilliant little treatise, *The Mystagogy*, claims merely to be filling in a few things left unsaid by Dionysius the Areopagite in the latter's *Ecclesiastical Hierarchy*, a claim which I believe to be true, though I am a minority of one among scholars who prefer to see Maximus as wholly re-writing and "correcting" the Areopagite. It is, though, incontestably true that the former presents his readers with a clearer picture than Dionysius, hence my choice of him here. In his *Mystagogy*, Maxiumus opens by presenting the church as a series of icons that represents, in the following order, God, the world, the human being ("man" or *anthropos*), the scriptures and the soul. Here we may discern a number of points touched on above, including: (a) the presence of God, which Maximus underlines through an opening discussion of apophatic theology, accentuating the mystery at the heart of the church; (b) creation, in the inclusion of the world as a category; (c) the "one new man" of Ephesians 2, which is Christ in the church, the *makranthropos*; (d) the inter-relation of Old Testament and New, as Maximus puts it, like the wheels one within the other of Ezekiel's vision of the chariot-throne; and (e) mystical union with God, in the section of the soul, as fulfilment of life in the church. The whole is based on the division of the church building into nave and sanctuary. Thus, for example, in *Mystagogy* 4, Maximus speaks of the human body as the nave, the soul as sanctuary, and the intellect *(nous)* as altar. Everything meets ultimately in the one mystery of the altar, at which we discover an anticipation of the resurrection, i.e., of the *eschaton*. The remaining and larger part of the treatise walks the reader through the eucharistic liturgy, from the entry of the clergy to communion, and builds on the opening passages to portray the church's worship as an icon – and a real communication – of the soul's encounter with, and growth into Christ. Once again, in Maximus we find an overlapping and coordination of the physical temple, the "inner man", the divine abiding, *Urzeit* and *Endzeit*, recognized in the sacramental presence and known in mystical experience.

Symeon the New Theologian carries on these themes particularly in his *Ethical Discourses*, with the most concentrated dosage in *Discourses* I-III and XIV. The first three comprise a kind of unity, beginning with creation and Eden, then touching on the fall, the incarnation, the renewal of creation, the "mystical marriage of God" with his church, with Mary Theotokos, and with the Christian in *Discourse* I. *Discourse* II again recapitulates salvation history, but stresses Paradise, Old Testamental Israel, and the church as *progressively more* real and efficacious icons of the *eschaton*. *Discourse* III concludes with the subjects of mystical union with God, based on an exegesis of 2 Corinthians 12:2ff., and the eucharist as, both of them together, a complementary and genuine reflection of, and participation in the world to come. In *Discourse* XIV, on liturgical celebration of the church's feasts, Symeon takes issue with a formalistic approach to corporate prayer and, typical both of his own personal emphases and of those of his monastic predecessors (such as Maximus), depicts the visible church at worship as an icon of the "inner man", guiding and shaping the latter for union with God. At the same time, the New Theologian insists again on the presence of Christ in the sacrament, a presence which the properly formed and inspired soul must recognize. Given this formation and this conscious participation in the eucharistic presence, he concludes with an evocation of the future age:

> If you celebrate the feast and so partake as well of the divine mysteries, all your life will be to you one single feast. And not *a* feast, but the beginning of feasting and a single Pascha, the passover and emigration from what is seen to what is sensed by the intellect, to that place where every shadow and type, and all the present symbols, come to an end, and where we... shall in purity rejoice eternally in the most pure sacrifice, in God the Father and the co-essential Spirit, always seeing Christ and seen by him, ever being with Christ, reigning with Christ, than whom nothing is greater in the kingdom of God...

Here, in the language of the Passover, of sacrifice, of "the place" (recall *hammaqom* above), and of the reign and kingdom of God, we encounter again the notes of Exodus: passover/pilgrimage, God as king, the "place" of divine presence, and the prescribed *cultus*. Elsewhere, Symeon assembles many of the other images of the church that we have met: "bride of Christ", Mary Theotokos, "the one, new man", the new Jerusalem, "the temple of God the King", God's "city and world". Throughout his thought, the protological, eschatological, mystical and sacramental aspects of the church are front and centre. At every point, his thought remains fundamentally ecclesial in its mysticism, and mystical in its ecclesiology, always turning around the unique mystery or sacrament of the Word made flesh and available to the believer, now, in the Spirit. His is thus as good an accounting of scriptural imagery for the church as may be found in medieval Orthodoxy, and, as he also marks the limits of my own competence, here my essay concludes.

NOTES

[1] *Images of the Church in the New Testament*, New Testament Library, 1960.
[2] New York, Harper & Row, 1987.

Contributors

REV. DR PAUL F. BRADSHAW is an Anglican priest-vicar of Westminster Abbey, England, and canon of the Episcopal Diocese of Northern Indiana, USA. He is also professor of liturgy at the University of Notre Dame, IN, USA, and a director of the University's London programme.

REV. DR EMMANUEL CLAPSIS, a priest of the Greek Orthodox Archdiocese of America (Ecumenical Patriarchate), is professor of systematic theology and dean of Holy Cross Greek Orthodox School of Theology, Brookline MA, USA. He has been vice-moderator of the WCC's Faith and Order commission.

DR NICHOLAS CONSTAS (Greek Orthodox Archdiocese of America, Ecumenical Patriarchate) is associate professor of theology at Harvard Divinity School, USA.

METROPOLITAN DANIEL CIOBOTEA of Moldavia and Bukovina, Romania, is associate professor in the department of Christian mission of the University Theological Institute in Bucharest, and professor of theology at the faculty of Orthodox theology of the University of Iasi. He has been a member of the WCC's Faith and Order standing commission.

REV. ARACELI EZZATTI, a pastor of the United Methodist Central Church, is a coordinator of programmes of theological education in Uruguay and has served as pastor to people in the marginalized areas of Montevideo since 1990. She has been a vice-moderator of the WCC's Faith and Order commission.

REV. DR ALAN D. FALCONER is an ordained minister of the Church of Scotland and pastor in St Machar's Cathedral, Aberdeen, Scotland. Professor of ecumenics and director of the Irish School of Ecumenics from 1974 to 1995, he was director of the WCC's Faith and Order secretariat from 1995 to 2004.

DR DONNA GEERNAERT, a Roman Catholic Sister of Charity, is the congregational leader for the Sisters of Charity (Halifax) and responsible for missions across Canada, the Eastern United States, Bermuda, the Dominican Republic and Peru. She is a member of the WCC's Faith and Order commission.

REV. DR TIMOTHY GEORGE (Southern Baptist Convention) is dean of Beeson Divinity School of Samford University in Birmingham, AL, USA, and an executive editor of *Christianity Today*. He is a member of the WCC's Faith and Order commission.

REV. DR CHRISTINE GLOBIG, a pastor of the North Elbian Lutheran Church in Germany, is lecturer in systematic theology and women studies at the Kirchliche Hochschule Wuppertal (Barmen School of Theology, Wuppertal). She has been involved in Faith and Order studies on koinonia and the community of women and men in the church.

REV. DR ALEXANDER GOLITZIN, hieromonk of the Orthodox Church in America, is professor of Eastern Christian theology at Marquette University, Milwaukee, WI, USA.

REV. DR WILLIAM HENN, a Capuchin-Franciscan friar and ordained priest in the Roman Catholic Church, is professor of ecclesiology, ecumenism and theological methodology at the Gregorian University in Rome. He is a consulter to the Pontifical Council for Promoting Christian Unity and a member of the WCC's Faith and Order standing commission.

REV. DR GERT JANSEN, a minister of the Protestant Church in the Netherlands, is a member of the consulting group on faith and ecclesial community of the Council of Churches in the Netherlands.

MRS SARAH KAULULE, a lay preacher in the United Church of Zambia, is chief vocational education and training officer for the ministry of science, technology and vocational training of Zambia, and a member of the board of governors of the United Church of Zambia. She is a member of the WCC's Faith and Order standing commission.

DR DIMITRA KOUKOURA, an Orthodox theologian from the Ecumenical Patriarchate, is assistant professor of homiletics and communication at the Divinity School of Aristotle University, Thessaloniki, Greece. She is a member of the WCC's Faith and Order commission.

DR NIKOS MATSOUKAS is emeritus professor of systematic theology, history of the ecumenical movement and philosophy at the departament of theology of Aristotle University, Thessaloniki, Greece.

Contributors

DR BERND OBERDORFER, an ordained minister of the Evangelical Lutheran Church in Bavaria, Germany, is professor of systematic theology at the University of Augsburg, Germany.

DR MARY O'DRISCOLL, a Roman Catholic Dominican sister, is professor of theology and head of the department of ecumenical studies at the University of St Thomas Aquinas, Rome, Italy. She is a member of the WCC's Faith and Order standing commission.

REV. DR CONSTANCE F. PARVEY, one of the first women ordained by Lutheran church bodies in North America, was a visiting professor at Vancouver school of theology, Canada, and taught feminist studies in the history department at Bryn Mawr College, Pennsylvania, USA. She directed the WCC's study on the Community of Women and Men.

REV. DR MARTYN PERCY, former director of the Lincoln theological institute for the study of religion and society at the University of Sheffield, and a canon of Sheffield cathedral (Anglican Church), is principal at Ripon College, Cuddesdon, Oxford, UK.

REV. DR JAMES F. PUGLISI, Roman Catholic minister general of the religious community of the Franciscan Friars of the Atonement, is director of the Centro Pro Unione and professor of ecclesiology, sacraments and ecumenism at the Pontifical Athaenum Sant'Anselmo, Rome, Pontifical University of St Thomas-Angelicum, Rome, Pontifical University Antonianium, Rome, and the San Bernardino Institute of Ecumenical Studies, Venice, Italy.

REV. ANTTI SAARELMA, a parish pastor in the diocese of Tampere, Finland, is a staff member of the Church Research Institute of the Evangelical Lutheran Church of Finland, and a member of the WCC's Faith and Order plenary commission.

REV. DR BARBARA SCHWAHN is a pastor of the Evangelical Church in the Rhineland, Germany (EKD), and a member of the WCC's Faith and Order commission.

DR TURID KARLSEN SEIM is a member of the Lutheran Church of Norway and vice-chair of its Commission on Doctrine. Currently she is a professor of theology (New Testament) at the University of Oslo and a member of the Commission on Unity between the Roman Catholic Church and the Lutheran World Federation. She is a vice-moderator of the WCC's Faith and Order commission

REV. DR HERMEN SHASTRI (Methodist Church of Malaysia) is general secretary of the Council of Churches of Malaysia, and a member of the WCC's Faith and Order standing commission.

DR MARY TANNER was a professor of Old Testament and Hebrew at Hull and Bristol Universities, England. She has been moderator of the WCC's Faith and Order commission.

DR URS VON ARX is professor of New Testament studies and history of Old Catholicism in the faculty of theology at the University of Bern, Switzerland.

IMPRIMERIE
LUSSAUD

L'impression et le façonnage
de cet ouvrage
ont été effectués
à l'Imprimerie LUSSAUD
85200 Fontenay-le-Comte

Dépôt légal 2ᵉ trimestre 2005
n° 3914
N° d'impression : 204 093